TOWARDS ENVIRONMENTAL SUSTAINABILITY?

Towards Environmental Sustainability?
A comparative study of Danish, Dutch and Swedish transport policies in a European context

EMIN TENGSTRÖM
Aalborg University

LONDON AND NEW YORK

First published 1999 by Ashgate Publishing

Reissued 2018 by Routledge
2 Park Square, Milton Park, Abingdon, Oxon, OX14 4RN
52 Vanderbilt Avenue, New York, NY 10017

Routledge is an imprint of the Taylor & Francis Group, an informa business

Copyright © Emin Tengström 1999

All rights reserved. No part of this book may be reprinted or reproduced or utilised in any form or by any electronic, mechanical, or other means, now known or hereafter invented, including photocopying and recording, or in any information storage or retrieval system, without permission in writing from the publishers.

Notice:
Product or corporate names may be trademarks or registered trademarks, and are used only for identification and explanation without intent to infringe.

Publisher's Note
The publisher has gone to great lengths to ensure the quality of this reprint but points out that some imperfections in the original copies may be apparent.

Disclaimer
The publisher has made every effort to trace copyright holders and welcomes correspondence from those they have been unable to contact.

A Library of Congress record exists under LC control number: 99073391

ISBN 13: 978-1-138-36540-7 (hbk)
ISBN 13: 978-1-138-36545-2 (pbk)
ISBN 13: 978-0-429-43073-2 (ebk)

Contents

List of Tables   *xi*
Acknowledgements   *xiii*
List of Abbreviations   *xiv*
Executive Summary   *xvi*

Introduction
  The background of the study   1
  The objectives, limitations and focus of the study   1
  The disposition of the book   3

1 Theoretical Points of Departure
  1.1 Transport policies for environmental sustainability   5
    1.1.1 Transport policies as an object of empirical investigation   5
    1.1.2 The concept of 'sustainability'   7
    1.1.3 Previous studies of transport policies for environmental sustainability   11
    1.1.4 The character of the present study   14
  1.2 Theory and method   15
    1.2.1 Understanding historical change   16
    1.2.2 Understanding societal processes of change   17
    1.2.3 Interpreting political texts   18
    1.2.4 Identifying the strategic elements of transport policies   20
    1.2.5 Analysing the role of the car, the key problem of transport policy   24
    1.2.6 My own previous studies of the role of the car   30

2 Global Environmental Aspects
  2.1 The objective, sources and disposition of the chapter   32
  2.2 The present transport sector: global environmental problems and international policy responses   33
    2.2.1 The present energy use of the transport sector - a threat to the environmental sustainability of transport systems?   33

    2.2.2 Greenhouse gases from the transport sector - a threat to global environmental sustainability?   36
    2.2.3 Are there other effects of the transport sector threatening environmental sustainability at the global level?   38
    2.2.4 International policy responses to present problems   39
    2.2.5 A summing up   40
  2.3 Global development of car ownership and car use   41
    2.3.1 Introduction: modernization and motorization   41
    2.3.2 A worldwide survey   42
    2.3.3 The case of Northern America   43
    2.3.4 The case of Western Europe   45
    2.3.5 The case of Eastern Europe   46
    2.3.6 The case of Latin America   47
    2.3.7 The case of East and South Asia   49
    2.3.8 A summing up   52
  2.4 Prospects for the future   53
    2.4.1 Energy futures and the risks of conventional development   53
    2.4.2 Future environmental impact of transport-related emissions   56
    2.4.3 The transition to carbon-low, carbon-neutral or carbon-free fuels   58
    2.4.4 Technological possibilities of the future   60
  2.5 Conclusions   60

3 The Changes of Danish, Dutch and Swedish Transport Policies
  3.1 Introduction   63
    3.1.1 Theory and method   63
    3.1.2 Previous studies   65
    3.1.3 Some basic facts about the three countries   66
  3.2 Danish transport policy in the period 1987-1997   67
    3.2.1 Introduction: transport policy before 1987   67
    3.2.2 The Transport Action Plan of 1987   67
    3.2.3 The Transport Action Plan of 1990   69
    3.2.4 The Traffic Plan of 1993   71
    3.2.5 After 1993: evaluation of results and controversies about measures   73
    3.2.6. The findings of the analysis   75
  3.3 Dutch transport policy in the period 1987-1997   77
    3.3.1 Introduction: transport policy before 1987   77
    3.3.2 Initiating a new transport policy in 1988   77
    3.3.3 The Transport Structure Plan of 1990   79

  3.3.4 Successive evaluations and revisions of the policy in
    1990-1997   82
  3.3.5 The findings of the analysis   84
 3.4 Swedish transport policy in the period 1987-1997 (1998)   85
  3.4.1 Introduction: transport policy before 1987   85
  3.4.2 The transport policy of 1988   86
  3.4.3 The changes made in 1988 transport policy in
    1991-1994   88
  3.4.4 Elaborating a new national plan 1995-1997   91
  3.4.5 The government bill on a new transport policy as of
    March 1998   94
  3.4.6 The findings of the analysis   96
 3.5 Conclusions   97
  3.5.1 How did the transport policies change?   97
  3.5.2 Why did the transport policies change?   98
  3.5.3 A new transport policy cycle initiated around 1990   101
  3.5.4 The first stages of the new cycle of transport policy   102
  3.5.5 The future of the new transport policy cycle   104

4 Differences Between Danish, Dutch and Swedish Transport Policies
 4.1 Introduction   105
  4.1.1 The aims, focus and research questions of the chapter   105
  4.1.2 The theoretical basis of the comparative analysis   106
 4.2 The transition to a more alarming view of the environmental problems of transport   110
  4.2.1 Some differences in the transition   110
  4.2.2 Explanations of identified differences   111
 4.3 The introduction and formulation of environmental sustainability as a political goal   114
  4.3.1 Political processes leading to the formulation of the goal of environmental sustainability   114
  4.3.2 The definition of 'environmental sustainability'   116
  4.3.3 The treatment of the conflict between different goals   117
  4.3.4 Explanations of identified differences   119
 4.4 The selection of intermediate objectives, policy instruments and concrete measures   122
  4.4.1 Introduction   122
  4.4.2 To influence the traffic volumes and the distribution among different transport modes   123
  4.4.3 To influence the level and composition of energy consumption   125

4.4.4 To influence the technical standard of the fleet of vehicles	127
4.4.5 To influence the environmental adaptation of new infrastructure	128
4.4.6 A summing up of identified differences and suggested explanations	129
4.5 Implementation and evaluation	131
4.5.1 Some differences in implementing strategies	131
4.5.2 Explanations of identified differences	133
4.6 The emergence of ecological modernization capacities in national transport policies: some differences and their explanation	134
4.6.1 The building-up of ecological modernization capacity in national transport policies	134
4.6.2 Explanations of differences in capacity building	139
4.7 Conclusions	140

5 The European Dimension

5.1 Introduction	143
5.1.1 The objective, focus and limitations of the chapter	143
5.1.2 Previous studies	144
5.1.3 The disposition of the chapter	145
5.2 Towards a harmonization of European transport policies	146
5.2.1 Towards a Pan-European Transport Policy - the role of the ECMT	146
5.2.2 Towards a Common Transport Policy of the EU - the role of the Commission	148
5.2.3 A first summing up	150
5.3 The role of the Common Transport Policy in national policies	150
5.3.1 Introduction	150
5.3.2 Denmark and the Common Transport Policy of EU	151
5.3.3 The Netherlands and the Common Transport Policy of EU	152
5.3.4 Sweden and the Common Transport Policy of EU	153
5.3.5 A second summing up	155
5.4 The Common Transport Policy: role and implementation	157
5.4.1 Introduction	157
5.4.2 The conflict between economic growth and environmental sustainability	157
5.4.3 The character of the decision-making in the Union	159
5.4.4 The role of the Principle of Subsidiarity	160

5.4.5 The problems of the implementation processes	161
5.4.6 A third summing up	163
5.5 Recent issues concerning transport and the environment	164
5.5.1 Introduction	164
5.5.2 The harmonization of national CO2 taxes	165
5.5.3 The energy use of the transport sector	166
5.5.4 The Auto/Oil Programme	167
5.5.5 The environmental effects of the TEN Programme	167
5.6 A final summary and some conclusions	168

6 A Critical Evaluation: Success or Failure?

6.1 Introduction	172
6.2 A critical evaluation of present national transport policies	172
6.2.1 Intermediate objectives aiming at environmental sustainability	172
6.2.2 Two timetabled targets	182
6.2.3 General conclusions: few successes, more failures	187
6.3 Explanations of the failures	189
6.3.1 A theoretical approach	189
6.3.2 The role of governments	190
6.3.3 The role of organized interests	193
6.3.4 The role of ordinary citizens	194
6.3.5 Concluding remarks	195

7 Policy Options for the Future

7.1 Introduction	196
7.2 The importance of an underestimated policy instrument	197
7.3 Four possible topics for dialogue or conflict	201
7.3.1 Lowering speed limits on the entire road-net	201
7.3.2 Increasing the use of carbon-low, carbon-neutral or carbon-free fuels	203
7.3.3 Stabilizing the motor vehicle transport volumes for individual mobility	205
7.3.4 Reducing the use of private cars	207
7.4 The potential socio-political basis for the suggested policy options	210
7.4.1 The core group: environmentally concerned people	210
7.4.2 The role of women in changing transport patterns	213
7.4.3 The role of people at present caught in a social dilemma	214
7.4.4 The role of people at present suffering from cognitive dissonance	215

7.4.5 A Norwegian empirical study of different lifestyles in transport	216
7.5 Concluding remarks	217

Sources and Literature

1 Primary sources	220
1.1 Official documents	220
1.2 Publications of various organizations	224
1.3 Statistical handbooks etc	225
2 Secondary sources	226
2.1 Bibliographies	226
2.2 Scientific literature and reports	226
2.3 Articles in newspapers and newsletters	241

List of Tables

3:1 Timetabled quantitative reductions of certain substances from the Swedish transport sector   95

6:1 The development of GDP (index 1986=100) and road passenger km (cycle km not included) and rail passenger km (index 1986=100) in the three countries   173

6:2 The number of cars (in ten thousands) and the car density (number of cars per 1000 inhabitants) in the three countries for five selected years   174

6:3 The development of passenger km by car (drivers and passengers) in the three countries compared with the development of GDP (index 1989=100)   175

6:4 The relation between public (bus+rail+ship) transport (figures to the left) and private (car+soft modes) transport (figures to the right) in the three countries (in percent of passenger km) for three selected years   176

6:5 The percentage of passenger km by cycle in the three countries for three selected years (the Swedish figures are estimated)   176

6:6 Energy consumption (in Mtoe) in the total transport sector and in road transport (consumption of diesel and petrol in parenthesis) in the three countries in three selected years   177

6:7 The percentage of cars in use equipped with catalytic converters for four selected years   178

6:8 The average energy efficiency of new petrol-driven cars measured as number of km driven per litre of fuel   178

6:9 The percentage of cars weighing 1100 kg or more for three selected years   179

6:10 The expansion of motorways in the three countries between 1990 and 1994 in absolute (km) and relative (%) numbers   180

6:11 The expansion of motorways in the three countries between 1970 and 1989 in absolute (km) and relative (%) numbers   180

6:12 Losses of more or less productive soil (in ha) in the three countries totally (until 1994) and during two different periods: 1970-1989 and 1990-1994   181

6:13 The development of emissions of NOx from road traffic in the three countries for four selected years   182

6:14a Emissions of CO_2 from road traffic in the three countries for four selected years (index 1986=100)   184

6:14b Emissions of CO_2 from road traffic in Holland compared to the number of vehicle km   185

6:15 Total emissions of CO_2 (in Kt) per capita, the percentage of the total emissions contributed by the transport sector (%) and per capita emissions (in Kt) in the transport sector in the three countries   185

6:16 A comparison of current per capita emissions of CO_2 in the transport sector in the three countries (in the year 1994) and a globally equitable share of the per capita emissions in the same sector by 2050   186

7:1 Estimates of direct and indirect effects of three different scenarios of speed reduction in Holland compared to the actual figures (=basic scenario)   202

7:2 Modal split in Holland (in percentage of total number of passenger km) for two years: actual figures for 1984 and estimated figures for 2010   212

Acknowledgements

The present study was carried out at Aalborg University in Northern Denmark in the period September 1995 - August 1998. It was financed by the Danish Transport Council in Copenhagen. Being a part time Research Professor (approximately half time), I was accepted as a full member of the Department of Development and Planning and its Traffic and Transport Group. Now that the task is completed, I want to express my sincere thanks for the way I was received, particularly to the members of the Traffic and Transport Group and its secretary.

During my stay at Aalborg, I also had the privilege of being able to discuss with a national group of reference. These discussions were not only of great help in many concrete questions but I was also able to profit from the intellectual stimulation of these contacts. The members of this group were: Dag Bjørnland, Bent Flyvbjerg, Henrik Gudmundsson, Susanne Krawack and Otto Anker Nielsen. I am very grateful for their help and support.

There are also quite a few colleagues and specialists who have read and commented on different parts of the study: Christian Azar and Karl-Erik Eriksson, Göteborg (chapter 2), T. van der Hoorn, The Hague (parts of chapter 3), Jørgen Kristiansen, Aalborg, (parts of chapter 3), Hans-Carl Nielsen, Copenhagen (parts of chapter 3), Staffan Widlert, Stockholm (chapters 3 and 4), Gunnar Falkemark, Göteborg (chapter 4), Martin Kroon, the Hague (chapters 3, 4 and 6), Carsten Hansen, Aalborg (chapter 6). I thank them all for their interest and many useful comments.

Gillian Thylander, Göteborg, has corrected my English in a careful way. I thank her warmly for her dedicated work, and particularly for her ability to understand what I really intended to express.

Finally, it should be underlined that the responsibility for all remaining errors and mistakes are exclusively mine.

List of Abbreviations

ACEA= Association des Constructeurs Européens d'Automobiles
BAT= Best Available Technology
CO= Carbon Oxide
CO_2= Carbon Dioxide
COREPER= Committee of Permanent Representatives (in Brussels)
CTP= Common Transport Policy (of the Europan Union)
ECMT= European Conference of Ministers of Transport
EEC= European Economic Community
EIA= Environmental Impact Analysis
EIS= Environmntal Impact Statement
EMC= Ecological Modernization Capacity
ERT= European Round Table of Industrialists
ERTICO= European Road Transport Telematics Implementation Coordination Organisation
EST= Environmentally Sustainable Transport
EU= European Union
EUROPIA= The European Petroleum Industry Association
FIA/AIT= Federation Internationale de l'Automobile/Alliance Internationale de Tourisme
GDP= Gross Domestic Product
GHG= Greenhouse Gases
IEA= International Energy Agency
IFR= International Road Federation
IIASA= International Institute for Applied Systems Analysis
IPCC= Intergovernmental Panel on Climate Change
LPG= Liquified Petroleum Gas
MaTs= Miljöanpassat transportsystem (=Environmentally Sustainable Transport System)
NGO= Non Governmental Organizations
NO_x= Nitrogen Oxides
NPP1= The First National (Dutch) Environmental Plan
NPP2= The Second National (Dutch) Environmental Plan
OECD= Organization of Economic Cooperation and Development
OPEC= Organization of the Petroleum Exporting Countries
OICA= Organisation Internationale des Constructeurs d'Automobiles

RIVM= The (Dutch) State Instititute for Public Health and Environmental Protection
SCB= Statistiska Centralbyrån (The Swedish National Bureau of Statistics)
SEA= Strategic Environmental Assessment
SEI= Stockholm Environmental Institute
SEPA= Swedish Environmental Protection Agency
SIKA= Swedish Institute for Communication Analysis
SOU= Statens Offentliga Utredningar (Reports of Swedish Investigative Commissions)
SVV1= the First (Dutch) Transport Structure Plan
SVV2= the Second (Dutch) Transport Structure Plan
TEN= Trans-Europan Networks
T&E= Transport and Environment (an environmental organization)
UN= United Nations
UNEP= United Nations Environmental Programme
UU= Utrikesutskottet (the Swedish Parliament's standing committe on foreign affairs)
VOC= Volatile Organic Compounds
WCED= World Commission on Environment and Development
WEC= World Energy Council
WWF= World Wide Fund for Nature

Executive Summary

The Character of the Study

The present publication is mainly an empirical study of Danish, Dutch and Swedish national transport policies in the period 1987-1997. It has its focus on the question to what extent current transport policies have been able to enhance environmental sustainability.

Empirical studies of transport policies are rare, at least in comparison with other kinds of transportation studies. For instance, scientific interest in suggesting new policy options for realising sustainable transport has been rapidly increasing during the last few years.

In the present study, the two approaches have been combined. The major part of it (chapters 3-6) consists of an empirical analysis of current transport policies in the three countries but, in the final chapter, the author suggests some policy options for the near future, intended to reduce the present unsustainable character of the national transport systems to some extent.

The basic idea behind the study was to make a comparison of transport policies in three North European countries selected for their reputation for well developed environmental policies: Denmark, the Netherlands and Sweden. Little attempt had been made to compare national transport policies previously.

On the other hand, a number of comparative studies of national *environmental* policies had been published during the last few years. Since its focus is on environmental sustainability, the present work is able to draw on theories used by such studies.

The Introduction: Objectives, Limitations and Focus

The main objectives of the study are

- to analyse the *theoretical points of departure* for a study of this kind
- to identify *global environmental considerations* for national transport policies
- to identify, describe and explain *changes in stated transport policies* in Denmark, the Netherlands, and Sweden in the period 1987-1997

- to identify, describe and explain *differences between stated passenger transport policies* in Denmark, the Netherlands and Sweden in the period 1987-1997
- to explore the *relations* between national transport policies and European transport policies
- to evaluate the *results* of the national policies in the perspective of environmental sustainability by contrasting stated policies and actual outcomes and to *explain the results* of the evaluation and
- to identify and describe *some policy options* for promoting the goal of environmentally sustainable transport.

The present study is limited in the sense that it deals only with passenger transport (mainly on land) and not at all with freight transport. Neither does it discuss policies or practices developed at regional or local levels but analyses only national policies. Besides the focus on environmental sustainability, the role of the automobile in the transport systems is another focal point of the study.

Chapter 1 Theoretical Points of Departure

In the first chapter, transport policy is defined as *'an authoritative allocation of values in society influencing the technical standard of vehicles, the development of the transport infrastructure and the behaviour of the transport users'*.

Here, the concept of 'sustainability' is also discussed. The history of this concept is summarized, the author's own interpretation of it briefly indicated and a survey of recent scientific literature on environmentally sustainable transport presented. Instead of formulating a more detailed definition of the concept of 'sustainability', the author provides the concept with a concrete content in relation to transport in the second chapter.

A general theoretical framework is also outlined, covering, very briefly, the questions how to understand historical change and how to interpret political texts.

The key question of the chapter is how to identify and describe the strategic elements of transport policies. They were found to be four:

- the policy-makers' perceptions of the problems of transport
- their formulation of goals and targets
- their selection of intermediate objectives, policy instruments and concrete measures and

- their views of the implementation and evaluation process.

These elements were discussed in some detail, and a number of concepts used in the study were presented.

In the final part of the chapter, a theoretical basis is laid for a discussion of the socio-cultural importance of the private car.

Chapter 2   Global Environmental Aspects

The second chapter provides the study with a global background based upon surveys of current scientific knowledge and on other information. At the same time, the concept of 'environmental sustainability' is given a concrete content in relation to transport. Some global environmental aspects that should be considered by national transport policies are described, based upon the assumption that a high level of car ownership and car use is likely to become a global phenomenon in the following decades (present trends in car ownership and car use in important regions of the world are surveyed). The entire argumentation is based upon the notion of a limited ecospace in terms of available natural resources, the climate system and terrestrial and maritime ecosystems.

In the long term (2020-2050), three threats against the sustainability of existing transport systems were identified: 1/ To provide a growing global fleet of motor vehicles with oil may turn out to be problematic after 2020 if the present trends in increased motorized transport and in discovering new rich oil fields persist. 2/ The consequences of the human impact on the climate (for which the transport sector is partly responsible) may be dramatic in the long term (2020-2050) having a strong impact on transport systems. 3/ Another, indirect, threat to the transport systems, being regional in its effects but global in its occurrence, is constituted by the emissions of various chemical substances from mobile as well as from non-mobile sources. These emissions may initiate developments that reduce the carrying capacity of natural ecosystems as well as the carrying capacity of ecosystems controlled today by human beings. Scenarios associated with any of the threats would have a serious impact on the sustainability of the transport systems.

In the medium term (2005-2020), two possible threats against passenger transport systems are identified. One is associated with the possibility that oil shortages will occur if oil is again used as a political weapon by OPEC (probably increasing its market share above the limit of 50% in the beginning of next century), or if long-lasting military conflicts are initiated in oil producing areas such the Middle East and Central

Asia. Limitations on fossil fuels following on such events will hit the transport sector harder than the oil crises in the 70s, as the share attributable to the transport sector has increased significantly since then. The other threat in the medium term (2005-2020) is represented by the possibility that new scientific knowledge will result in a worldwide consensus that the total emissions of CO_2 and other greenhouse gases must be reduced more rapidly than considered necessary today. In this case, too, politically initiated measures intended to reduce the emissions of greenhouse gases would hit the transport sector seriously.

The conventional development of global energy use will give rise to a prolonged and deep social crisis in the world, according to a future study initiated by the Stockholm Environmental Institute. Therefore, substantial changes in global energy use will be necessary. As to transport, a successive shift from a fossil-fuelled transport system to a non-fossil-fuelled system is estimated, in the present study, to be a process full of problems even if it takes place under favourable conditions. The social shaping of new technological systems has been shown to be a very complex process. Existing technological systems tend to give priority to conservative rather than to radical solutions. The introduction of new energy sources, new energy carriers and new vehicle technology will therefore have to overcome difficult barriers.

Theconclusion was drawn that any solution to the current unsustainable character of existing transport systems cannot be based exclusively on technological innovation, particularly when one considers both the time restrictions and the expected expansion of the global fleet of motor vehicles.

Chapter 3 The Changes of Danish, Dutch and Swedish Transport Policies

The third chapter initiates the empirical part of the study. It was found

- that the national transport policies of Denmark, the Netherlands and Sweden have become less fragmented than before
- that certain themes have been more emphasized in transport policy in the 1990s than in the 1980s
- that the environmental problems have been perceived as more serious than before
- that the package of policy instruments has been somewhat enlarged
- that the internalization of external costs of transport has been much in focus

- that the possibility of enhancing technical development at the European level has been looked upon as a means of reducing the environmental problems of transport
- that the role of integrated transport networks has been regarded as essential for the economic development of Europe and, finally,
- that a greater interest than before has been shown in the implementation and evaluation of transport policies.

The explanations of some of these changes are based on the idea that the interest in a certain transport policy issue fluctuates over time in a cyclical manner. Theories of this kind were presented, separately, by a British and a Dutch scientist in 1987. Three of the major changes in Danish, Dutch and Swedish transport policies are explained as cyclical phenomena in the present study. These issues are the increased interest 1/ in road safety 2/ in upgrading of the railway system and 3/ in expansion and upgrading of road infrastructure (with the exception of Holland). Various factors contributing to this renewed political interest were indicated:

- changed perceptions of the problems of transport
- new technical possibilities
- pressure from lobbying organizations
- a political will to stimulate a weak economy and
- a political will to enhance European integration.

However, the most important change in the transport policies of the three countries is that environmental sustainability was formulated as a new goal in 1990 in Denmark and Holland and somewhat later in Sweden. The introduction of this new issue initiated a new cycle in the transport policies of the three countries. The change is explained by:

- the political importance of the report of the Brundtland Commission
- the alarming experience of the unexpected expansion of the ozone hole above Antarctic leading to the signing of the Montreal Protocol
- the increasing public awareness of the risks of an increased greenhouse effect (studied by IPCC, the Intergovernmental Panel on Climate Change which was established in 1988) and, finally,
- the end of the Cold War around 1990, which provided an opportunity for new approaches to defining the global problems of the future.

A cycle in transport policy consists of five stages, according to one of the theories mentioned above:

1   a pre-problem stage
2   a stage of 'alarming discovery and euphoric enthusiasm'
3   a stage characterized by realising the costs of significant progress
4   gradual decline in interest
5   a post-problem stage.

The new cycle in Danish, Dutch and Swedish transport policies, based on the issue of "sustainability", undoubtedly moved from the first to the second stage around 1990. Its further development in the 1990s can be described as a transition from stage 2 to stage 3.

Chapter 4   Differences between National Transport Policies

At the outset of this chapter, I present the hypothesis that there are only fairly unimportant differences to be found between Danish, Dutch and Swedish transport policies in the period 1987-1997. The reason for this view was that, in the previous chapter, a number of striking similarities in the changes of transport policies had appeared. However, the hypothesis turned out to be false to some extent, as some significant differences were actually identified. After all, no major surprise appeared. In the introductory section, a set of possible explanatory factors were indicated with reference to recent comparative studies of *environmental* policies.

A first significant difference was observed in the transition to a new and more alarming view of the environmental problems of the transport sector. Denmark and the Netherlands made this transition much more rapidly than Sweden. This difference between Sweden, on the one hand, and Denmark and the Netherlands, on the other, is related, primarily, to different political and administrative cultures and procedures, secondly, to the role of Green organizations in the Danish case and to geography in the case of the Netherlands (which being already partly below the present sea level feels more threatened than others by the greenhouse effect).

There were also some significant differences, this time between all three countries, in the national policy-making processes leading to the introduction and formulation of environmental sustainability as a new goal in transport policy. These differences were related to how the new policy was initiated, elaborated and made acceptable to different interests. The definition of environmental sustainability was, on the other hand, almost the same in the three countries. In contrast, it was found that there were certain differences in dealing with the inherent conflict between the goal of environmental sustainability and the traditional goals in transport policy. This conflict was openly admitted and described in Dutch political documents but more or less overlooked or denied in the Danish and Swedish ones.

The identified differences in policy formulation clearly reflected differences in political and administrative cultures. These differences were described in some detail. However, some other factors also seemed to have played a certain role, for instance, in the Swedish case, its weak economic development. The importance of certain actor groups (car industry, transport interests, Green organizations) was found to have varied between the countries, but the influence of such actors on the national policy-making is often difficult to trace.

The selection of intermediate objectives, policy instruments and measures to attain the new goal did not exhibit any significant differences. The only major exceptions to this general rule were found in the Netherlands, where one intermediate objective was to restrain the increase of transport volumes and to develop real alternatives to the private car and where there was a restrictive attitude to the expansion of road infrastructure. These differences were attributed mainly to the high population density of the area.

Concerning the implementation and evaluation of transport policy, there were again significant differences between all three countries. First, the Dutch way of implementing and evaluating was found to be much more refined than the Danish and Swedish counterparts. Second, the Danish way of implementing is much more decentralized than the Dutch one. This decentralization has deep historical roots. Implementation of transport policies in Sweden has become somewhat more decentralized in the middle of 1980s.

The final evaluation of the 'ecological modernization capacity' (EMC), a concept introduced in comparative studies of *environmental* policies, resulted, in the case of the *transport* policies of the three countries, in the conclusion that the Dutch transport policy appeared to be superior to the Danish and Swedish transport policies in terms of *strategic proficiency*, to some extent also in its *innovation capacity* and, finally, in its way of *consensus building*.

The background to the Dutch precedence was found in the Dutch tradition of handling the problems generated by the neighbourhood of the North Sea. The use of the system of canals for various purposes has fostered a political culture of cooperation at the national level.

Chapter 5 The European Dimension

The main objective of this chapter is to explore how and to what extent the Danish, Dutch, and Swedish transport policies have been influenced by European transport policies.

As a background, the general tendencies of harmonizing national transport policies in Europe are surveyed. Apart from spontaneous imitation of the transport policies of other European countries, the influence of the European Conference of Ministers of Transport (ECMT) and that of the transport policy of EC (EU) is studied. The effect of the two first factors is little known today. The question of the influence of the EU's Common Transport Policy is, on the other hand, answered by the present study.

The interpretation of Danish, Dutch, and Swedish transport policy documents of the 1990s indicates that the national politicians express both some fear of losing their independence in transport policy matters and some hope that they will, within the EU, find support for their ambition to enhance environmental sustainability. They exemplify their expectations by referring to harmonized taxes and to harmonized technical standards and emission levels. They also refer to the use of some kind of technology-forcing at the European level to promote the development of energy-efficient and environmentally friendly vehicles in Europe.

The analysis of the policy-making in the Union and of the implementation of its Common Transport Policy showed, however, that there are a number of circumstances which are not in favour of supporting the creation of environmentally sustainable transport systems in the Union. In EU documents, the inherent and unsolved conflict between economic growth and sustainable transport is openly admitted but not analysed in a way which permits the selection of priorities.

The present rules for decision-making are a barrier to policies aiming at reducing the current unsustainability of the European transport systems. Important actors (such as car industries, oil industries and some NGOs) are seldom in favour of a policy for sustainability. These actors are able to interfer with the decision-making within the EU (through lobbying) and with the implementation (by refusing to cooperate).

These general observations were thereafter tested by means of a discussion of some recent issues concerning transport and the environment within EU:

- the suggested harmonization of CO_2 taxes

- the intended reduction of the energy use of the transport sector
- the actual implementation of the Auto Oil Programme aiming at an improvement in the air quality and, finally,
- the desired but not realised strategic environmental assessment (SEA) of the Trans-European Networks (TENs).

It was found that no obvious success was in sight in any of the selected issues.

The general conclusion of the analysis in this chapter is that the national transport politicians have been caught in a kind of a social trap. They cannot solve the problems of current unsustainable transport systems exclusively at the national level

- as the problems are not confined within the national borders
- as the present rules of the Union have set certain limits on the use of environmental laws that can be interpreted as trade barriers and
- as even successful transport policies in some countries are not enough to solve the problem of the unsustainable transport systems in the Union.

At the same time, the national politicians cannot act at the level of the Union

- as a certain proposal may be rejected by reference to the principle of subsidiarity
- that a decision in the Union may have to be unanimous according to the present rules and
- as the implementation of a possible decision may be blocked by influential actors at the European level.

The author therefore claims that the national politicians tend to be unable to develop and implement policies aiming at the construction of sustainable transport systems (the effect of an *institutional failure*). The creation of transport systems in the Union which are efficient, safe, equitable and sustainable in the long term requires, in the view of the author, the allocation of more political power to genuine European institutions such as the European Parliament and the Commission.

Chapter 6 A Critical Evaluation of the Results

In the next chapter, the real outcomes of the national transport policies in Denmark, the Netherlands and Sweden are compared, not with the ultimate goal of environmentally sustainable transport, but with four selected intermediate objectives. The evaluation was based almost exclusively on quantitative data. The limited reliability and comparability of available data necessitated a guarded interpretation.

Two successes were identified. The emissions of NOx had been substantially reduced in the three countries. The primary reason was, of course, the mandatory introduction of catalytic converters. The ultimate cause of this success was, however, the initiative of the US Government to use technology-forcing as a political instrument to solve the problems of certain emissions from motor vehicles. After a substantial time lag, the new technology was introduced in European countries.

The second success story was the reduction of transport *growth* in the Netherlands. This reduction may be seen as a result of the national transport policy. The actual reduction was, however, interpreted as insufficient by the Dutch authorities.

In contrast to the number of successes, the number of failures in relation to the intermediate objectives is substantial. These failures relate to four intermediate objectives and one quantitative target (concerning the emissions of CO_2):

1. Despite the political will to influence the transport volumes (in size and/or distribution among different transport modes)
- transport volumes are still increasing (somewhat less rapidly in the Netherlands)
- car density has been increasing (with the temporary exception of Sweden as an effect of weak economic development in the first half of the 1990s)
- passenger kilometres by car are still increasing
- the share of the public transport versus private transport is not being strengthened (except a minor increase in Holland)
- the role of the bicycle has not been strengthened.

2. Despite the political will to influence the energy consumption of the transport sector
- the use of energy in the transport sector shows a stable upward trend (with a temporary (?) exception in Sweden 1996 and 1997)
- the dominance of fossil fuels is still unbroken
- the per capita emissions of CO_2 are higher than the indicated targets and far from being acceptable from a global egalitarian perspective.

3. Despite the political will to influence the technical standard of the

fleet of motorcars
- the trend towards improved energy efficiency has been broken
- the percentage of cars heavier than 1100 kg is increasing
- the emissions of CO_2 from the transport sector have increased significantly.

4 Despite the political will to influence the environmental adaptation of new infrastructure
- losses of productive soil are still substantial as an effect of the building of new motorways (to a somewhat lesser degree in the Netherlands, where the total losses are, however, impressive)
- the attempts to apply environmental impact assessment in road building have been a failure.

The explanation of these failures is found to be rather complex. It is first reasonable to talk about *government failures* (but in another sense than in the language of economists). In the view of the author, the Danish, Dutch and Swedish governments have failed

- to analyse the inherent conflict between the new goal of environmental sustainability and the traditional goals in transport policy (efficiency, safety and equity)
- to renew the package of policy instruments
- to analyse the barriers to the implementation of the new goal in transport policy and
- to develop an ecological modernization capacity (EMC) in the field of transport and environment.

The present rules of the European Union are also regarded as a factor which does not support the national policies aiming at a reduction of present unsustainability of transport systems. A part of the government failures has therefore its roots in the *institutional failure* of the European Union (see above under chapter 5).

The development of the transport system is not only due to political decisions. The influence of strong actors such as industries, transport companies, trade unions etc has to be taken into consideration. It was found that the way these actors perceive the problems and possibilities of the transport system is an obstacle to a concerted effort to reach the goal of environmental sustainability. Their *interaction failures* are regarded as an additional explanation of the short-comings in transport policy.

In a similar way, the role of ordinary citizens as consumers and voters is interpreted as another explanation of current failures in the field of transport policy. The citizens are not always willing to integrate the alarming information about the transport system, the climate system and the ecosystems into their view of their daily life (a kind of *acceptance failure*). The problems of the "system-world" seem to be distant, while the problems of their own "life-world" are always present.

Chapter 7 Policy Options for the Future

In the final chapter, the author claimed that there are, after all, certain ways of reducing the unsustainable character of present passenger transport at the national level. Some policy options are available immediately but the possible success of a revised national transport policy necessitates the involvement of the ordinary citizens.

It is argued that such an involvement can only be initiated by means of genuine communication between the policy-makers (and their experts) and the ordinary citizens. It is also claimed that such a communication will bring about both dialogues and conflicts. These forms of human interaction may, in their turn, open up new possibilities in transport policy. Four possible policy options were suggested as topics for the communication between policy-makers and the citizens.

The first option deals with how to reduce present speed limits as well as how to reduce the actual speed on different types of roads. It is possible to define an optimum speed in socio-economic sense. This is lower than the actual speed limits in the three countries. The result of a speed reduction would be decreased energy consumption in transport but, at the same time, a certain loss of transport efficiency measured in time. If the new speed limits were not respected, it would be possible, with the assent and political support of those accepting the reduced speed limits, to introduce the compulsory use of technical devices such as cruise control.

The second option is to mobilize ordinary citizens to begin a voluntary transition from fossil fuels to renewable fuels. This change can not be so impressive in the period 2000-2015, as there is no consensus yet as to what kind of alternative fuels should be favoured in the long term. However, a number of alternative fuels will be available on the market in the near future. The most important effect of such an initiative would be to anticipate, mentally, a major change in the time to come. Such a major change cannot be ruled out in the medium term (2005-2020) and seems to be inevitable in the long term (2020-2050).

The third option is to achieve stabilization of transport volumes even in periods of economic growth. This could be achieved through voluntary agreement with the citizens ('a social contract'). If this initiative fails, it would be possible, with the assent and political support of those citizens who were willing to achieve the objective by voluntary means, to introduce sharp economic instruments to cut the increase in passenger transport.

The fourth option is to propagate and support the idea of converting private car ownership to membership of car clubs. This measure would reduce both the transport volumes and the energy consumption substantially even if many car-less people may join the clubs. This change would reduce transport efficiency in some cases (through switching from car use to use of public transport or cycling/walking) and increase the same efficiency in other cases (through reduced congestion). It would also favour road safety and, possibly, increase the equity of the transport system. The total effect would probably be increased social well-being if measured in the entire population. The success of the fourth initiative cannot be secured by compulsory means but can be substantially facilitated by means of economic incentives.

In the final section of the chapter, an attempt is made to map the potential socio-political basis for the suggested policy options. First, it is possible to claim that the core group is constituted by people who are environmentally concerned. Many of these people are members of environmental organizations. It was shown that Danish, Dutch and Swedish environmental organizations have expressed views which seem to be in support of the four suggested policy options.

Secondly, it is claimed that quite a few citizens can be expected to support the same policy options - if their present feeling of being caught in a social dilemma is dispersed by the policy-makers. Some of those who are now suffering from cognitive dissonance in relation to their car use could also be expected to support the same options if they are deeply convinced of the negative effects of an unsustainable transport system. Arguments are presented indicating that women in general seem to show more support than men for transport solutions which entail using other forms of transport than the car. A Norwegian study of lifestyles in transport gives some empirical confirmation of the theoretical arguments used.

Finally, the author claimed that a transport policy revised in the way described seems to be a very important feature in democratic societies confronting "the sustainability transition". Transport policy may even become a paradigmatic case of this process if based upon the involvement and commitment of the ordinary citizens.

Introduction

The background of the study

Since the industrial revolution economic growth has, among many other things, led to a high level of individual mobility and a high level of car ownership in the OECD countries. Increasing individual mobility and growing automobility are therefore two societal phenomena which are closely connected with the development of modern societies. The present trends are expected to continue in the future. There is no level of saturation in sight, not even in the most motorized OECD countries.

Cars, vans, lorries and buses are driven on roads and streets. Today's road transport systems, particularly in highly urbanized regions, are associated with a number of serious problems: increasing congestion, unacceptable levels of road injuries, aesthetic intrusion on sensitive urban and rural environments. To this are added a number of serious environmental effects of traffic on local and regional ecosystems and on the global climate, as well as on local land resources and on the global reserves of natural resources. A high degree of vulnerability to disturbances in energy markets is also typical of the transport sector. The question of the long-term sustainability of present transport systems has therefore aroused increasing scientific and political attention.

In the next few decades, many countries outside the present OECD area are also likely to become more and more motorized, in some countries and regions at a very fast rate. Motorization and automobility may successively become global phenomena. Such a development will create new challenges to the national transport policies in the OECD countries as well, as an increased impact on the biosphere and an expanding demand on global resources of fuels will add new aspects to the problems of the transport sector of each country. A policy for transport systems which are sustainable in the long term is therefore an essential element of any attempt to create favourable global preconditions for what is called 'sustainable development' in the terms of the Brundtland Commission.

The objectives, limitations and focus of the study

Against this background, it is justified to put two questions about the current transformation of national transport policies: how do they change over time and to what extent do they include measures to influence the long-term development of the transport systems in the direction of environmental sustainability?

To answer these questions, one possible approach is to make some case studies. In this study, the cases of Denmark, the Netherlands, and Sweden have been selected. The reason for this selection is primarily that these countries have a good reputation for environmental awareness. They are all members of the European Union, the official transport policy of which is announced in 1992 to promote 'sustainable mobility' (see below 5.2.2).

The time period under scrutiny is the decade from 1987 to 1997, the beginning of the period being the year of the publication of the Brundtland Commission's report *Our Common Future* and the end being the year of the completing of the collection of material for the study (with the exception of the Swedish Government's new bill on transport policy as of March 1998).

The scope of the study is limited in some respects. The first limitation is that it deals exclusively with *passenger transport on land*. There are some doubts if such a limitation is advisable, as freight transport and passenger transport are closely interrelated: cars, buses and lorries are driven on the same roads; it is the total amount of emissions from all sorts of motor vehicles that has an impact on the environment etc. I claim, however, that the role of ordinary citizens is much more important in the field of passenger transport than in the case of freight transport. In my view, this fact requires particular attention to the problems of road passenger transport. This reason has to do with my belief that a solution of the problems of passenger transport, in contrast to the problems of freight transport, necessitates the involvement of the ordinary citizens (the arguments behind this belief will be presented later).

Another limitation of the study is its *concern with national transport policy*. In Denmark, the Netherlands, and Sweden, there is a three-level administrative structure in issues related to transportation: the national level, the regional level (county) and the local level (municipality). This study will focus on the national level, as it is believed that this level is still the most important one in setting and implementing new goals and introducing major changes in transport policy.

Particular emphasis will be put on *the role of the automobile* in the transport system. The reason is the increasing use of cars, which makes it more difficult to solve the problems of present road transport systems.

The main focus of this study will, however, be on the *question of environmental sustainability* of road passenger transport. The empirical background for this emphasis will be elaborated in the following chapter.

Introduction 3

A second important focus is *the European dimension of national transport policies*, as the trend is towards harmonization of national transport policies in Europe. In short, the main objectives of the study are seven:

1 to *analyse the theoretical points of departure* for a study of this kind

2 to identify *the global environmental aspects* that have to be considered by national transport policies

3 to identify, describe and explain *changes in stated transport policies* in Denmark, the Netherlands, and Sweden in the period 1987-1997 focusing on road passenger transport and on the question of environmentalmental sustainability

4 to identify, describe and explain *differences between stated passenger transport policies* in Denmark, the Netherlands and Sweden in the period 1987-1997 (with the focus on environmental sustainability)

5 to explore *the relationship* between national and European transport policies

6 to evaluate *the results of the national policies* in the perspective of environmental sustainability by contrasting stated policies and actual outcomes and to *explain the results* of the evaluation and

7 to identify and describe *some policy options* for promoting the goal of environmentally sustainable passenger road transport in the near future.

The disposition of the book

The book is structured and organized in accordance with these seven objectives. In the first chapter, I describe the scientific setting in which the present inquiry has been carried out and discuss some theoretical points of departure for the following chapters. In the second chapter, I identify global environmental aspects that should be considered by national transport policies aiming at sustainability and illustrate what 'environmental unsustainability' means in relation to transport.

In chapter 3, I present an analytical description of the changes of stated Danish, Dutch and Swedish transport policies in 1987-1997. In chapter 4, I also make a comparative analysis of the stated transport

4 Towards Environmental Sustainability?

policies of Denmark, the Netherlands and Sweden (in the same period). In chapter 5, I discuss the relationship between the national transport policies of the three countries and European transport policy (a concept which has to be defined in the beginning of this chapter). In chapter 6, I evaluate the current transport policies of the three countries and discuss the results and, finally, in chapter 7, I present some suggestions for national policy options in the near future.

1 Theoretical Points of Departure

1.1 Transport policies for environmental sustainability

A comparative, empirical study of national transport policies is a fairly uncommon kind of scientific research. An important exception is represented by a recent study of British and Dutch transport planning and policy (Haq, 1997). The background of the prevailing disinterest in empirical and comparative studies deserves some introductory remarks. The scientific interest in 'sustainable transport' is, on the other hand, increasing. However, the notion of 'sustainable', being today a much disputed concept, needs to be discussed before entering upon my own analysis. These comments will be followed by a survey of some recent studies of 'sustainable transport'. Some remarks on the character of the present inquiry will finish this section.

1.1.1 Transport policies as an object of empirical investigation

It is a remarkable fact that empirical studies of transport policies are fairly rare. By tradition, transportation studies have been decionistic in the sense that they have been carried out on the assumption that better information to decision makers will result in better decisions. A brochure of the Swedish Transport and Communications Research Board (KFB), which is in present use, illustrates this by claiming: 'Politicians and other decision-makers sometimes need information based upon scientific results in order to be able to take the right decisions in due course' (my translation). Transportation studies have therefore been very much dominated by planners, technical and statistical expertise and by economists.

Empirical studies of past and present national transport policies (of the kind represented by chapters 3-6 of the present study) are, thus, not very many. Some publications dealing with Danish, Dutch and Swedish transport policies will be presented in connection with the analysis of current transport policies (in chapter 3).

Transport is often seen as a derived demand in the same way as the amount of passenger and freight traffic is seen as determined by structural factors (people have to move to reach their working places and to different services etc, products have to be moved to the neighbourhood of the consumers etc). It is quite obvious that there are factors beyond the control of transport policy makers which have an impact on the development of transport.

It is therefore possible to study transport policy both as an integrated part of a government's policy and as a sector policy. A reason for the first alternative would be that the objective of transport policy has traditionally been to assist economic growth and social development by reducing transport costs and by making transport more efficient, safe and equitable. Transport policy is therefore closely related to other policy fields such as economic, industrial, regional and social policy. In recent decades, it has also become closely associated with environment policy and energy policy.

Notwithstanding the importance of these facts, I have chosen the second alternative. The reason is, that it would be more difficult to identify changes in transport policies, if they are looked upon as a part of more comprehensive policy packages. And a comparison between transport policies of different countries would be made inoperable. In my analysis, I will, however, refer to environment policy in many cases, as my main focus is the environmental sustainability of transport systems.

Environmental policy has been defined by Lennart J. Lundqvist, a Swedish political scientist, as 'courses of action to regulate polluting activities, to regulate the occupation of space, and to regulate the extraction of raw materials, all with the purpose to prevent the deterioration of, to maintain, or to improve, the quality of the natural environment' (Lundqvist, 1996a, p 16).

Transport policy as a sector policy has been defined by another Swedish political scientist as 'an authoritative allocation of values in society influencing the structure of the transport system and the behaviour of the transport users' (Sannerstedt, 1979). I think that this definition should be modified somewhat to cover the content of transport policies in the 90s. I therefore suggest the following definition: *an authoritative allocation of values (material as well as immaterial) in society influencing the technical standard of vehicles, the development of the transport infrastructure and the behaviour of the transport users.*

Transport policy may be studied as formal policy (the political principles as they are expressed in basic political documents) and as *Realpolitik* (the actual outcome of the policy in terms of budget decisions and other specific decisions). I have chosen the first alternative, as I am looking particularly for significant changes in the perception of the problems of the transport sector, in the formulation of new goals in transport policy and in the views of how to reach these goals. However, I will not completely refrain from assessing the policies under study and I intend to do it by comparing the formal policies with the actual outcome. This assessment will be carried out in the last chapter but one.

As my main interest in this study is the emergence of transport policy for sustainability, I have now to confront the problem of how to define the concept of 'sustainable' in a transport policy context.

1.1.2 The concept of 'sustainability'

It is well-known that the frequent use of the concept of 'sustainability' in political contexts was initiated by the publication of *Our Common Future*, the report of the World Commission on Environment and Development (WCED), commonly known as the Brundtland Commission, in 1987. It is less well known that the term 'sustainable development' was already coined in 1980 by two NGO:s, the International Union for Conservation of Nature and Natural Resources (IUCN) and the World Wide Fund for Nature (WWF) together with the United Nations Environmental Programme (UNEP). In a *World Conservation Strategy*, three objectives for living resource conservation were outlined by these organizations:

- the maintenance of essential ecological processes and life-support systems
- the preservation of genetic diversity and
- the sustainable utilisation of species and ecosystems (quoted from Hardoy et al. 1992, p 177).

The first use of the term 'sustainable development' was therefore based on the idea of environmental sustainability. The report of the WCED, entitled *Our Common Future*, enlarged the concept to include the idea of social and economic sustainability. Its definition of the concept of 'sustainable development' is often repeated: 'to meet the needs of the present generation without compromising the ability of future generations to meet their own needs'. One may therefore distinguish between a broad definition ('socially, economically and environmentally sustainable development') and a narrow one ('environmentally sustainable development'). In political documents, there is a variation in the use of these definitions. The increased political interest in the term 'sustainable development' initiated an intensive scientific debate on how to operationalize the concept. Though many publications on the topic appeared, no clarification was reached by the beginning of the 90s (Lélé, 1991). There is still no clarification in sight.

The scientific interest in the discussion about the definition of the concept now appears to be declining. Some scientists avoid the concept completely as being too vague.

The debate on the definition is complicated by several circumstances. First, if the narrow definition is chosen, then comparatively well-defined criteria or indicators can be formed (for instance, Holmberg et al. 1994). With a broader definition it is difficult to suggest well-defined criteria.

Secondly, some economists (Pierce et al. 1994) have introduced a distinction between 'weak sustainability' and 'strong sustainability' (see also *Climatic Change 1995 - Economic and Social Dimensions of Climate Change*, pp 40sq). Weak sustainability (advocated by some economists) means that any depletion of natural capital will be offset by other forms of natural capital or by various forms of man-made capital. Strong sustainability presupposes, on the other hand, that at least some natural capital cannot be replaced by other forms of capital, and that it must therefore be preserved. Pierce and his collaborators refer to 'the multiple services that natural capital provides', for instance, 'assimilation capacity for industrial wastes, supply of biological diversity, role in modulating climate and maintaining clean air and water, maintenance of fertile soil etc' (*op.cit.* pp 468sq). There are 'no real substitutes' for these services.

In the following discussion, a more detailed distinction has been suggested, namely between 'weak sustainability' and 'very weak sustainability', the latter term meaning that all natural resources can be replaced by human capital in the form of artefacts created from nature. The complementary distinction between 'strong sustainability' and 'very strong sustainability' refers, in the first case, to the necessity of applying the Precautionary Principle as a general rule and, in the second case, to the necessity of establishing a steady state economy in the long term (O'Riordan, 1996).

A third circumstance makes the discussion difficult. Most scientists associate the concept of 'sustainability' with important ethical dimensions. The idea behind this is that one has to consider both intergenerational equity and intragenerational equity in defining what 'sustainable development' really is. Concerning intergenerational equity, the question of time horizon is raised. Intragenerational equity is associated with the allocation of natural resources to the increasing world population (both in terms of energy and materials and in terms of sinks for emissions). This discussion leads to the introduction of the idea of a limited ecospace.

The political problems of what is called the 'sustainability transition' in democratic societies has recently initiated another scientific discussion. It is claimed that, as there is no single way to a sustainable society, it is reasonable to concentrate in politics on the question how to achieve 'a society that is less unsustainable' (O'Riordan, 1996, p 140). I do agree and I will, in the following, focus on how the present unsustainability of the transport sector can be reduced.

Since the UN Conference on Environment and Development in Rio in 1992, it has been emphasized in the political debate that each sector of society should develop in a sustainable way. This turn of the discussion has also increased the interest in discussing 'sustainable transport', as the transport sector is generally regarded as highly unsustainable in its present state. There are, however, some objections to this way of dividing the issue: it is obvious that no sector can be 'sustainable' in isolation. I completely agree, but in the discussion on how to reduce the unsustainability of the transport sector, it is assumed that any changes will take place within the framework of general transition to a 'sustainable society'.

The political interest in 'sustainable transportation' raises the same questions as the case of 'sustainable development'. There is again a choice between a narrow and a broad definition. A narrow definition is, for instance, suggested by Kågeson (1994) and a broad definition by Gudmundsson and Höjer (1996). The broad definition is also preferred by the World Bank *(Sustainable Transport*, 1996) and by the Canadian Centre for Sustainable Transportation *(Definition and Vision of Sustainable Transportation*, 1997).

The concept 'environmentally sustainable transport' (EST) is, however, often used. It has been defined by OECD as: 'Transportation that does not endanger public health or ecosystems and meets mobility needs consistent with (a) use of renewable resources at below their rates of regeneration and (b) use of non-renewable resources at below the rates of development of renewable substitutes' (*Pollution Prevention and Control: Environmental Criteria for Sustainable Transport*, 1996, p 54).

In the following, it is not my intention to contribute to the scientific clarification of the concept but primarily to study how the concept of 'sustainability' is used and defined in political texts. However, in order to investigate the significance of the concept in political texts, I have to present the significance of the concept in my own analytical language. The various reasons why one has to distinguish clearly between the political language and the analyst's own language will be presented below (1.2.3).

My first point is to claim that what is sustainable in transport is not certain artifacts (such as vehicles) but the transport system as a whole. The reason is that the meaning of 'sustainable' refers to some ability of reproduction: a system may be sustainable if its components are replaced over time. An ecosystem such as a forest may be sustainable over long periods if its trees are harvested at the proper time and at appropriate intervals. The influx of solar energy is the driving force behind the sustainable character of the forest. A transport system which is sustainable in the long-term consists of components which can be replaced successively by human actors and is provided with some sustainable energy supply.

Secondly, I will choose the narrow definition of the concept of sustainability, i.e. I will deal only with environmental sustainability. For analytical purposes, there are some advantages in choosing such a narrow definition. Furthermore, to me it is a basic fact that environmental sustainability has to be seen as the very precondition for other forms of sustainability (such as economic, social and cultural sustainability). Accepting the notion of a 'limited ecospace', I also claim that both the question of intragenerational and the question of intergenerational equity has to be founded on the idea of environmental sustainability.

Thirdly, I will take the concept of 'environmental sustainability' in its strong sense. There are, in my view, very good arguments for claiming that there are natural resources that cannot be replaced by alternative natural resources nor by man-made resources. The function of certain important ecosystems and the function of the global climate are such resources. On the other hand, I will not use the concept in the sense of 'very strong sustainability', as I think that this is a question for to-morrow. Today it is, for practical reasons, more important to discuss how to reduce the present unsustainable character of all modern societies.

Finally, I claim that a sharp distinction should be observed between 'a sustainable transport system' and 'sustainable mobility' the concept introduced by the EU Commission in the new Common Transport Policy of the Union (of December 1992). The concepts 'sustainable transport' and 'sustainable mobility' are sometimes taken as synonyms (for instance by Kågeson, 1994). It is, in my view, something quite different to strive for 'sustainable mobility' instead of striving for 'a sustainable transport system', as long as the level of mobility is not defined. As I see it, the level of mobility of peole has to be adapted to the carrying capacity of an environmentally sustainable transport system.

Instead of elaborating a more precise definition of a 'strong environmentally sustainable transport system' I will, in the following chapter, illustrate what 'environmentally unsustainable' really means in connection with transport. I will do this by identifying a number of global environmental aspects that should be considered by national transport policies aiming, in the short term, at the reduction of present unsustainability of transport and, in the long term, at the creation of sustainable transport systems. These aspects are related to the limits of the environment, for instance the air quality, the function of terrestrial and maritime ecosystems, the availability of natural resources (for instance, of fossil energy) and, last but not least, the function of the climate.

There are also some problems associated with this way of arguing. Ecosystems and climate systems change naturally over time but are also influenced by human activities to a greater or lesser degree. Some human influence might reduce the sustainability of the system. One of the difficulties of applying the concept of environmental sustainability is therefore to distinguish between natural and man-made changes of different systems.

Another difficulty has to with the fact that sciences like ecology, climatology and physical resource theory cannot make precise predictions of what will happen when a certain system (for instance, a terrestrial ecosystem) is exposed to serious environmental stress for a long period. They are able to predict that some changes will occur but not when and in what direction. A special source of concern is the fact that the changes in a system may be linear or non-linear. In the second case, it might turn out to be very difficult for human beings to adapt to the new situation. If so, this could compromise the ability of future generations to meet their needs. These facts create a fundamental uncertainty in assessing the environmental problems of transport.

1.1.3 Previous studies of transport policies for environmental sustainability

Studies on the theme of sustainable transport or sustainable mobility represent a new and rapidly expanding field of research, difficult to survey. Two comprehensive bibliographical surveys of such studies have been published by the Library Services of the Transport Research Laboratory in Crowthorne (Berkshire). The first issue (entitled *Sustainability in Transport*) covers the years 1991-1994 and the second issue entitled (*Sustainability in Transport Update*) covers the years 1995-1997. I refer to these surveys which include publications mainly in English. Some of the listed publications will be mentioned briefly here, and others will be added to the British surveys.

In the majority of the publications, different policy options for sustainable transport or planning instruments for sustainable traffic are discussed. Some of the publications are future studies. Very few are empirical studies of actual policies. I begin my presentation with those dealing with policy options at the national level.

An early publication entitled *Transport Policy and the Environment* (Barde and Button, 1990) was initiated by OECD. It contained six national case studies (USA, Western Germany, France, the Netherlands, Greece, and Italy).

In a report entitled *Modifying our volume of traffic: the primary route to sustainable transport* (1992), three British transport researchers, P.B. Goodwin, G.P Parkhurst and G. Stokes, argue that the total volume of traffic should be the primary concern in transport policy. They recommend matching demand to supply through road pricing and claim that environmental costs are real economic costs and that environmental benefits have a real economic value.

In a book entitled *Travel sickness. The need for a sustainable British transport policy* (1992), J. Roberts and some other authors advocate a new coherent transport policy for Great Britain. In the first section of the book, they identify the objectives and targets that have to be reached to achieve a particular quality of life. In the second section, they analyse ways of achieving these objectives and targets. In the final section, they examine particular means of transport and their contribution to the achievement of the objectives. In the very last chapter, John Adams discusses how to move towards sustainable transport policy. The key question is to reduce the demand for motorized transport:'The challenge now is to reverse the process by which we have become dependent on an unsustainable level of mobility. The skills of transport planners should be turned to the task of 'trip degeneration'- reducing the length and number of motorized trips' (*op.cit.* p 332).

Scenarios for road traffic in Britain have been presented by S. Peak and C. Hope in an article entitled *'Sustainable mobility in context. Three transport scenarios for the UK'* (1994). Taking the uncertainly surrounding the plausibility of predicted increases in traffic on UK's motorways, they explore three alternative scenarios and identify (what they regard as) a workable interpretation of sustainable mobility which they translate into a quantitative target scenario for 2025.

A Dutch study has made 25-year projections of the environmental impact of current traffic trends in the Netherlands (van Wee, 1996). A sustainable transport system would require stronger emphasis on both technical and non-technical measures, as present environmental targets will not be met, if present policy is implemented.

A Swedish group headed by P. Steen has analysed the possibility of creating a long-term sustainable transport system in Sweden by 2040 (Steen et al. 1997). The realisation of such a system requires both technical and non-technical measures. Another Swedish study, published by the Swedish Transport and Communication Research Board, presents a scenario entitled *An environmentally sustainable transport system in Sweden* (Brokking et al. 1997).

A Nordic study was initiated in the early 90s by the Nordic Council of Ministers and its Group for Environment and Transport (Jensen, 1993). Here, the problems of the transport sector were analysed in a European and a global perspective. Two strategic options were identified: a system change and the development of present transport systems. The political implementation of strategic measures was discussed.

Some studies deal with the question of sustainable transport at the European level. In a book entitled *Transport for a Sustainable Future. The Case for Europe* (1994), J. Whitelegg emphasizes the necessity of discussing sustainable transport systems in a global perspective (p 11). Stating that a sustainable world cannot be built upon current inequitable patterns of consumption, he argues that sustainability 'involves an equity dimension' (p 6). Many of the arguments in favour of sustainability today are, according to Whitelegg, mere rhetoric and based on the hope that the problems will be solved by means of technology (such as catalytic converters) so that 'changes of behaviour can be avoided' (p 154).

In a paper entitled *'From Growth to Equity and Sustainability: Paradigm Shift in Transport Planning?"* (1992), I. Masser, O. Svidén and M. Wegener analyse the question of European transport futures by setting up three alternative scenarios. One of these is a growth scenario characterized by a high-tech and market-economy-orientation and is associated with the political ideals of many current Conservative governments in Europe in the beginning of the 90s. The second scenario shows the impact of policies that intend to reduce inequalities in society. When these policies are in conflict with economic growth, consideration of equal access and equity is supposed to be given priority. This scenario is associated with policies typical of Social-Democrat governments. The third scenario is based on values such as quality of life and environmental concern. When economic activities are in conflict with environmental objectives, a slower rate of economic growth will be accepted. This scenario is associated with the Green parties.

There are also a number of publications which deal with the question of 'sustainability' in general terms. In a short article, *'Roads toward environmentally sustainable transport'* (1994), P. Nijkamp focuses on the barriers preventing the achievement of policy objectives of reconciling the economic interests of the transport sector with environmental constraints. Empirical evidence from various countries is put forward to demonstrate that current megatrends in transport are completely at odds with a sustainable development and that they also lead to high social costs.

14 Towards Environmental Sustainability?

In USA, the scientific interest is very much focused on technical possibilities of making the energy use of transport more efficient. The American Council for an Energy-efficient Economy has published two studies which are of interest here. One is entitled *Transportation and Energy: Strategies for a Sustainable Transportation System* (Sperling and Shaheen, 1995). A number of energy and vehicle alternatives as well as of alternative fuels and emission reduction policies are reviewed. The role of choices made by citizens, planners and policy-makers is emphasized. In another book, *Transportation, Energy, and Environment: How Far Can Technology Take US?* (DeCicco and DeLucchi, 1997), American experts present analyses of various technical opportunities. They also discuss the prospects for the realization of these opportunities both in the near term and the long term.

The Transportation Research Board has recently published a third study focusing on the environmental effects of motorized transportation: *Towards a Sustainable Future: Addressing the Long-term Effects of Motor Vehicle Transportation on Climate and Ecology* (1997). Here, the complexity of the problems is addressed in an impressive way.

Finally there are two empirical studies of actual transport policies worth mentioning in this context (more studies will be mentioned in chapter 3). An anthology, entitled *Transport, the Environment and Sustainable Development* (Bannister and Button, eds, 1993), includes some analyses of policy responses to the environmental problems of transport in three countries, the UK (D. Banister), the USA (E. Deakin) and the Netherlands (P. Rietveld). Gary Haq's recent book *Towards Sustainable Transport Planning* (1997) aims to 'examine the differences between the national transport and environmental policies of two Member States' (i.e. Britain and the Netherlands) within the policy framework provided by the European Union (p 55).

1.1.4 The character of the present study

Most of the publications mentioned can be classified as analyses of policy options. As already indicated several times, there are very few empirical studies of national transport policies. The present study is an empirical and comparative analysis of Danish, Dutch and Swedish transport policies in the 1990s. Such a study can be carried out in various ways.

Transportation studies constitute a multi-disciplinary field of research, but few studies in this field are interdisciplinary in the sense that their authors draw on different traditions of methodology and theory. The present study belongs, however, to this last category. To me, such an approach is quite natural, as I have been involved in interdisciplinary cooperation for the last 25 years and was a professor of the new interdisciplinary field of Human Ecology for about ten years. The focus of this scientific field is the relationship between human societies and nature. Transport and mobility are important aspects of this relationship.

This study is somewhat untraditional in another sense, too, as it is based upon an outspoken humanistic attitude 1/ to human beings 2/ to human society and 3/ to nature.

The first statement means that I do not believe that future actions of human beings are predictable on the basis of their position in a social structure or their belonging to a certain culture. It is impossible to knowhow they will adapt to new situations, how they may rethink the ways of solving problems and how they may change their values and their ways of living when confronted with new problems. Making projections based on models of present human behaviour is, in my view, of limited interest.

The second statement means that the author does not believe in any grand theory of societal change. In my view, it is necessary to handle the intellectual analysis of societal processes in a less ambitious way. What I mean by this will be elaborated below (1.2.1-1.2.2).

The third statement means that the author has an anthropocentric view of man's place in nature. Admitting that human beings are part of nature and that the well-being of other species should be seen as important to members of the human species as well, I claim that human beings have certain rights ('human rights') and duties that other species do not have. Among other things, the responsibility for the future of the ecosystems belongs only to human beings.

1.2 Theory and method

I will start each of the following chapters by discussing my approach to the themes they present from the theoretical and methodological point of view. In this introductory chapter, I will deal with some more general theoretical and methodological aspects which are, implicitly or explicitly, referred to in the book. I will deal with how to understand historical change (1.2.1), how to understand societal processes of change (1.2.2), and how to interpret political texts, which is my basic methodological approach (1.2.3). In the central passage of this paragraph, I will discuss how to analyse the strategic content of political exts describing transport policies (1.2.4). Finally, I will consider the theoretical aspects of the social and cultural role of the automobile, as I regard its present use as the key problem of transport policy (1.2.5).

1.2.1 Understanding historical change

The development of transport systems and transport policy-making are elements of historical processes. Some theoretical idea of historical change is therefore necessary. As I indicated above (1.1.4), I am sceptical about grand theories - be they non-Marxist or Marxist - pretending to be able to explain historical change. I think that it is necessary to have less ambitious aspirations when confronting the complexity of social, economic, and cultural change.

In my view, the macro-sociological idea of modernization, today very much in vogue, offers an adequate framework for understanding the history of Western societies during (at least) the two last centuries as well as the history of developing countries today. This concept describes (but does not explain) processes of change characterized by a transition from a traditional, rural and agrarian society to a rationalistic, urban and industrial society.

I referred to this transition in the very first paragraph, where I described the background of my study very briefly, stating that increasing individual mobility and increasing automobility are two phenomena closely linked to the process of modernization. Later in this chapter, I will touch upon the same concept when I discuss concepts such as 'quality of life' and 'lifestyle'.

There is, however, no consensus among sociologists on what 'modernization' and 'modernity' really is. I think that this lack of consensus does not exclude the use of these concepts for descriptive purposes. An interesting approach to such a descriptive use is to be found in a recent study of European modernity written by the Swedish sociologist G. Therborn. His book is entitled *European Modernity and Beyond. The Trajectory of European Societies 1945-2000* (1995).

Therborn identifies four different types of modernization processes. The European one is characterized by class conflicts. The modernization of North and Latin American has rather been a story of political emancipation from England and Spain/Portugal. A third type of modernization is exemplified by Japan, where local elites have been able to modernize the country in a politically independent way. The fourth type of modernization is found in previous colonies, where local elites have been the instruments of foreign political and economic interests promoting a partial modernization.

The modernization process, initiated in Europe towards the end of the 18th century, is now spreading worldwide. The much debated question of 'development' can be translated into 'modernization'. At the same time when modernity is beginning to be globalized, the whole process of modernization is being exposed to critical passages associated with the globalization of economy and the increasing negative impact on the global environment. It is motivated to talk about 'a crisis of modernity'.

Quite a few sociologists take the view that the beginning of a crisis is already here. *The Encyclopaedia Britannica*, which can be supposed to represent some common view of sociologists, describes this character of modernity as follows: 'Since its inception, modernity has worn two faces. One is dynamic, forward-looking, and progressive, promising unprecedented abundance, freedom, and fulfilment. The other, equally visible face is grim, revealing the new problems of alienation, poverty, crime and pollution'.

In the present historical situation, some unpleasant details of the negative side of modernity are clearly visible.

1.2.2 Understanding societal processes of change

To understand and explain societal processes is the key question in social science. A never-ending discourse on the role and importance of 'actors' (agents) and 'structures' has been going on for decades among scientists. It is not necessary, however, to look upon these concepts as mutually exclusive. Actors and their actions may be analysed in terms of structures. Structures may be analysed in terms of actors. If so, actors are seen as part of structures and structures as parts of actors. Normally, however, structural analysis and studies of actors are carried out in separate projects.

This can be exemplified by the ongoing sociological discussion of modernity and modernization. According to an interpretation made by the German sociologist U.Beck in the book *Risk Society. Towards a New Modernity* (1992), ongoing modernization leads to unintended risks. He claims that present modernity is therefore reflexionfree, a kind of autonomized modernization (Beck, Gaudiness and Lash, 1994, p 176). His opponent, the British sociologist A.Giddens, takes the view that 'the more societies are modernized, the more agents (subjects) acquire the ability to reflect on the social conditions of their existence and to change them in that way' (*ibid.*). He also says that 'individuals have become ever more free of structure; in fact they have to redefine structure or, even more radical, reinvent society and politics' (*op.cit.* pp 176sq). I will return to Giddens' ideas later in this chapter as well as in the final chapter.

My own study is mostly actor-orientated, but the role of structures will also be taken into consideration. The kinds of actors dealt with are national governments, political parties, local political authorities and national agencies, trade unions, NGO organizations, international organizations etc. Such actors represent collective units of action, conceptually found between the level of social structures and the level of individual actors. A collective actor is characterized by a shared interpretation of reality and a programmatic orientation towards a common goal. Through the coordination of the actions of their individual members, societal actors are provided with an action potential which may be used in concrete activities leading to a specified goal, which has, as a rule, to be compatible with the values embraced by the organization in question.

The actions of these collective actors are based upon their views of the world. According to a theory developed by some French social psychologists with S. Moscovici as the leading name (for an introduction to the theory in Swedish see M. Chaib and B. Orfali, 1996), these views can be seen as 'social representations' of the real world. The theory says that people create their social representations through communication with other people in order to understand and master the world. Their representations are based upon experience and are associated with models for thinking and acting which are typical of the social environment to which the individuals belong. The social interaction consists of everyday communication between ordinary people but also of institutional communication in school, professional life, politics and mass media. The patterns of thought which are developed are typical of different social classes, professional groups and geographical environments. They have been shaped (through omissions, additions and perversion) in a way that satisfies the needs and interests of the group and they are not exposed to the kind of critical scrutiny that scientific statements usually are. Once the social representation of a certain phenomenon is created, it is mostly sustained by means of feelings of sharing the same social experience. Social representations of political questions are often articulated in political texts.

1.2.3 Interpreting political texts

Political texts have a rhetorical character. Their aim is to convince and persuade the readers or listeners about the views of the politicians and their parties. To convince is to appeal to somebody's intellect, to persuade is to appeal to somebody's feelings. In classical rhetorical theory, there was no clear distinction between these two concepts (in Latin, *persuadere* means both 'convince' and 'persuade').

The interpretation of a political text produces, therefore, information about how the politicians want to be understood: what perceptions they pretend to have of current problems and other circumstances, what goals they pretend to strive for, what kind of policy instruments they pretend to be willing to use and, possibly what results they believe (or say that they believe) will follow from their policy.

Political documents are produced in a certain context and with a certain aim. They are parts of the policy-making process, and they are often very interesting from the point of view of the history of political ideas. The wording of the texts has sometimes been elaborated by civil servants, but the politicians are, of course, responsible for the content. The interpretation of political texts is hampered by some theoretical and methodological difficulties (Vedung, 1977 and Vedung, 1982). First of all, it is important to distinguish between the political language and the language of the analyser. Political language is characterized by its tendency to prefer statements which can be given manifold meanings. Furthermore, its semantic content is very complex: it is informative, evaluative, prescriptive and performative. The analyser's language, on the other hand, is characterized by its way of questioning and of answering the questions and by the theoretical perspective chosen. Its semantic content is mostly informative and evaluative, in some exceptional cases, also prescriptive.

An analysis of a political text is either content-orientated or functionalistic. The first kind of analysis is concerned with the clarity, logic, relevance, consistency of the ideas embedded in the text and with their empirical validity. The purpose of the functionalistic analysis is to explain the occurrence and origin of the ideas mentioned in political texts.

The analysis of this study is both content-orientated and functionalistic. Its aim is to find out *how* formal transport policy was expressed in political documents in Denmark, the Netherlands, and Sweden in the period 1987-1997 and to explain *why* stated transport policies changed in this period and *why* there are some differences between the national transport policies of the three countries. For both purposes, it is necessary to focus on what can be identified as the strategic elements of the policies.

1.2.4 Identifying the strategic elements of transport policies

In order to get hold of the significant features of a textual presentation of a transport policy, it is important to focus on the strategic elements of the policy in question. The concept of 'strategy' is, originally and etymologically, a military term. It is traditionally defined as consisting of 'conceptions of means and ends'. The strategic elements of formal policies (in this case transport policies) are, I will claim, four:

1. The perception of the problems of the transport sector.
2. The formulation of goals and targets intended to eliminate or reduce the problems perceived.
3. The selection of what kind of means should be used in order to reach the goals and attain the targets.
4. Expressed views of how to implement and evaluate the policy.

In the following, I will discuss the theoretical aspects of these four elements of political strategies.

The perception of the problems of transport. In the perspective of cognitive sociology, there is no such thing as an undisputable fact. Facts are seen as social constructs. A complete relativism must not follow from such a view. It is true that all facts have been constructed in a socially and historically conditioned context and we cannot get out of this context. But any statement, any interpretation of reality claiming validity is open to testing, and there are social procedures ensuring the validity. In brief, 'facts' in astrology are not the same as 'facts' in astronomy.

This view, applied to transport policy, means that current perceptions of the problems of transport are the result of a social construction process in which many actors may have taken part: scientists, transport experts, vehicle producers, transportation stakeholders, green actors, and, last but not least, the media. Such views may be parts of the social representations typical of different social groups (see above 1.2.2). The result of the social construction of problems in transport is the existence of different perceptions of the problems which compete with each other.

The formulation of goals in transport policy. The formulation of goals and objectives in transport policy is a genuine political task. Political goals have very much to do with ideology and values. One of the questions to be addressed in this study is to what extent present transport policies in Denmark, the Netherlands, and Sweden are based upon a distinct ideology.

The overriding goal of transport policy is often said to be mobility (compare the present goal of the Common Transport Policy of the European Union: sustainable mobility). Mobility is hardly a goal in itself, but rather a means to reach other objectives in life (for instance, a necessary condition for a flexible labour market, a fair distribution of public service, a rich supply of leisure activities etc). It is reasonable, therefore, to claim that the overriding goal of transport policy is not mobility, but accessibility. This view is also sometimes expressed in political documents (see, for instance, below 3.3.3). In my view, however, it is possible to boil down the traditional goals in transport policy to only three:

1 Efficiency - defined as minimizing the costs in money and time to reach one's destination.

2 Safety - defined as minimizing the risks of transport both for those transported and those exposed to the effects of transportation (in this concept I include minimizing negative health effects of traffic emissions and traffic noise).

3 Equity - defined as maximizing the access to various destinations for individuals of different ages, gender, income, residence and physical status.

The goal of 'accessibility' is, according to my interpretation, included in the combined goals of equity and efficiency.

New goals may be added to the traditional ones. In recent times, goals related to the protection of the environment have been added. An increasing number of goals may lead to a growing number of possible conflicts between different goals.

Politicy goals are sometimes operationalised and translated into timetabled quantitative targets. The reduction of the emissions of a certain substance from the transport sector by a certain percentage before a certain time limit is an example of such a target.

The selection of intermediate objectives, concrete measures and policy instruments. The implementation of a policy can sometimes be based on certain intermediate objectives. Transport policy is no exception. Influencing the modal split is an example of a usual intermediate objective. To reach the ultimate goal and the intermediate objectives requires, however, always the use of concrete measures and policy instruments.

It is impossible to introduce a sharp distinction between concrete measures and policy instruments. The reason will appear in a moment. Here, I will present my own classification of concrete measures and refer to a classification of policy instruments recently suggested by a political scientist. In accordance with the definition of transport policy (see above 1.1.1), I will claim that there are:

1. Measures intended to influence the current technical standard of vehicles and the technical development of such vehicles (these measures are often called "technical fixes").

2. Measures intended to influence the standard and structure of the transport system as a part of the urban and regional structure (these measures are sometimes called "planning fixes").

3. Measures intended to influence the behaviour of transport users.

In the first group I include a/ the spreading of best available technology (BAT) and b/ the influencing of technological development by means of publicly funded research or by means of so-called "technology-forcing" (exemplified by the development of the catalytic converter through the action of the US government and the present conditions for the sale of zero emission vehicles in California). Rules for public purchasing can be used to influence the technological development indirectly. In the second group I include ordinary urban and regional planning (physical planning) but particularly the planning of transport infrastructure (including investments in systems for public transport). The third group consists of taxes, fees, subventions, various regulations and information. In my view, these measures should be seen simultaneously as policy instruments.

In a recent article, the Swedish political scientist E.Vedung points to the fact that the question of policy instruments is 'neglected in the research and discourse of political science and public administration' (Vedung, 1998). After having reviewed some possible approaches to the categorization of policy instruments, he suggests 'a trifold scheme of regulation, economic means and information'.

Regulation is divided by Vedung into subcategories such as prescriptions and proscriptions (i.e. prohibitions of various kinds). Economic means include incentives (grants, subsidies, reduced-interest loans, credits etc) and disincentives (taxes, fees, tariffs etc). Information as a policy instrument can be 'transmitted' in a mediated way (through television, radio, newspapers etc) and in an interpersonal way.

In transport policy, economic disincentives are frequently used: 1/ vehicle taxes (acquisition taxes and annual ownership taxes) 2/ fuel taxes 3/ mileage taxes or fees ("road pricing") 4/ road tolls and 5/ parking fees. These instruments have very different advantages and disadvantages. Fuel taxes are a perfect instrument for dealing with the problem of carbon dioxide, as the emissions of this substance is proportional to the fuel consumed. Road pricing has the advantage of being a flexible instrument for internalizing many external costs, which may differ in time and space, such as local pollution, congestion and noise.

A similar classification has been suggested by the Danish political scientist P.Munk Christiansen. He distinguishes between legal, economic and informative instruments but adds voluntary agreements, for instance with industry (Christiansen, 1996b, p 92).

Views expressed on the implementation and evaluation of the policy. The implementation of a policy is the crucial part of the political process. Its success is dependent primarily on the political feasibility and the efficiency (including cost-efficiency) of selected measures and policy instruments and on the administrative efficiency of the national agencies and regional and municipal political bodies which are expected to carry out the policy in practice. Government failures are therefore not rare in this area. (see e.g. Himanen, Nijkamp and Padjen, 1992). Secondly, the implementation process is influenced by different barriers to the policy.

There are, in my view, barriers of three different kinds to transport policies for sustainability (Tengström et al. 1995, pp 103sq). Structural barriers are the first category. All technological systems have a certain inertia in their very construction. This means that it is difficult and time-consuming to introduce alternative technologies, even if this would be an unanimous wish of all relevant actors. It has been estimated that it would take around 30 years after a strategic decision to convert the present car fleet into one running on some alternative fuel (Svidén see Tengström, 1992, p 110). A technical system may also be seen as socio-technical one with strong well entrenched professional and financial interests defending its existence and its way of defining and solving problems (Bijker et al. 1987).

The second kind of barrier is actor-orientated. Collective actors in the field of transport demonstrate, often openly, that they are far from enthusiastic about certain elements of a government's transport policy. They do everything to 1/ avoid a certain issue being put on the political agenda 2/ influence the decision-makers during the policy-making process (through lobbying) and 3/ obstruct the implementation of an actual decision. The power of obstructing actors is not insignificant (Flyvbjerg, 1991 and Flyvbjerg, 1998).

The third kind of barrier might appear when political decisions aim at changing the use of the automobile. These barriers have to do with the social and cultural embeddedness of the motor car. Ideas of restricting the role of the car in the transport systems are often met by very negative attitudes from the general public and from the associations organizing the interests of the car owners. The practical usefulness of the car is not the only reason behind their resistance. The symbolic meaning of the car and its use has a certain value in our culture. There are, therefore, good reasons for going deeper into the question of the cultural embeddedness of the automobile (see below 1.2.5)

The implementation of a political decision has to be evaluated. Two different paradigms in the implementation and evaluation of transport policy and planning have been identified (Flyvbjerg, 1984). One called 'programmed implementation' draws on natural sciences and is mainly expert-orientated. It emphasizes the advantages of high accessibility over long distances in an overall one-mode transportation system. The other paradigm, 'adaptive implementation' draws on social sciences and builds upon the idea that the transport users should be active participants in the process with an influence on both implementation and evaluation. The method is mostly applicable in relation to specific problems at the local level.

1.2.5 Analysing the role of the car, the key problem of transport policy

Transport policies aiming at the creation of efficient, safe, equitable and environmentally sustainable passenger transport systems are, above all, confronted with the problem of the increasing use of private cars. I therefore see the present role of the car as the key problem of transport policy strategies and I have analysed some aspects of this problem in my previous studies (see below).

In the following analysis of the transport policies of Denmark, the Netherlands, and Sweden, I intend to focus very much on how the problem of increasing car use is perceived and what policy conclusions are drawn from this. In this part of the introductory chapter, I will, therefore, dwell upon some theoretical aspects of studies of the role of the car in society and culture.

The role of the car in society and culture. During the last few years, it has become an accepted notion that a car is something more than a vehicle that can be used for the rational and comfortable transport of people. Important steps in elaborating this view can be credited to the American researcher James Flink (particularly in the book *The Car Culture*, 1975) and to the German researcher Wolfgang Sachs (the English version of his book is entitled *For Love of the Automobile. Looking*

Back into the History of Our Desires, 1992 - the German edition already appeared in 1984). Important contributions have recently been made, for instance, by Liniado (1996) and Hagman (1999). The private car may represent and symbolize such cultural values as status, freedom, togetherness, masculinity, wealth, youth etc. The social and cultural embeddedness of the car is to day an established scientific fact.

This embeddedness represents, however, a strong barrier to a necessary change of its role in future transport systems. This fact raises questions about the role of the automobile in what is seen as 'quality of life' as well as in current lifestyles and lifestyle changes.

The automobile and quality of life. Indicators of a high standard of living traditionally include statistics on car ownership in a country. The average individual mobility can also be quoted as an indicator of a high standard of living and asa result of modernization. The car ownership of a country is mostly proportional to the GDP/capita, at least in market economies. Present car use is also closely associated with modern views of what is 'quality of life'.

This concept was introduced in the political debate in Europe in 1974. (For instance, the French government established a Department for quality of life in that year). The aim of using the concept was to highlight the fact that real welfare could not be described exclusively in quantitative material terms. Those who attempted to define the new concept in a more precise way never reached any consensus. Still, 'quality of life' is, in my view, usable as a descriptive concept to indicate that there are elements of welfare and well-being that cannot be easily translated into quantitative material terms.

It does not seem to be impossible to develop indicators describing the impact of car use on the quality of life (but this is beyond the scope of this study). Without having access to such indicators, it can anyhow be assumed that individual access to a safe, well-functioning and comfortable car is an important element in the quality of life in the view of modern man. The high level of mobility by car is a means of reaching various places of interest influencing the individual professional and private life. The car brings him/her there and may also offer some joy during the trip. Some people even seem to be emotionally involved in their individual cars (in contrast to their feelings for other artifacts such as washing-machines and TV-sets).

In a unified Europe, the role of individual mobility and car use will certainly become a frequent issue. In a survey of the transport policy of the Union, the concept of 'quality of life' is used in a description of the future problems of passenger transport:'Community citizens are also demanding a quality of life which includes easy travelling across borders, a high level of safety, and last but not least, more environmentally friendly modes of transport. These expectations have to be met at all levels of decision' (Schinas and Vinois, 1993, p 146).

At the same time, however, the development of a transport system heavily based upon automobiles can be assumed to reduce the quality of life of many people. Noise from the vehicles, the creation of barriers through the construction of new roads, new threats to the safety of their children are some of the negative factors influencing the quality of life of many citizens.

Another aspect of the relation between transport in general and the quality of life was discussed by Torsten Hägerstrand, the famous Swedish geographer, in a paper entitled *'Transport in the 1980-90 decade - The impact of transport on the quality of life'* (1974). In this paper, Hägerstrand claims that an average of 9 hours is used daily used for sleep and personal care, 1 hour for eating, 8 hours for work and about 2 hours for private administration, care of private property and similar activities. Time for mobility has to be taken from the remaining 4 hours. Thus, transport has to compete with activities such as social intercourse and other leisure activities (reading, theatre performances, concerts).

Thus, a high level of mobility accomplished by means of cars is, in my view, not only a part of the quality of life but also represents a threat to other important aspects of the same quality of life, for instance to the life outside the vehicles. A similar opinion was expressed by the British Royal Commission on Environmental Pollution (1994). It was claimed that it is necessary 'to improve the quality of life, particularly in towns and cities, by reducing the dominance of cars and lorries and providing alternative means of access' (quoted from Haq, 1997, p 77).

The automobile and lifestyles. A private car may also be associated with the lifestyle of its user. Introduced in the scientific literature by the psychologist Alfred Adler and the sociologist Max Weber in the beginning of this century, the concept of 'lifestyle' was never in frequent use before the 1960s. At that time, some environmentalists began to talk about the necessity of creating "alternative lifestyles" for the sake of the environment. The concept was, however, soon appropriated by marketing people for advertising purposes.

Today, there is a somewhat hesitant attitude to the use of the concept in modern social science. Some scientists avoid the concept completely. Others continue to discuss its definition. There seem, however, to be some common elements in suggested definitions. The concept includes a unifying aspect (some consistency is assumed between different aspects of the objects to which the concept of 'lifestyle' is referring), a differentiating property (one lifestyle can be distinguished from another) and, finally, lifestyle is closely related to comprehensive patterns of behaviour (Uth, 1996).

In my own use of the concept, I will follow the definition of the concept proposed by two Swedish sociologists, Lööv and Miegel. They distinguish between three different but interrelated levels at which aspects of human life can be studied in terms of 'lifestyles': a structural level, a positional level and an individual level (Lööv and Miegel, 1989).

At the structural level, they are able to identify differences between countries, societies or cultures. They use the term 'ways of living' when referring to such collective lifestyles (think, for instance, of "the American way of living"). The second level, the positional level, concerns differences between classes, groups, subcultures etc in a given social structure. Here, they use the term 'forms of life' to indicate the collective lifestyle of some social category (think, for instance, of "the bourgeois form of life"). Finally, at the individual level, human beings express their personality and identity. Here, Lööv and Miegel use (individual) 'lifestyle' as their term of reference (think, for instance, of examples such as "Mr A has a lifestyle which is threatening his health").

Lööv and Miegel believe that all lifestyles express different kinds of human values. They distinguish between outer-orientated values (material and aesthetic values) and inner-orientated values (ethical and religious/metaphysical values). At the structural level, there is a (maybe very limited) number of common basic values serving as the basis for human interplay and coexistence. At the positional level, there are, instead, considerable variations in values between different social groups. At the individual level, the variations of values are, of course, innumerable.

To me, this way of defining 'lifestyle' makes it a useful concept. It makes analyses of complex cultural patterns feasible. I only want to add that lifestyle in the sense indicated above can often be recognized by an external observer. As we can recognize a person's handwriting by means of a kind of pattern recognition, we are also able to recognize individual lifestyles as well as collective lifestyles (at the structural and positional levels) by a similar pattern recognition.

It is not so common in current social science to link lifestyle to patterns of mobility and car use. To me, however, it is evident that car use and degree of mobility cannot be excluded from the description of both collective and individual lifestyles. A definition of travel-related lifestyle has recently been offered by a Danish sociologist, Thyra Uth: 'the individual's pattern of those cognitions, emotions and actions connected with personal transportation that contribute to the personal and social identity of the individual' (Uth, 1996, p 541). This definition may be easily applied to the three levels identified by Lööv and Miegel: A certain car use may, for instance, be seen as an expression of the American way of living, or of a middle class lifestyle or of a certain person's individual lifestyle.

The very fact of car ownership may serve the purpose of expressing one's lifestyle. It is a well-known fact that a material product can be used to communicate messages to other people (see, for instance, Berge, 1995). An artifact has to have three properties to be used in this way. First, it has to be visible to external observers. Secondly, the artifact has to be available in variable forms in order to have a differentiating function. Finally, it has to be able to be given a personal touch, i.e. it can be used to denote a standardized image of the user.

To communicate the message about one's *individual lifestyle*, I believe that all these three properties of the car are activated. The car not only makes its owner visible in the street or on the road, but it also has something to say about the owner's social position and, under certain circumstances, about the owner's personal identity. The car owner's *lifestyle at the positional level* is indicated primarily by the visibility of the car but, above all, by the differentiating function of its make. Finally, *the collective way of life* in a given society may be realised by the visibility of one's private car: in USA, for instance, a person who is seen moving without a car will be interpreted as behaving in an untypical, non-American way. In the Soviet Union, ostentatious use of a private car was once interpreted as anti-Soviet behaviour.

The automobile and lifestyle changes. The most problematic aspect of the concept of 'lifestyle' is that it is not linked to any well-developed social theory presenting an idea of a mechanism behind changes of lifestyles. There are, however, some sociological approaches of interest.

Lifestyle changes have been associated by sociologists with the invention of basically new technical artifacts. The invention of the car is a classical example of such a lifestyle change (Berner, 1981). With access to a car, people were able to develop new, more flexible and mobile lifestyles than before.

Lifestyles changes are, more generally, believed by sociologists to be initiated by imitation (Lindén, 1994). Lifestyles can be transferred from well-to-do people to less privileged people, and, in another structural dimension, from men to women of a similar social class. Lifestyles are, however, mostly transferred between generations, from elderly people to young people (today also vice versa?).

The expansion of car use, typical of a modernized society, has been attributed to imitation (Lindén, 1994). Lifestyle changes are initiated through imitation at all levels (in the sense of the definition proposed by

Lööv and Miegel).A whole society may, at a certain historical date, imitate foreign lifestyles based on car-use (for instance Japan under the American occupation after World War II, see Plath, 1990 and Maruo, 1992). Social groups often imitate, for instance in car ownership, the lifestyles of other groups ranking higher in the societal hierarchy. Young male individuals sometimes try to imitate some film idol (for instance, imitating the way the hero of the film drives his car).

The lifestyle of an individual changes during his/her lifetime. This also applies to automobile use. The role of the car in the years of childhood, teenage and youth and in the family life of middle-aged people has been studied in an empirical Swedish study (Heurgren, 1995). The analysis was made from a gender perspective and was based on interviews with people belonging to the middle class. The importance of the car for their lifestyle was found to vary significantly over time.

Are there any indications of increasing interest among ordinary people to problematize their present lifestyles? In his book *Modernity and Self-Identity* (1991), the British sociologist Anthony Giddens takes the view that some people have initiated what he calls 'the reflexive project of the self'. According to Giddens, it is therefore motivated to talk about 'life politics' at the level of the individual: 'Grappling with the threats of the earth's ecosystems is bound to demand coordinated global responses on levels far removed from individual action. On the other hand, these threats will not be sufficiently countered unless there also is reaction and adaptation on the part of every individual' (*op.cit.* p 222).

In my interpretation of these ideas, new lifestyles which are formed by reflexive actions are probably based more upon 'inner-orientated' values than on 'outer-orientated' values (in the terms of Lööv and Miegel). In relation to car use, for instance, this means that such lifestyles changes would possibly reduce number of car-dependent people in a given population.

In the present debate on changes in the transport systems, lifestyle changes are sometimes mentioned as necessary elements in a process of transformation. Let me quote just one example from a report published by OECD and the European Conference of Ministers of Transport (ECMT) on *Urban Travel and Sustainable Development* (1995): '*lifestyles* (the italics are mine) and technology of western countries and the direction of the development in the rest of the world will have to change' (p 19).

Such lifestyle changes are, however, difficult to link to the political alternatives of today. Giddens takes the view that 'life-political problems do not fit readily within existing frameworks of politics, and may very well stimulate the emergence of political forms which differ from those hitherto prominent, both within states and on a global level' (*op.cit.* p 228).

1.2.6 My own previous studies of the role of the car

During the last decade, I have spent some time on studies of the role of the car in society. In my first contribution to this theme, a book entitled *The Use of the Automobile: its Implications for Man, Society and the Environment* (1992), I tried to define and describe this comprehensive field of research in a worldwide perspective.

After this I turned to the political aspects of car use. In an empirical study, entitled *Private Cars and Political Decision-makers. An Historical Survey and a Critical Review of Current Transport Policy* (1993) and, based on secondary sources, I analysed how political decision-makers in the history of selected countries have looked upon the automobile and how they have responded to the problems associated with its use. I found that the politicians in many countries were sceptical, from the very beginning, to the spreading of motor cars but that they, as a rule, accepted the innovation not later than 1910. They confined their own role in relation to private cars to reducing the number of road accidents by issuing laws and other regulations for car use and to expanding the road infrastructure by using their right of taxation (in contrast to the expansion of railway systems, which were often financed by private money).

Under these circumstances, car use expanded rapidly in the USA between the two world wars. In some European countries, the politicians supported motorization but only that of the middle class (for instance, in the UK), while in others (such as Nazi Germany), they consciously stimulated the spreading of cars to others than well-to-do people as a way of reducing class conflict (the idea of '*das Volkswagen*' was intensively propagated by Adolf Hitler). In the Communist countries, on the other hand, the politicians tried to restrict car use and to keep it as a privilege for a small political and administrative elite.

After World War II, mass automobility was accepted and stimulated by the politicians in most Western European countries. In some countries (Britain and Norway are two examples), the politicians still hesitated, for different reasons, in the 50s but accepted the mass use of the car around 1960. During this decade, the attitude of the Soviet regime also changed to private cars and their production was increased. The same applies to Japan. In the late 50s, the car industry, also stimulated by the Japanese government, began to build up its production capacity, and great schemes for the building of motorways were initiated by the same government in the 60s.

After the second half of the 1960s, when the awareness of the difficult problems caused by mass mobility increased, the politicians of the US introduced technology-forcing as a new instrument in transport policy. In European countries, the politicians made more use of economic incentives to influence the technology of cars, the size of the car fleet and the use of cars.

In the final part of this study, I analysed a number of official documents on transport policy from different countries and continents, all dating from the years 1989-1992. This enabled me to claim that the politicians of that time were well aware of the increasing problems of road transport, but that they seemed to be unable to elaborate well-structured strategies to meet these challenges. As a general rule, they also seemed to pay too little attention to the implementation of their transport policies and how the barriers to this implementation could be overcome.

In the second empirical study, which I made in collaboration with Elisabet Gajewska and Marie Thynell, entitled *Sustainable Mobility in Europe and the Role of the Automobile. A Critical Inquiry* (1995), we took the Common Transport Policy of the European Union (of December 1992) as our starting-point for a study of the implementation of the Common Transport Policy.

Actors (political, industrial, NGOs etc) relevant to the transport policy in Europe were identified. The perceptions of these actors were analysed concerning the problems of road transport, as well as their views on the goals of transport policy and the measures to be used to implement the policy. The analysis focused on the role of the automobile in the transport systems.

We found that the present situation of road transport in Europe could be seen as an *interaction failure*, i e the most important actors in the field of transport have not been able, in their own interest, to initiate a process leading to the creation of efficient, safe and sustainable transport systems. One of the origins of this interaction failure was lack of agreement in the actors' perceptions of the problems. I will return to these ideas later in the present study (in chapters 5 and 6).

2 Global Environmental Aspects

2.1 The objective, sources and disposition of the chapter

The primary objective of this chapter is to provide the following description and analysis of Danish, Dutch and Swedish transport policies in the 90s with a more detailed background (than the one presented in the Introduction). This background will be both globally and long-term orientated.

Secondly, I intend to illustrate, in a concrete way, what 'environmentally unsustainable' really means in connection with transport. This will enable me to identify some global environmental aspects that should be considered by national transport policies.

Similar but far from identical studies have been carried out by OECD *(Pollution Prevention and Control: Environmental Criteria for Sustainable Transport*, 1996) and by the American Transportation Research Board (*Toward a Sustainable Future: Addressing the Long-Term Effects of Motor Vehicle Transportation on Climate and Ecology*, 1997).

It should be said at once that my survey is based upon the idea of the existence of a limited 'environmental space' (or ecospace), consisting of the biosphere of the Earth with the available amount of renewable and non-renewable resources of energy and materials, of agricultural land, forests and water resources that can be used without depriving future generations of the resources they will need. The creation of equitable and sustainable transport systems all over the globe has to be based on the notion of such a limited ecospace.

The objectives of the chapter will be realised in three steps.

1 As a first step, an outline will be given of present knowledge of the use of energy resources in the transport sector today and its impact on the global and regional environment. The present political responses to this problem will also be briefly reviewed. The main sources are surveys of current energy use and of climatological and ecological developments, some of them initiated by the Intergovernmental Panel on Climate Change (IPCC).

2 Secondly, against a background of the ongoing modernization of Human societies (on the concept of 'modernization' see 1.2.1), the

current trends in car use and car ownership in some selected regions will be surveyed. Here, the main sources are OECD-reports, scientific reports (some of them unpublished), recent news-paper articles and various statistics.

3 Finally, the implications of increasing road transport for global energy demand and for the global environment will be discussed (the present environmental impact of the transport systems is analysed in an article entitled '*Global Environmental Degradation: The Role of Transport*' by K. Button and W. Rothengatter, 1993). The sources of this part of the following chapter are 1/ future studies and 2/ estimates of the future environmental impact and of future technological possibilities.

When dealing with the future, I will make a distinction between the short term (up to 2005), the medium term (up to 2020), the long term (up to 2050) and the very long term (up to 2100). The discussions will lead to some conclusions about global environmental aspects that should be considered by national transport policies.

2.2 The present transport sector: global environmental problems and international policy responses

2.2.1 *The present energy use of the transport sector - a threat to the environmental sustainability of transport systems?*

The energy use of the global transport sector is at present heavily dominated by oil products (the figures below are quoted from *Global Transport Sector Energy Demand towards 2020*, a report made by the Norwegian oil company Statoil for the World Energy Council in 1995). In the case of the OECD, the oil products claimed 99%, the remaining 1 percent being covered by electricity, gas and coal (p 9).

The oil products (mostly petrol and diesel) consumed in the transport sector accounted for 58% of all oil products consumed worldwide in the beginning of the 90s (according to an assessment made by the IPCC in 1994). Of the final oil consumption within OECD, the transport sector was responsible for 59.4% (1990). The estimates for the non-OECD countries are less exact *(ibid.)*.The total oil consumption of the transport sector (apart from international maritime traffic, which is not included in current statistics) was heavily dominated by road transport. Its share of the total transport sector oil consumption was 82.5%. Next came air traffic with 13.3% *(ibid.)*.

In the period 1970-1990, there was a steady growth in oil use in the transport sector despite the two oil shocks in the 1970s. Transport was in fact the only growth sector, as industry and other users have been reducing their dependence on oil as an energy source. The average annual growth of the oil consumption in the OECD transport sector was 2.4% in this period. The average annual growth of the oil consumption in the same sector was higher outside OECD, but the OECD countries still accounted for two thirds of global transport energy consumption in the beginning of the 90s (*op.cit.* pp 9sq).

Thus, the whole transport sector is extremely dependent on the oil market for its energy input. This input has been growing for a long time. The relative importance of the transport sector in the total oil consumption has also increased substantially. According to the Norwegian report, the future of the oil market will therefore be largely determined by the developments of the transport sector (*op.cit.* p 112).

What will happen if there is a strong increase in the oil demand (for instance, through rapid motorization of less developed countries) in the short and medium term? The potential respond of the oil market to an increased demand is regarded as being comparatively good, at least up to 2020. There are substantial proved reserves of oil. New technology also makes it profitable to exploit more oil from old sources. If growing demand leads to higher oil prices, this, too, will increase the number of oil reserves worth exploiting. Therefore, the Statoil company takes the view that, for the foreseeable future, 'oil supply will not be a constraint to continued transport growth, but instead be fully sufficient to meet even a strong increase in oil demand up to the year 2020' (*op.cit.* p iv).

A more pessimistic view was recently presented by Campbell and Laherrère in *Scientific American* (March 1998). They claim that the 'global production of conventional oil will begin to decline sooner than most people think, probably within 10 years' (Campbell and Laherrère, 1998). They base their view on the facts 1/ that official statistics on oil reserves are distorted and misleading, 2/ that 80% of the oil that flows today comes from sources identified before 1973 and 3/ that advances in geochemistry and geophysics have made it possible to map productive and prospective fields 'with impressive accuracy', which means that large areas of the globe must now be seen as being of no interest in the perspective of oil production.

In the long (2020-2050) and very long term (2050-2100), even Statoil believes that the situation might turn out to be serious. Since the middle of the 80s, it has been increasingly difficult to identify new rich fields. This has resulted in growing costs 'arising from the increased geological problems associated with finding new fields, resulting from the depletion of easily accessible oil fields' (*Global Transport Sector Energy*

Demand towards 2020, p 35). These costs may, at least to some extent, be counterbalanced by new and more cost-efficient technology for the exploitation of oil sources (*ibid.*).

However, there are, according to the same source, already some serious uncertainties associated with the oil provision of the transport sector in the short and medium term. The OPEC organization is expected to regain a 50% market share in the beginning of the 21st century (*op. cit.* p 35). Therefore, oil may again be used as a political or economic weapon by this organisation. Another circumstance worth mentioning is that substantial parts of the proved reserves of oil are located in politically and socially unstable regions such as the Middle East and Central Asia. The Middle East area has been a politically hot area for decades. Prolonged internal and external conflicts may reduce the oil production substantially both in the short and medium term. Saudi Arabia (from which country USA imports 25% of its oil) is a feudal state which is expected by some observers to collapse in the near future (Aburish, 1996).

Another politically unstable area, Central Asia, also has rich oil reserves that are attracting the attention of Russia, USA and China (see the survey in *The Economist* 1998-02-07). The crucial question is how to bring the oil to the consumers in other parts of the world. American and Saudi-Arabian oil companies are making attempts to bring the oil via Afghanistan to ports in Pakistan. Iran and Russia are cooperating to counteract this initiative. According to Henry Kissinger, Russia is trying to channel the oil export via Russian territory in order to ensure a strong position in the event of a new oil crisis *(Dagens Nyheter* 1997-04-17). China has recently signed an agreement with Kazakhstan to exploit the Uzen oilfields in that country and transport the oil to China by means of a new pipeline and by tankers to Iran, from where it will be shipped further (*The Economist* 1997-08-16).

Therefore, new energy crises of the kind that occurred in the 70s cannot be ruled out during the first two decades of next century, particularly not if the global demand is growing as a result of the rapid increase in the number of motor vehicles. The sector's increased share of the total consumption of oil also means that a possible future oil crisis will hit the transport sector harder than in the 70s.

Thus, owing to its present great dependence on oil products, the transport sector is running a risk of facing politically initiated oil crises in the short (up to 2005) and medium term (to 2020), and a risk of facing oil shortage in the long term (2020-2050) and very long term (to 2100).These risks have led to ambitious research and development programmes in many countries to produce alternative fuels (for instance, biomass-derived alcohols and gaseous hydrocarbons) and alternative motor technologies (mostly electric cars). General Motors announced, for instance, after the Kyoto meeting that it will be able to produce fuel cell electric cars by 2004, its chairman claiming that '(n)o car company will be able to thrive in the next century if they rely solely on internal combustion engines' (*Global Environmental Change Report* X:2 January 30, 1998).

2.2.2 Greenhouse gases from the transport sector - a threat to global environmental sustainability?

It is now a well-known fact that the human contribution to the emissions of greenhouse gases (GHG) influences the concentration of such gases in the atmosphere (see, for instance, Bolin, 1993). Measurements of the concentration of carbon dioxide (CO_2) began in the late 1950s. At this time, the level was 315 parts per million volume (ppmv), which may be compared with the 280 ppmv in the preindustrial era. The level was rising in the 1950s by 0.6 ppm per year (Keeling et al. 1985). Today, the level is 360 ppm and the increase is 1.6 ppm per year. That man-made emissions of other greenhouse gases (methane etc) were also contributing to enhancing the greenhouse effect was not completely understood until 1985 (Bolin, 1997, p 171).

The anthropogenic enhancement of the natural greenhouse effect is now perceived as a serious problem. The situation has been continuously monitored since 1988 by an Intergovernmental Panel on Climate Change (IPCC). Its first report, entitled *Climate Change*, appearing in 1990, was very guarded in its statements. In its second report, published in December 1995, *Second Assessment Report*, the panel was more affirmative, stating that 'the balance of the evidence suggests a discernable human influence on global climate' (*Climate Change 1995: The Science of Climatic Change*, p 4).

The risks are still very difficult to assess. There are, for instance, some doubts about the models used by the IPCC. Furthermore, the observed global temperature increases may be interpreted as natural variations of the climate.

The **OECD** publication *Global Warming: Economic Dimensions and Policy Responses* (1996) summarizes what can be said about the uncertainties linked to the present human impact on the climate. These uncertainties relate to

- the amount of current and future anthropogenic emissions of GHG
- the relation between these emissions and the changes in the atmospheric concentrations of GHG

- the relation between the rise in the atmospheric concentration of GHG and climate change
- the impact of climate change on economic and ecological systems
- the difficulties of predicting climate change, partly because elements of the climate system may be chaotic (*op.cit.* pp 143-154).

The last statement means that the first-order effects are known but that there is uncertainty about higher order effects. Therefore, some very dramatic consequences cannot be ruled out. Higher temperatures may, for instance, lead to 'the disintegration of the West Antarctic ice fields, which could result in a sea level rise of up to six meters' on a timescale of several centuries (*op.cit.* p 152).

However, some effects of human influence on climate appear likely and these effects are added to and embedded in natural climate variations. Some rise in sea level is probable (higher temperatures lead to the melting of ice and snow cover and also to thermal expansion of ocean water). This would lead to widespread flooding of low-lying coastal areas. A change in rainfall in arid areas is another kind of changes that may influence land use in a negative way in certain areas. If precipitation increases in polar regions, this could change the salinity of sea water and thereby affect ocean currents (for instance, the Gulf Stream) with substantial effects on local climates. Extreme weather patterns may develop (*op.cit.* p 152). The greenhouse effect could also accelerate the depletion of stratospheric ozone (Rodhe, 1997, p 164).

Although the effects of a climate change on terrestrial ecosystems are difficult to predict, they should, according to quite a few specialists, be taken seriously if we want to avoid 'adverse effects on the people living in these ecosystems' (Walker, 1996, p 604). Despite all uncertainties, it is generally believed that there is a distinct risk that an unfettered increase in GHG emissions 'will have serious consequences, and that many of the likely impacts of climate change are irreversible' (*Global Warming*, p 14).

Since CO_2 is the principal GHG, responsible for more than half of the global warming effects from the accumulation of man-made GHG, political attention centres on how to limit the emissions of this gas. The share of transport in emitting CO_2 is considerable, around 22%, and is rapidly growing (*Climate Change 1995. Impacts, Adaptations and Mitigation of Climate Change:Scientific-Technical Analyses 1996*, p 681). The emissions associated with the production of vehicles and the construction of infrastructure are not included in this figure. The actual percentage is therefore higher. The production of cars, for instance, is estimated to require around 10% of the energy used during the lifetime of the car (Erikson et al. 1995).

2.2 3 Are there other effects of the transport sector threatening environmental sustainability at the global level?

The greenhouse gases have attracted most interest in the global perspective, as they are seen as the greatest potential threat to the long-term sustainability on a global scale. There are, however, some other emissions, particularly of sulphur oxides (SOx) and oxides of nitrogen (NOx), which should also be taken into consideration here and to which transportation contributes substantially. These emissions are usually seen as causing regional (or local) problems. Emissions causing regional or local problems worldwide may also be seen as "global" but in another sense than the GHG.

The global emissions of SOx and NOx have recently been estimated (Graedel et al. 1995; Rodhe et al. 1995). The annual man-made emissions of SOx (almost entirely the result of the combustion of sulphur containing fossil fuels and the smelting of metal sulphide ores) are about 65 million tons of sulphur (whereas the natural emissions are about 25 million tons). The annual man-made emissions of NOx (almost completely related to the combustion of fossil fuels) are in terms of nitrogen about 22.5 million tons (the corresponding figure for the natural emissions is 15-20 million tons). These emissions could contribute to the successive accumulation of effects that will change or worsen the physical and biological conditions for production and diversity on the global scale in the medium or long-term perspective.

The transport sector as a whole emits a substantial percentage of the total emissions of SOx and NOx. It therefore contributes significantly to the *acidification* of arable land, forests and lakes in large areas around the world. This impact on terrestrial and marine ecosystems will remain for 50-100 years after a complete stop of emissions of the substances contributing to acidification (Bertills and Hanneberg, 1995).

The unintended production of NOx, typical of present transport systems, also contributes, together with the use of fertilizers, to the *eutrophication* of forests, lakes and seas in many regions in the world. The future consequences of this eutrophication are difficult to predict.

Emissions from motorized vehicles give rise to *ground-level ozone,* which threatens vegetation as well as human health (respiratory problems), and this kind of ozone is also one of the greenhouse gases. This problem is most pronounced in summer time and in certain geographical areas of the world.

Transport infrastructure also has a heavy impact on the landscape in motorized countries *transforming large areas of soil into infertile surfaces*. This loss of arable land may prove to be a serious loss in the long-term perspective. At the same time, road and rail traffic *reduces bio-*

diversity by creating barriers to the mobility of various species and by exposing them to other disturbances (noise etc). The density of the road-net plays a role here as well as the size of the roads. The future consequences of these disturbances are difficult to predict but may become serious (for instance, Bolund, 1996).

2.2.4 International policy responses to present problems

With the problems and risks of greenhouse gases in mind, 157 governments signed a treaty at the Earth Summit in Rio (1992), a treaty called a "Framework Convention on Climate Change" (FCCC). This document commited the governments who signed it to immediate action. The objective of FCCC was to achieve 'stabilization of greenhouse gas concentrations in the atmosphere at a level that would prevent dangerous anthropogenic interference with the climate system' (Article 2).

Several principles and ways of achieving this objective were suggested in the document (a summary is to be found *in Global warming: Economic Dimensions and Policy Responses,* p 11). Economic efficiency and international equity were looked upon as two important principles. Joint implementation was seen as necessary, as unilateral responses would probably prove ineffective. The concept of 'joint implementation' 'alludes to policies which allow Parties to achieve the commitments of the convention among a wider coalition of countries through allowing a redistribution of abatement costs so as to make participation attractive' (*ibid.*).

The joint implementation may be based on taxes or on tradable emission quotas. Both ways have advantages. In the case of carbon taxes, the revenue collection and use may remain under the control of each government. A global carbon tax fund is another alternative (*op.cit.* pp 49sqq). The introduction of quotas would mean the creation of a link between efficiency and equity. Quotas may be allocated either in proportion to emissions shared a given year (for instance 1990) or in proportion to world population shares a certain year (*op.cit.* p 50). The first principle is called 'grandfathering' and the second 'egalitarian' The following measures were indicated for preventing climate change:

1. emission mitigation options (such as raising energy efficiency and fuel substitution
2. GHG sequestration and removal of carbon dioxide (through biomass growth or through the capture of carbon dioxide from large emitters such as power plants in order to be stored in empty oil or gas wells)
3. some geo-engineering measures (*op.cit.* pp 21sqq).

The report also identified and described some important elements of appropriate policy responses (*op.cit.* pp 31sqq). Apart from basic climate research (to reduce uncertainty) and research and development on mitigation and sequestration, the main elements of an appropriate policy were said to consist of improving energy efficiency (a kind of "no-regrets policy") and policy-making under uncertainty including, for instance, the use of economic instruments to favour a shift to carbon-low (such as natural gas), carbon-neutral (for instance, biomass) or carbon-free energy sources (for instance, wind power).

In the case of transport and particularly with respect to motor vehicles, there are substantial problems to overcome. Of increased energy efficiency it is said:

> Transport is an end-use sector characterized by rapid growth of energy demand. Most of the expected energy-saving in transport is based on improved fuel efficiency of vehicles. The long-term technical potential here is large, but there is often a trade-off between fuel efficiency and other vehicle characteristics... The use of electric vehicles, the introduction of speed limits, increased use of public transport and tele-commuting may also provide considerable energy savings, but there is a trade-off with performance, mobility and other transport characteristics relevant to consumers. This implies that such measures are far from being perfect substitutes for present technology and are therefore difficult to evaluate in a cost-benefit analysis (*op.cit.* pp 99sq).

At the international meeting in Kyoto in Japan in December 1997, a new step was taken. Most of the industrialised countries committed themselves to a reduction of their emissions of important greenhouse gases (CO_2, N_2O, methane, and some others) in relation to the base year 1990. The emissions should be reduced by on average 6-8% over the years 2008-2012. However, it can be doubted whether these commitments will be realised. There are also still (spring 1998) some doubts about the willingness of the US Congress to ratify the agreement.

2.2.5 A summing up

Thus, there is good reason to believe that the environmental sustainability of the present transport sector is threatened by several factors. Some of these threats may be visible in the medium term 2005-2020 (for instance, in the form of new oil crises) or in the long term 2020-2050 (in the form of shrinking oil resources, climate changes or ecological disasters). Some of these developments may 'compromise the ability of future generations to meet their own needs'. Hitherto, the international political responses to these threats have been hesitant, even if the conferences in Rio in 1992 and in Kyoto in 1997 are steps on the road towards more sustainability-orientated policies.

The reason for the hesitant political attitude is that particularly the question of climate change exposes the decision-makers to 'a set of formidable complications: large uncertainties, the potential for irreversible damages or costs, a very long planning horizon, long time lags between emissions and effects, a global scope, wide regional variation, and multiple greenhouse gases of concern' (*Climate Change 1995: Economic and Social Dimensions of Climate Change 1996*, p 21).

2.3 Global development of car ownership and car use

2.3.1 Introduction: modernization and motorization

The aim of this section is to survey the present trends in car ownership and car use. It should, however, be kept in mind that the current growth of world trade is expected to result in expanding volumes of freight transport, which will also have a heavy impact on the global environment. However, the expansion of car ownership leads to much more far-reaching changes, as it influences the lifestyle of many people in a more direct way, i.e. in terms of increased individual mobility and car use.

The survey will be given against a background of the current globaization of modern life. In the theoretical discussion in the first chapter, the concepts of 'modernity' and 'modernization' were introduced to describe present historical change (1.2.1). When traditional, mostly rural and agrarian societies are transformed into modern, rationalistic, urban and industrial societies, this change is accompanied by successive motorization of the transport sector. Individual mobility increases and the number of private cars is multiplied. This modernization process is now becoming global.

There are certainly a number of strong driving forces behind motorization and the increased use of cars all over the world. First, both the automotive industry and motorization *per se* are regarded by many governments as important elements in the process of industrialization. This statement refers both to open, liberal economies and to more regulated development strategies (exemplified below by Brazil and China).The car industry has often been regarded as the "motor" of national economies.

Secondly, with the exception of centrally planned economies, car ownership seems to be clearly correlated to GNP/capita, although with a certain delay (Tanner, 1983). This expansion in the number of cars is associated with a transfer of lifestyles from rich people to less rich people as well as from rich countries to less rich countries, the transfer in the second case mediated by local car using elites and by films and television (Lindén, 1994). If suppressed by ideological arguments as in regions dominated by the former Soviet Union, the demand for privately owned cars can explode when the economy is deregulated, and car ownership may even exceed the expected level as correlated to the GDP/capita (as in Poland, see below 2.3.5).

Thirdly, increasing car use often leads to urban sprawl, which in its turn stimulates still more car use. This interaction between car use and changing urban structure is a strong driving force behind increasing car use in already highly motorized countries (exemplified below by USA).

Population growth, the high divorce rate leading to the split up of families and households, the entrance of many women on to the labour market, and the fact that recently retired people are becoming more active and more mobile than in earlier generations are also important social factors accounting for the expansion of car use.

Finally, increased speed (by using a car compared to using public transport) also results in increased mobility, as the average travel time seems to be constant on a global scale (Schafer and Victor, 1997).

2.3.2 A worldwide survey

In the middle of the 1990s, the total number of motor vehicles (with four or more wheels) worldwide was approximately 600 million. 80% of these 600 million, or about 450-480 million, were automobiles (including privately owned passenger vans). Only 10% of all automobiles and 20% of all lorries and buses were running in countries outside OECD. The number of two- or three-wheeled vehicles, which are particularly common in industrializing countries, was about 100 million (*Towards Clean Transport*, 1996, p 17).

In the 90s, the number of motor vehicles in the world has grown much faster than the world population, close to 5% compared to 2% (*op. cit.* p 17). Maurice Strong, the Secretary General of the UN Conferences in Stockholm 1972 and in Rio 1992, commented in the Swedish newspaper *Dagens Nyheter* (1990-09-13) that the world community is now confronted not only with a population explosion (as in 1972) but also with a car explosion. In OECD countries, the annual increase in the number of motor vehicles is less than 1% but around 10% outside OECD (*Towards Clean Transport*, 1996, p 17). In absolute numbers, this means that the two figures are almost equal: around 5 million each.

This increase in the number of vehicles has been accompanied by a more intensive use of each motor vehicle (in terms of vehicle kilometres travelled). In OECD countries, road traffic increased by about 40% in the 1980s, corresponding to an average annual rate of increase of 3.4%, while the increase in the number of vehicles was less than 1% (*op. cit.* p 17).

The number of motor vehicles in the world is generally expected to reach 1 billion by 2010 (*op.cit.* p 17). If development follows historical patterns in the long term and if car ownership in industrializing countries reaches, for instance, half the present North American rates by 2060, the number of automobiles in the world will exceed 2.5 billion at that time. Given the present trends, the total distance travelled by automobile (compared to 1985) will increase sevenfold and fuel consumption will more than treble (*op.cit.* p 19). At present rates of growth, however, the non-OECD countries are expected to reach the level of American automobilization by 2085. This would mean that the world's car fleet would reach the 6 billion mark at that time *(op.cit.* p 24).

This general picture of present worldwide road transport and its expected future is based upon figures from OECD and IEA. In the following paragraphs, it is my intention to select some important regions (such as Northern America, Western Europe, Eastern Europe, Latin America, East and South Asia) to find out more about the present trends at the regional level.

2.3.3 The case of Northern America

USA was the first region in which mass mobility by car was established. It occurred in the period between World War I and World War II. USA is today the most motorized country in the world. The car density is approaching 600 cars per 1000 inhabitants. In 1985, there were 131 million cars in the country and this figure grew to 146 in 1993 (*Transportation Energy Data book*, table 1.1. - the figures for 1994 and 1995 are not comparable with the figures of the preceding years). In Canada, there is a similar trend. The number of cars increased from 11 million in 1985 to 13 million in 1995 (*op. cit.* table 1.1.).

The mobility of American citizens almost doubled (from 12 000 km a year) between 1960 and 1990 (Schafer and Victor, 1997). Distances travelled by road were approximately 16 700 km per capita in 1990 (Raskin and Margulis, 1995, p 58).

There is no level of saturation in sight in USA, neither as to the number of cars (one person may own and use more than one car) nor as to the vehicle kilometres travelled. There are several factors behind the increase in vehicle km (source: a report in Swedish entitled *Hållbara transportsystem i USA,* 1996, pp 9-11):

1. There are more people absorbed by the labour market (particularly women have increased their professional activities).
2. There are more households per unit of the population (younger people move from their parents and many married people divorce).
3. The urban sprawl has continued (many people have moved to the suburbs and the distances between home and work have increased).
4. Many work-places have moved to the suburbs.
5. The daily commuting goes more often from suburb to suburb, which leads to increased car use (public transport offers no alternatives).
6. The costs of car use has been decreasing in comparison with the costs of public transport.
7. The percentage of commuters using public transport has fallen successively since 1980 and is now 5.3%.
8. Car occupancy has decreased, particularly during the 80s, when car sharing was reduced because the number of cars *per household* increased.

All these trends lead to:

1. increased energy use per unit passenger transport, partly dependent on increased use of privately owned "light-duty-trucks" or vans (the energy-efficiency of such vehicles is less than that of ordinary automobiles)
2. increased dependence on imported oil
3. increased emissions of carbon dioxide and
4. increased time loss due to highway congestion.

Summing up these trends, it is reasonable to claim that there is no level of saturation in car use in sight in North America. Efforts are therefore being made to reduce the unsustainable character of the present transport system (a summary of these efforts are to be found in *Hållbara transportsystem i USA*, 1996).

However, no sustainable solution of the problems of providing the expanding fleet of motor vehicles with energy has been put forward. In the foreword of the latest edition of the *Transport Energy Data Book* (no.17), it is said:'Unfortunately, the transportation sector's dependence on oil has not changed'. Rather US dependence on imported oil had increased substantially. The net imports as a percentage of US petroleum consumption grew from 33.4% in 1986 to 46.2% in 1996 (*op.cit.* table 2.2).

2.3.4 The case of Western Europe

Mass mobility by car was established in Western Europe much later than in the USA. It occurred only after World War II, in the late 50s and in the 60s. In 1985 there were 121 million cars in Western Europe (Pemberton 1988). The figure for 1993 was 160 million (*OECD Environmental Data Compendium, 1995*). However, European mobility differs from that in America (Orfeuil and Bovy, 1993). There is a greater reliance on public transport and soft modes (walking, cycling) than in USA. There is therefore a clear difference in car ownership and car use. In 1990 there were 572 cars per 1000 inhabitants in the USA, while the corresponding figures were 416 in France, 472 in Italy, and 353 in Great Britain (*World Road Statistics 1990-1994*). At the same time, the average distance travelled by road was approximately 9 500 km compared to 16 700 in the USA (Raskin and Margulis, 1995, p 58).

The current dominating trends in Western Europe are the following (Bleijenberg and Dings, 1997):

1. The volume of passenger kilometres increased between 1970 and 1994 by 3.1% per year (a minor part of this increase, 0.7%, is caused by population growth - thus the increase in travel distance per person was around 2.4%).
2. The car transport share of total passenger transport increased from 76% in 1970 to 82% in 1994 (the car transport share rose on average by 0.3-0.4% a year).
3. Car occupancy is probably slowly decreasing (no average figures for Western Europe as a whole available).
4. The specific energy consumption of a given type of car has been reduced by 1-1.5% per year but the overall upgrading of car technology (the cars become faster, heavier and more comfortable) increases the specific energy consumption by (0.5% per year), the net reduction thus being between 0.5 and 1%.

These trends have meant that European passenger traffic has increased its oil consumption and carbon dioxide emissions by 2-3% per year.

The creation of the internal market within the European Union is expected to result in lower prices of cars and petrol, and this will in turn generate more car traffic (see below chapter 5). The weak economic development in the European Community in the 1990s has, however, reduced this risk, at least for a while. Instead, the European car industry is suffering from over-production at present. A thorough reconstruction of this industry is to be expected during the next few years (*The Economist*

1997-03-08).

There is good reason to believe that the saturation level of car use and individual mobility is still far ahead in Western Europe. The problems of present motorization are therefore far from being solved in the European Union (Tengström et al. 1995). This question will be dealt with in more detail below (in chapter 5).

2.3.5 The case of Eastern Europe

The automobilization of the former Soviet Union and the Soviet-dominated Eastern Europe was kept back for ideological reasons for a long period of time. Communist ideals did not include extended car use as an expression of individualism and conspicuous consumption. The famous motorization programme for the Soviet Union, launched by Stalin in November 1929, focused therefore on the role of the lorry in society (Tengström, 1993, p 21). The existing cars were intended for the privileged elite. In the middle of the 60s, however, Prime Minister Kosygin announced a new car policy. The production of cars in the Soviet Union and Eastern Europe increased significantly from that date and between 1977 and 1984 the car fleet in Eastern Europe grew rapidly at a rate of 8.3% per year (*op.cit.* p 26).

A comparison of Eastern and Western Europe in 1987 just before the big change from planned to market economy in the region still shows, however, significant differences in car ownership: an average number of 130 cars per 1000 inhabitants in Eastern Europe as opposed to 360 cars in EEC of that time. In 1990, the average distance travelled by road in Eastern Europe was around 2 200 km per capita compared to 9 500 in Western Europe (Raskin and Margulis, 1995, p 58). There were also big differences in the length of motorways related either to the number of cars or to the number of inhabitants (Orfeuil and Bovy, 1993).

Since 1989 there has been a rapid increase in car ownership and car use in some of the Central and Eastern European countries (the statistics are not complete). The domestic production of cars is increasing in some of the countries. The Russian car industry, for instance, seemed to have recovered from the transition to a market economy in 1997 and the vehicle output has been steadily increasing since 1994 (*The Economist* 1997-08-23).

Taking Poland as an extreme example of what can happen in Eastern Europe after the transition to a market economy, we may learn about possible futures in this part of Europe. At the end of the 60s, there were still only 0.5 million cars in this country and a car density of 14 per 1000 inhabitants (Gajewska, 1994, p 33). In the 1970s, the number of cars increased in Poland to 2.4 million and in the 80s to 5.2 million, resulting in a car density of around 135 per 1000 inhabitants (Gajewska, 1994, p 41 and p 48).

Since 1989 the Polish car fleet has expanded at a very rapid rate. In five years, from 1990 to 1995, the number increased from 5.2 million to 8 million. In 1994, the car density in Poland was 185 cars per 1000 inhabitants (*World Road Statistics 1990-1994*). The development of roads, car production (60% of cars in use are produced in Poland) and increased car use are regarded as important elements in the present Polish strategy for rapid economic growth and in its official transport policy (launched in 1993 and treated by the Polish Parliament in 1995). The upgrading of the transport system is also looked upon as a necessary precondition for the future integration of Poland into the European Union (Gajewska, 1998 and Menes, 1997).

The car has become a symbol of the new liberty. The present average mobility of the Polish people is still comparatively low. It is therefore reasonable to assume a substantial increase during the years to come both in car ownership and car mobility in Poland. By 2010, the number of cars in Poland is officially expected to reach a level of 12-15 million (Gajewska, 1998).

The environmental impact of motor transport has been underestimated by the authorities so far. A study from the "Institute for Sustainable Development" in Warsaw claims that '(a)cceptance and implementation of the official transportation policy would leave sustainable development requirements completely by the wayside' (*Alternative Transport Policy in Poland*, 1997, p 16).

Thus, in the medium and long term, it seems probable that the number of cars and individual mobility will substantially increase in Central and Eastern Europe as well as in the former Soviet Union. The environmental impact of this increasing motorization and automobilization will certainly be quite serious.

2.3.6 The case of Latin America

Motorization began comparatively early in some Latin American countries, for instance, in Argentina. In Brazil, General Motors and Ford established assembly factories as early as 1920s. The importance of upgrading the road infrastructure when establishing national entities was emphasized by political leaders in the second half of the 20s. In the middle of the 90s the average distance travelled by road in Latin America was, however, still very low, approximately 1,500 km per capita, to be compared with the corresponding figure in North America, about 16,800 km per capita (Raskin and Margulis, 1995, p 58).

The economic development of the region after World War II has been hampered by protectionism and various structural factors leading to high inflation, political instability and foreign debt, even if there have been periods of rapid economic growth in certain countries. In 1991, a new era seemed to have begun. In this year, the formation of a Common Market (not yet completely free), called "Mercosur" in Spanish and "Mercosul" in Portuguese, was agreed upon by Argentina, Brazil, Uruguay and Paraguay. A trade agreement has been concluded with Chile. The emerging common market covers an area with about 300 million people. In December 1995, the member states of Mercosur also agreed on a five-year plan for the establishing of a perfect free-trade area and a customs union (see '*A survey of Mercosur*' in *The Economist* 1996-10-12). The following analysis will focus on the situation of Mercusur, particularly the Brazilian development.

The modernization and expansion of the motor industry constitute one of the most visible achievements of Mercosur during the first half of the 90s. This is, however, not only an effect of free trade but also of a conscious industrial policy and of infrastructure projects. As some governments in other parts of the world, the governments of the member states of Mercosur regard the motor industry as too important to be left completely to the market forces (Thynell, 1998). In the middle of the 90s, many car makers were, however, enticed by the growing market and were putting money in their Mercosur plants in the hope that the tariff walls would be lowered. Newcomers such as Honda, Toyota, Chrysler, Hyundai were also establishing factories in the region (*The Economist* 1996-10-12). The economic crisis in late 1997 has, however, increased the uncertainty about the future relation between the state and the market *(The Economist* 1997-12-13).

The case of Brazil will be used to illustrate the historical development of passenger road transport in Latin America since World War II in more detail (Thynell, 1998). In the second half of the 50s, President Kubitscheck decided to speed up the development process in Brazil by using the automotive industry as its motor. He invited foreign car companies to establish a complete system for production of motor vehicles (not only assembly factories) in the country and several European and American companies accepted this invitation. President Kubitscheck also decided to open up the huge interior of the country with its rich natural resources by an extensive road-building programme and by founding the new capital Brasilia far away from the coast to integrate the interior regions in the development of the country. This remarkable urban project was planned for car use as the main mode of transport.

During the military regime in Brazil between 1964 and 1985, the government continued the extensive road building programme. The same government also favoured the automotive industry in different ways but kept rigid control of its investment decisions. In the late 70s, in response to rapid increase in the price of imported oil, the government initiated a Brazilian alcohol fuels programme, based upon the production of ethanol from sugarcanes. The programme resulted in a dramatic increase in the use of ethanol instead of petrol.

The Brazilian economy went through a period of rapid economic growth (7% in average) between 1956 and 1979. This development (sometimes looked upon as a "Brazilian Miracle") represented the largest growth among Newly Industrialized Countries at that time. The automotive industry seems to have been one of the most important factors behind this development. After the fall of the military regime in 1985, a transition to a more liberal, capitalistic economy was initiated. The Color government reduced, for instance, the taxes on imported vehicles in several steps. In 1994, the domestic production of motor vehicles reached a new all time high level of 1.5 million units and there were around 13 million motor vehicles in use. The annual production was expected to reach 2.5 million by 2000 (*The Economist* 1996-10-12).

The number of cars is increasing all over Latin America (*World Road Statistics 1990-1994*). The existing cars are used more intensely than in Europe, most of them in urban areas. The distribution of cars among the population is very unequal. In some parts of the cities, car density is probably as high as 350 per 1000 inhabitants (the average in OECD countries in 1987 was 330 cars).

The environmental effects of transportation growth in the entire region of Latin America are substantial. Transportation accounts for 55% of the region's total oil consumption and for 35% of energy-related regional CO_2 emissions. Many cities in the region are exposed to unrestrained, rapid growth, leading to low-density patterns of settlement. This results in increased CO_2 emissions as transport demand rises. At the same time, CO_2 sinks are removed when arable and forested land is used for housing, industrial plants and roads (Zegras, 1996).

2.3.7 The case of East and South Asia

The first Asian country to become motorized was Japan. Confronted with the American way of life after World War II during the occupation period (1945-1952), many Japanese were fascinated by Western car culture. In the late 50s, the Japanese car industry began to expand and the first motorway was constructed in 1959. From then onwards, the Japanese state and industry collaborated closely to motorize Japan and to expand the motor industry (Maruo, 1992). Japan was the biggest car producing country in the world in the early 1990s (12.5 million vehicles in 1992). Its own car fleet is also expanding. In the middle of 1960s, there were 2 million cars in Japan, a figure that grew to 17 million in 1975, to 27 million in 1985 and to 44 million in 1995 (*Transportation Energy Data Book* - table 1.1). In 1993, the number of cars in domestic use per 1000 inhabitants was, however, still comparatively low (329), i.e. much lower than in Germany (464) or in the USA (564).

Some other East Asian countries that are rapidly industrializing, for instance in Malaysia and Singapore, have followed the Japanese example and increased their use of motor vehicles during the last few decades quite substantially. A particularly rapid increase in car ownership is demonstrated by South Korea, from 2 million in 1990 to 5.1 million in 1994 (*World Road Statistics*). This country has also become one of the big car producers with a production of around 1.7 million vehicles, thereby approaching the production volume of the Italian automotive industry. Indonesia, Thailand and Philippines represent another category of countries where the increase in the number of motor vehicles has recently begun.

A slow-down in the rapid economic development of the South-Asian "tiger" economies was noticed in the first half of 1997 (*The Economist* 1997-03-01). The dramatic financial crisis beginning in the summer of 1997 was first regarded as threatening economic growth only in the short term (*The Economist* 1997-09-06). The escalation of the crisis towards the end of 1997 raised the question 'How far is down?' (*The Economist* 1997-11-15). The future of the motorization of South-Asia is at present (spring 1998) somewhat obscure, but it is generally believed that the tiger economies will recover in the not-too-distant-future (see the survey of East Asian economies in *The Economist* 1998-03-07).

More important than the present economic crisis in Eastern Asia are the future possibilities of motorizing India (approaching 1 billion inhabitants) and China (trying to stabilise its population at 1.3 billion). In India, the number of cars is still very small. In 1985, there were only 2 cars per 1000 inhabitants, a figure which had risen to 3 cars by 1990.The total fleet consisted of 1.2 million cars in 1985 and of 3 million in 1995 (*Transportation Energy Data Book* - table 1.1.). These low figures may be explained by a very strongly regulated economy. The substantial middle class who could pay for a car were put on the waiting list for a domestic car or had to pay very high import taxes on foreign cars. The economic growth was around 4% in the period 1960-1990 ("the Hindu rate of growth"). This comparatively low growth resulted in many people still living under the poverty line (328 million according to the World Bank) in the middle of the 90s ('*Survey of India*', in *The Eco-*

nomist 1997-02-22).

In 1991-1993, a series of economic reforms gave a new impetus to the Indian economy. Parts of the economy were deregulated and this change initiated a period of rapid economic growth, since 1994 as much as 7%. If the economic deregulation is permitted to continue, it is believed that this would allow an average economic growth of 9-10%.

Such a growth rate would probably stimulate car use and car production significantly. Even if a bicycle and then a scooter are the first investments of an Indian family making some more money, the selling of cars can be expected to increase in the future. Joint ventures have already reorganised the production of cars (many new brands), upgraded the technical standard of the vehicles and are discussing an expansion of the production (*The Economist* 1997-08-16).

The existing infrastructure is not adapted to any car expansion, however: endless jams are a part of Indian everyday life, particularly in the cities. The present air pollution problems in India are mostly caused by scooters, 3-wheelers and buses and to a much less degree by cars. This situation represents a serious health problem in India. A great number of people are said to die annually from air pollution (Sharma and Roychowhury, 1996).

In the People's Republic of China, motorization was not given priority in the first decades of its history. In 1980, there were only 350 000 cars in the entire country. This figure had grown to 1.6 million by 1990 (*Transportation Energy Data Book* - table 1.1.). However, in July 1994, a new motorization policy was launched in China. It was based on the view that the car industry would be the motor for national economic development. The expression used in *China Daily* on July 5th 1994 was: 'the car industry is expected to become the economic pillar (of the country) before 2010'. Foreign car producers are invited to invest in China under specified conditions. The production is expected to grow from 1.3 million motor vehicles (including more than 300 000 cars) in 1993 to 3 million units in 2000 (of which 50% are assumed to be cars). As the car fleet is expected to grow from 1.7 million in 1991 (including light buses) to 6 million in 2000 and 20 million in 2010, the expansion of the production is assumed to continue (Gakenheimer, 1995).

In 1994, there were 3.5. million cars in China (*Transportation Energy Data Book* - table 1.1.). In the same year, there were 3.8 million cars in Taiwan *(World Road Statistics 1990-1994)*. The growth rate of cars in the People's Republic of China was however 18% in the period 1985-1995 (*Transportation Energy Data Book* - table 1.1.).

The future demand for cars is, of course, difficult to estimate. It will be determined by the rate of economic growth, by income distribution and by the prevailing consumer policy. Estimates made by an official

Chinese institute based upon surveys of upper income families arrive at a demand of about 4-4.5 million cars by 2000 (which is 3.5 times the expected production that year). For the year 2005, the Chinese institute estimates a demand of about 15.5. to 16.5 million (Gakenheimer, 1995).

If the planned expansion of the Chinese fleet of motor vehicles is realised, such a development will expose the infrastructure and the urban structure to enormous strain. Ralph Gakenheimer, who has studied these questions for the World Bank is, however, very much impressed by the Chinese will and ability to manage the problems of increasing traffic: 'In fact, if you were to take the best traffic management practices from all over the world and implement them all in one place - that's what you will find in many of the cities of China' (quoted from an interview with Gakenheimer in *Transportation* 1995:39). However, the environmental challenge of Chinese motorization is, to my knowledge, less well covered in the current studies of Chinese development, and I doubt whether Gakenheimer had paid due attention to the environmental aspects of traffic growth when he arrived at his conclusion.

2.3.8 A summing up

There are, as we have seen, many indications that global car ownership and car use will increase in the next few decades in highly motorized regions (North America and Western Europe) as well as in less motorized regions (Eastern Europe, South America and Eastern and South Asia). Some developing countries may be rapidly motorized. In a recent American survey based on historical data, global mobility is expected to double between 1990 and 2020 and again almost double between 2020 and 2050 (Schafer and Victor, 1997).

The car industry itself is more sceptical about a rapid increase in the number of cars. The dominant problem of the automotive industry, as it is perceived by the industry itself (see for instance *ACEA Newsletter* 41, 1997), is a significant over-capacity in production capability and, as a consequence, shrinking profitability. The industry worries about the emergence of "mature markets", where old cars are simply replaced, and about over-production in new markets in Asia and Latin America (see *The Economist* 1997-05-10). The concern of the industry is, however, mostly short term orientated. In the middle term (2005-2020), the same industry may very well be involved in a process of rapid expansion unless a major world crisis in economic or political terms arises.

Assuming that the real increase in car ownership and car use will approach the levels estimated at the OECD Conference in Mexico City in 1995 (see above 2.3.2), such an increase (at least 2.5 billion cars by

2060 and possibly 6 billion by 2085 and a corresponding increase in car mobility) would have a tremendous impact on the environment and the energy resources. The environmental sustainability of a global car fleet consisting of 2.5 billion vehicles and of a 'sevenfold increase in the total distance travelled by automobile' was denied at the Conference: 'Even lower rates of increase would result in dramatic, unsustainable increases in world oil consumption' (*Towards Clean Transport*, p 19).

About the possibility that the non-OECD countries would reach the present level of automobilization of North America by 2085, which they would do at present rates of growth, it is said in the same report:

> A dilemma for non-OECD countries is that present rates of growth are too low to provide early parity with North Americans, as least as measured in terms of access to and use of automobiles, but they are too high to be considered as even remotely sustainable in the medium and long term (*op.cit.* p 24).

Estimates of this kind prompt the following questions: What are the prospects for the future energy supply of the transport sector? What are the prospects for the environmental impact of an expanding global fleet of motor vehicles? What are the prospects for a transition to alternative (carbon-free) fuels and alternative vehicle technologies? These questions will be the themes of the following section.

2.4 Prospects for the future

The objective of this section is to highlight some aspects of the future which should also be considered by national transport policies. In order to do this, I will present two different types of future studies of the global energy supply and a study of the risks of conventional development (2.4.1), describe the current debate on the negative impact of emitted substances on the environment much of which can be blamed on the transport sector (2.4.2), discuss the conditions for a future transition to carbon-low, carbon-neutral or carbon-free fuels (2.4.3) and, finally, touch upon the question of a radical transformation of the present technologi-cal system for road transport (2.4.4).

2.4.1 Energy futures and the risks of conventional development

Quite a number of global energy scenarios have been developed during the last few years. I have selected two of them: 1/ *Global Energy Perspectives to 2050 and Beyond*, published by the World Energy Council (WEC) and International Institute for Applied Systems Analysis

(IIASA) in 1995 (quoted as "WEC/IIASA") and 2/ *Global Energy in the 21st Century: Patterns, Projections and Problems*, written by P. Raskin and R. Margulis (quoted as "Raskin and Margulis") and published by the Stockholm Environmental Institute (SEI), also in 1995.

In the World Energy Council study (elaborated in conjunction with IIASA), the focus is on the long term (to 2050) and the very long term (to 2100). The world population is expected to reach 10 billion by 2050 and nearly 12 billion by 2100. Substantial social and economic development is supposed to take place in the meantime, particularly in "the developing world".

Six different scenarios are elaborated to illustrate alternative energy futures. Three of them are associated with a very high rate of economic growth and technological progress. The primary energy demand in all these scenarios rises considerably, the resource availability is without problems and the technology costs are supposed to be low. There is no constraint on emissions of CO_2 either. In one scenario (A1), there is a large supply of oil and gas available and these fuels dominate to the end of the 21st century. In another scenario (A2), the oil and gas resources are supposed to become successively scarce, why a massive return to coal takes place. In the third scenario (A3), a rapid phase-out of fossil fuels and a transition to nuclear and renewable energy technologies take place, largely for economic rather than environmental reasons.

A "middle course" future is illustrated by only one scenario (B) in the WEC/IIASA study. It is based upon more modest estimates of economic growth and technological development. Here, too, developing countries are supposed to have more prosperous conditions than today but they are expected to develop more slowly and less uniformly than in the first three scenarios (A 1-3). The future energy supply is similar to the present one in its composition, but the level is much higher. There is no constraint on emissions of CO_2. Oil and gas maintain a significant share of the global primary energy mix up to 2070. A successive transition from fossil to alternative fuels is expected to be feasible. The technology costs and technology dynamics are supposed to be at a medium level.

The two remaining WEC/IIASA scenarios (C 1-2) are "ecologically driven". In these cases, it is assumed that there will be an 'unprecedented aggressive international cooperation focused explicitly on environmental protection and international equity'. A broad range of measures (such as "green taxes") are used to encourage energy producers and consumers to utilize energy more efficiently and increase their use of renewables. The CO_2 emissions by the year 2100 are supposed to have been reduced to one third of today's level, by means of carrots rather than of sticks. One of the scenarios (C1) is based on the view that nuclear power is a transient technology which will be entirely phased out by the end of the new century. In the other scenario (C2), a new generation of nuclear reactors is developed which gain widespread social acceptance, particularly in areas with high population densities that limit the potential supply of renewables.

According to WEC/IIASA, these scenarios should not be seen as forecasts but as internally consistent projections checked by formal models (p 1). One of the important results of the study is, in my view, its conclusion that the energy future beyond 2020 will be determined before that date 'because of the long lifetimes of power plants, refineries, and other energy investments' (p iv).

In the Stockholm Environmental Institute (SEI) study, Raskins and Margulis have examined the energy implications of a long-range global conventional development scenario, in which the future economic development pattern of developing regions is assumed to be analogous to the historical development of the present OECD countries (thus, a kind of business-as-usual scenario).

The SEI scenario is fairly similar to the B scenario in the WEC/IIASA study: by the year 2050, it is assumed that the world population will have nearly doubled relative to 1990, the GDP/cap. more than doubled and the world GDP quadrupled. The energy input per unit of GDP is expected to decrease substantially as a result of increased energy efficiency and as a result of a global shift to less energy-intensive activities. Despite this, energy use will increase by a factor of 2.5 over the period. Emissions of CO_2 will remain almost the same per energy unit as in 1990, and the total emissions of this greenhouse gas will therefore grow by a factor of just over 2.5 over the period.

Fossil fuels are expected to dominate in the global energy balance as they do today, but there is also a substantial increase in the absolute expansion of renewable energy as well as of nuclear energy. The demand for coal is expected to increase by a factor of 4.1 between 1990 and 2050 (with Chinese coal demand skyrocketing by a factor of seven). The oil demand will more than double by the year 2050.

With this future business-as-usual scenario in mind, the two authors identify a number of factors which may influence global development:

1 Problems arising from the depletion of oil resources may lead to higher prices and geopolitical tensions caused by the geographically uneven distribution of oil and gas resources.
2 Substantial barriers to the expansion of nuclear energy may be set up due to concerns about costs, safety, waste disposal and security issues.
3 Constraints on the full potential of hydroelectric facilities may become a reality due to ecosystem disturbance and human displacement.

4 The risks of significant climate changes may be more serious than now due to global increases in GHG emissions from energy combustion.
5 Limits to the expansion of traditional fuels in rural environments may turn out to be an important constraint in many less developed countries.
6 Increased local and regional pollution will be an effect of higher energy use.

The basic conclusion drawn by Raskin and Margulis is that a business-as-usual scenario is improbable, at least in the long term, because of the uncertainties enumerated above.

In another SEI study, the socioeconomic and political consequences of business-as-usual developments have been analysed (Gallopin et al. 1997). A dozen environment and development professionals have explored some possible images of the next 50-100 years. Failure to address the challenges posed by a conventional development would probably result in chains of events where even the winners may become losers owing to a number of vicious circles. The outcome of this downward spiral would depend on how powerful actors perceive the threats and how they respond. One alternative future would be a world where the most powerful actors try to create 'bubbles of wealth' (or a "fortress world"). Alternatively, the powerful elites will be unable to resist the violence arising from extreme inequality. In such a case, the result would be a general breakdown (a "breakdown world"). A massive change of values and new lifestyles would, however, lead to a 'planetary deal' trying to establish a sustainable level of material consumption per capita. That level being reached, economic growth would cease or become dematerialised (a "new sustainability paradigm world").

One of the main results of this study, which highlights the necessity of choosing energy future very soon, closely coincides with the conclusion of the World Energy Council claiming that 'the choice of the world's post-2020 energy systems may be wide open now. It will be a lot narrower by 2020' (WEC/IIASA, p iv).

2.4.2 Future environmental impact of transport-related emissions

According to both the WEC/IIASA study and the SEI study, it seems very probable, in a business-as-usual future, that the emissions of CO_2 will increase in both the short and medium term. According to the Swedish chairman of IPCC (Bolin, 1993, p 86), the concentration of CO_2 would increase as much between 1990 and 2025 as it did in the whole period from the beginning of industrialization up to 1990. The contribution from the transport sector will be substantial if motorization is globalized in the way described in the previous section.

The future political responses to these problems are uncertain. At present, stricter international agreements to reduce the use of fossil fuels are counteracted at the international level by the oil-producing countries representing strong production and export interests and by the USA representing strong consumer and import interests (Bolin, 1997, pp 191sq). It is probable that the emissions of CO_2 will continue to dominate in the debate on the emissions of greenhouse gases, as the emissions of other such gases (methane etc) are more difficult to reduce.

The key problem is that it takes a very long time to stabilize the levels of concentrations of CO_2 in the atmosphere. It is generally believed that *the emissions of CO_2 remain in the atmosphere 100 years or more* (*op.cit.* pp 187-189). It has therefore been estimated that a stabilization of the concentration of CO_2 in the atmosphere for instance at the level of 450 ppmv (the level of today is 360 ppmv) requires a reduction of the global CO_2 emissions to a level which is below the level of today (i.e. <360ppmv), achieved not later than by around 2050. A stabilization at the level of 550 requires a corresponding reduction below the level of today not later than by about 2100 (*op.cit.* p 187). If these levels of stabilization are to be attained in time, all the estimated levels of emissions described in business-as-usual scenarios have to be reduced significantly (*op.cit.* p 189).

According to Bolin, the necessary reduction of the emissions of CO_2 would be difficult to perform for two reasons:

1 Present population growth will increase the demand for energy.
2 Current trends in the energy demand in developing countries are dominated by the use of fossil fuels: in East Asia, the emissions of CO_2 are now increasing by 5% annually (*op.cit.* Pp 188sq).

The situation is aggravated by the following circumstance: if the emissions of CO_2 are reduced by burning less sulphurous oil and coal, the emissions of sulphur aerosols (in the form of particles) would also be reduced, which would, in its turn, reduce the present reflection of solar radiation carried out by the particles, and this reduction would, in its turn, immediately accelerate the greenhouse effect (*op.cit.* pp 189sq).

Some estimates made by the Norwegian oil company, Statoil, may be taken as an example of how the actors in the oil market look upon the future situation. Statoil takes the view that alternative fuels are not expected to gain significant market shares in the transport sector's demand before 2020 and that the emissions of CO_2 will therefore be proportional to the energy use of this sector *(Global Transport Sector Energy Demands towards 2020*, p 112). At the same time, however, the report argues 'that population growth and urbanization inevitably mean that *local pollution* problems will soon reach thresholds of reaction, leading to considerable changes in current urban transport trends' (*op.cit.* p 126). Concerning global warming, the report underlines the difficulties in reaching international agreement, as long as scientific evidence is inconclusive as to the effects of the concentration of CO_2 in the atmosphere. Despite this, it concludes, however, that '(i)t should not be ruled out that this situation could change markedly within the time framework of the report (2020)... Even in the absence of a scientific consensus view, the potential gravity of global climate change merits precautionary measures already today' (*op.cit.* p 126).

The global emissions of other air pollutants such as SO_x and NO_x (to which the transport sector contributes considerably) are declining in Europe at present (Bleijenberg and Dings, 1997). On the other hand, they will increase dramatically in the next few decades, given the present trends, particularly in Eastern and Southern Asia but also in parts of South America and Africa. The emissions of sulphur are estimated to be doubled by 2050 and thereafter somewhat decline, whereas the emissions of NO_x are estimated to double by 2050 and nearly triple by 2100 (Graedel et al. 1995; Rodhe et al. 1995). By 2050, the emissions of sulphur will probably 'exceed the critical load for acidification of soils and surface waters not only in Europe and North America but also in large parts of Asia, Africa and South America'. The emission of NO_2 'will lead to additional stress on terrestrial ecosystems in many parts of the world both through its acidifying effect and through a potential overfertilization of some plant species'. The surface concentrations of ozone 'may well turn out to be an even more serious problem in tropical regions' (Rodhe et al. 1995, p 48).

These developments may have serious consequences for the conditions of human life. Ecosystems exposed to environmental stress may reduce their carrying capacity in a dramatic way. They are complex systems which may flip surprisingly when sufficiently perturbed (Wiman, 1992).

2.4.3 The transition to carbon-low, carbon-neutral or carbon-free fuels

The transport sector seems to be caught in a difficult dilemma. One way of getting out of this dilemma is to initiate a transition to carbon-low (for instance, natural gas), carbon-neutral (for instance, biofuels) or carbon-free energy sources (for instance, electricity generated by means of hydropower). According to an OECD report entitled *Toward Clean and Fuel Efficient Automobiles* (1992), there are certainly a number of candidates as substitutes for petrol and diesel (such as natural gas, liquefied petroleum gas /LPG/, ethanol, biomass fuels, methanol from gas or coal, hydrogen, and electricity).

There is, however, no given main candidate. Giving priority to solving air pollution leads to recommendations to use natural gas, LPG, methanol or electricity. If global warming is the main concern, a dramatic reduction of the overall consumption of fuels may be the only option in the short and medium term. The main concern is, on the other hand, that the available amount of alternative fuels based on alternative primary energy sources would not respond to expected global demand at reasonable costs. Furthermore, all presently known alternative sources and alternative energy carriers have a number of disadvantages.

A transition to methanol based on biomass will, for instance, require huge areas for its production. All alternatives are more expensive than petrol and diesel, given the oil price of today and the technology and production processes of today. Some of them require (given the present technology) a substantial input of oil-based fuels when they are produced and processed (for instance fuels made of biomass). None of them is ready for global implementation in the short term. The possibilities of converting car fleets to electric cars is closely connected with the question how the electricity needed will be generated (hydropower, biomass or nuclear power?), a topic which is politically sensitive.

Thus, the current prospects for phasing out fossil fuels in the transport sector are poor owing to the complex problems associated with such a procedure. There seems to be a common view among various actors that the present (spring 1998) low oil price is efficiently blocking the emergence of alternative markets for carbon-low, carbon-neutral or carbon-free fuels. This is a problem both for the handling of the risks of global warming and for the handling of the problems of national vulnerability to future oil crises (Helby, 1997, p 108).

A recent analysis of alternative fuels and other options for the reduction of CO_2 emissions can be quoted as an example of current views among scientists. The author claims that 'currently available options (of alternative fuels, my comment) are applicable mainly for a few selected scenarios rather than on a global scale, and even then primarily for local air pollution issues only'.

On the other hand, 'a number of additional options (such as increasing the efficiency within a given mode of transportation, and switching to more efficient modes) are presently available to policy-makers that could serve as tools to effectively tackle the greenhouse emissions problem from automobiles' (Sagar, 1995, p 270).

2.4.4 Technological possibilities of the future

In the long term (2020-2050) and very long term (2050-2100), however, it is quite possible that new vehicle technologies and new alternative fuels (based upon new energy sources) will be available (for a survey see, for instance, Sperling and Shaheen, 1995). Scientists speculate about the future possibilities of direct solar energy as the basic energy source, hydrogen as the main energy carrier and fuel cells as a possible vehicle technology (the possibilities of hydrogen and fuel cells reaching the market were reviewed in two articles in *The Economist* 1997-10-25). Technicians and environmentalists (for instance, "Friends of the Earth") believe in the possibilities of cutting the overall resource use by a factor of 10 or more and, at the same time, increasing the quality of life globally (see *Ten Times Better: Fair Shares in Environmental Space*, published by "Friends of the Earth").

Many economists have an optimistic view of technical development. Some of them assume that substitutes exist or could be found for all kinds of resources, and they also point to the fact that economic history indicates that no single resource is indispensable (see above 1.1.2). The evidence of economic history during the last 200 years is certainly impressive in this respect, but its results cannot be extrapolated into the future without very good arguments.

A number of studies in the history and sociology of technology (inspired by Bijker el al. 1987) indicate, however, that the social shaping of new technological systems is a very complex process. One important aspect of this complexity is that established socio-technological systems have a certain momentum which makes the transition to more radically different technologies very difficult. Existing systems tend to solve salient problems in more or less conservative ways. The socio-technical preconditions for the introduction and expansion of radical solutions seem to be far from favourable. There are therefore some serious arguments against the possibility of "technical fixes" of the dilemma of the transport sector.

2.5 Conclusions

The main aim of this chapter was to identify global environmental aspects that should be considered by transport policies aiming at the creation of favourable preconditions for environmentally sustainable transport systems, permitting equitable transport behaviour at the global level. Some conclusions can now be drawn from the preceding paragraphs.

In the long term (defined as the period 2020-2050), the current transport systems will probably turn out to be unsustainable. This statement is based on three strong arguments.

First, a direct threat to the transport sector is associated with its future energy supplies. To provide the growing global fleet of motor vehicles with fossil or alternative fuels (or electricity) is associated with great problems for the indicated period.

Second, it is well-known that the transport sector contributes substantially (more than 22% of the total emissions) to the concentration of CO_2 in the atmosphere. The consequences of the human impact on the climate system, which are added to and embedded in the natural variations of the climate, may become clearly visible only in the long term (2020-2050). At that time, it will probably be too late to act in order to avoid serious effects on the human condition. There are therefore very good arguments for already taking political actions in the short term (see, for instance, Johansson, 1997 and Azar and Rodhe, 1997).

Third, there is also another threat to the long-term sustainability of existing transport systems. It is regional in its effects but global in its occurrence. In quite a few regions of the world, the emissions of substances such as SO_x and NO_x from the transport sector (together with the emissions from non-mobile sources) have a negative impact on the function of terrestrial and maritime ecosystems (on which human survival and well-being depend) and reduce their capacity to deliver ecological services to human beings. The effects of the present influence on ecosystems are in some cases irreversible, in some cases reversible, but only after a long period (50-100 years). Particular concern is associated with the fact that ecosystems are complex systems which may flip surprisingly when sufficiently perturbed and, through non-linear changes, reduce their carrying capacity in a dramatic way. The sensitivity, adaptability and vulnerability of these systems will be decisive for the future of humankind.

The expected expansion of motorized transport, particularly outside but also within the present OECD, will, if it is realised, accelerate the breakdown of ecological sustainability. The global consumption of fuels in the transport sector will be increased considerably by the expected expansion and so will the total amount of emissions of substances harmful to the climate system and the ecosystems. The global fleet of cars was already in 1989 regarded as an important biogeochemical factor by the International Geosphere-Biosphere Programme *(A Study of Global Change*, 1989).

In the medium term (2005-2020), the sustainability of present transport systems may also be threatened. One possible cause would be politically initiated oil shortages. Middle East and Central Asia are important production areas which are politically instable. Internal and external military conflicts may lead to disturbances in the exploitation and the transport of oil and result in turbulence on the oil market. Passenger transport systems based on intensive car use may be particularly exposed to sudden and possibly long-lasting energy supply crises. Politically initiated restrictions on oil consumption will hit the transport sector harder than in the 70s, as the share of the total oil consumption attributable to the transport sector has increased significantly since then.

Another possible scenario is based on the fact that, in the medium term (2005-2020), one cannot exclude that new scientific knowledge will create worldwide consensus about the necessity to stabilize the concentration of CO_2 in the atmosphere in a much more rapid way than is expected today. Politically initiated restrictions on the use of fossil fuels based on international agreements will follow in such a case.

A shift from present fossil-fuelled transport to non-fossil-fuelled transport in the future would, on the other hand, be a gigantic step full of problems even if it took place under very favourable preconditions. At present, there is no alternative energy source nor any alternative energy carrier in sight which are able to cover the increasing demand of the global transport (some technology based on direct solar energy as the primary source might be a future possibility). New scientific knowledge about the social construction of technological systems shows, however, that radical technical solutions are often very difficult to implement.

Therefore, any solution to the problem of making existing systems less unsustainable which is based exclusively on technical development (a "technical fix") seems improbable, given both the time restrictions and the expected expansion of the global transport systems.

3 The Changes of Danish, Dutch and Swedish Transport Policies

3.1 Introduction

3.1.1 Theory and method

The objective of this chapter is to identify, describe and explain how stated transport policies have changed in Denmark, the Netherlands and Sweden in the period 1987-1997. The reasons for limiting the period under scrutiny were presented in the Introduction. The focus will be on national policies for passenger transport with particular emphasis on the question of environmental sustainability, as also indicated in the Introduction. Possible differences between the countries will not be emphasized here, as they will be the main topic of a comparative analysis in the following chapter.

Since the source material here comprises the transport policies as expressed in basic policy documents, the main focus of this chapter is on the policy-making process rather than the implementation of the policies. An attempt to compare the *strategies* with the real *outcome* will be made in the last chapter but one. What follows in this chapter is therefore not a structural analysis of transport policies but rather a study of the policy-making process as it appears in stated transport policy strategies.

My main method is, therefore, *interpretation of political texts* (on the problems associated with the interpretation of such texts, see above 1.2.3). The main research material comprises written documents such as government bills, records from Parliamentary sessions, reports from governmental commissions and from different transport and environmental agencies, etc.

In order to grasp the strategic elements of a given political text, I will apply the definition of 'strategy' which was presented in the first chapter. In accordance with this definition, the findings of the analysis will be presented as integrated parts of four strategic elements: 1/ the policy-makers' varying perceptions of the problems of the transport system 2/ their formulation of strategic goals in transport policy 3/ their selection of intermediate objectives, policy instruments and concrete measures and 4/ their expressed views of the implementation and evaluation process.

The results of this analytical description will produce answers to the question *how* stated transport policies have changed in Denmark, the Netherlands and Sweden in the period 1987-1997. To answer the question *why* transport policies have been changed requires a more theoretical approach.

Some theoreticians have attempted to explain changes in government transport policies. Two contributions, both published in 1987 (and thus not influenced by the actual changes in the period 1987-1997), are of relevance here: le Clercq (1987) and Starkie (1987), the first author basing his view upon empirical studies of the history of Dutch transport policy, the second one on the history of British transport policy. Both discuss the emergence of new issues in transport policy and the decline of other issues, leading to the modification of goals and objectives. They are also concerned with the varying popularity of different policy instruments.

Le Clercq thinks that transport policy issues 'exhibit a pattern of "upswings" and "downswings"'. The idea is that attention paid to a transport issue (for instance, interest in infrastructure investments) fluctuates over time in a cyclical manner. The fluctuation is associated not only with economic cycles (for instance, when economic growth leads to increased congestion) but also with changes in the underlying views in society (for instance, attitudes to new technologies). According to le Clercq, such a policy cycle may be analysed in terms of policy formulation, planning and implementation.

Starkie takes a similar view (with reference to Downs, 1972) that 'public attention rarely remains focused upon any one issue for very long' He therefore talks about 'issue cycles', each of which can be divided into five stages of varying duration. Starkie distinguishes between 1/ the pre-problem stage 2/ 'alarmed discovery and euphoric enthusiasm' 3/ a stage characterised by the realising of the cost of significant progress 4/ gradual decline of interest and 5/ the post-problem stage.

Both le Clercq and Starkie claim that not only traditional but also new issues are exposed to upswings and downswings. Le Clercq takes the view that new problems, new technologies, new interest groups and new developments in society give rise to new transport policy cycles, because governments have to react to the pressure of these factors in one way or another.

Starkie claims that new problems do not necessarily become an "issue" but require some dramatic event, highlighted by the media. The role of interest groups is thereby often crucial in building up pressure. Exposed to intensive and lasting pressure, the old policy collapses. The policy reaction to the built-up pressure depends on various factors such as 1/ the character of the issue 2/ the current levels of aspiration and 3/ the availability of policy instruments adapted to the new issue. Starkie also suggests that processes leading to the collapse of existing transport policies may be analysed by means of the catastrophe theory presented by the French mathematician Réné Thom. Thus, discontinuous change can be given a mathematical description.

3.1.2 Previous studies

Empirical studies of Danish, Dutch and Swedish transport policies are rare. This fact reflects, at least in the case of Denmark and Sweden, that transportation studies have mostly been seen as a source of necessary information for policy makers rather than a kind of critical analysis of really existing transport policies (see 1.1.1).

In Denmark, transportation studies are a rather late phenomenon. A survey of previous transport policy in Denmark was published in 1993 (*Dansk Transportpolitik - en oversigt*). This appears to be the only empirical study hitherto.

In the Netherlands, the situation is somewhat different. Le Clercq analysed Dutch transportation planning from the middle of the 50s to the middle of the 80s in a paper entitled '*Dynamics in transportation Planning: an Overview*' (1985). A case study of Dutch transport policy and the environment up to 1990 (Vleugel et al. 1990) is included in an anthology of six case studies from 1990 (Barde and Button, 1990). The present Dutch transport system has been described by Kerver, Jansen and Bovy (1993) and Dutch transport policy in the 90s has been analysed by Rietveld (1993), by Schrama and Klok (1995), by Kroon (1997) and by Haq (1997).

In Sweden, empirical studies of transport policy are also relatively few: There is one survey used as a text book in transport studies (Holmgren, 1994), one dissertation dealing with the transport policy decision of 1963 (Sannerstedt, 1979) and one dealing with the transport policy both of 1963 and 1979 (Wedin, 1982).

At the Universities of Uppsala and Umeå, a large research programme entitled "Transport and Communication History" has recently been initiated. The aim of one of the reports (Andersson-Skog and Ottosson, 1994) is to illustrate the usefulness of institutional theory in studies of the transport sector, taking the Swedish railway and the growth of Swedish motorized society as examples. In another report, the relation between the Road Authority and representatives of car interests is discussed (Gerentz, 1995).

3.1.3 Some basic facts about the three countries

Before entering upon the analysis, some basic facts about Denmark, the Netherlands and Sweden could be useful for readers not so familiar with these countries.

Denmark is a small country (about 44.000 square km in size) situated at the Northern edge of the European continent. It is surrounded by the North Sea and the Baltic and is bordered by Germany in the South. It is a transit area for traffic to and from Norway, Finland and Sweden.

Denmark's land area is split up into a number of islands of various size and one large peninsula (Jutland). Eighty-five per cent of the population (of about 5.12 million) is urban (in 1988). The population density is about 120 inhabitants per square km. There is only one major metropolitan area (Copenhagen), while there are some cities of medium size (Århus, Odense and Aalborg).

The Netherlands is situated at the North-western edge of the European continent and it covers a surface of 41.863 square km. It borders on the North Sea in the North and West, on Belgium in the South and Germany in the East. About half of the land area is below sea level. The population density is high (444 inhabitants per square km). Ninety per cent of its population (of 15.1 million in 1992) lives in cities.

The urban agglomeration called "Randstad", including Amsterdam, the airport Schiphol, The Hague (the capital) and Rotterdam, with about 6 million inhabitants is particularly traffic-intensive. There are also quite a number of cities with over 100 000 inhabitants (such as Groningen, Enschede, Nijmegen, Maastricht, Eindhoven, Tilburg, Breda, Dortrecht).

The Netherlands is a transit country for large quantities of goods (the "Gateway to Europe") and for many tourists. The effects of the Common Market have reinforced the Netherlands' particular role of being a transit country.

Sweden, a part of the Scandinavian peninsula, has a relatively large land area (approximately 450 000 square km). The average population density is very low (19 inhabitants per square km). Specific transport problems are associated with remote and sparsely populated areas.

The majority of the population (8.8 million in 1995) is concentrated in the southern part of the country. In 1980, eightythree per cent of the population was living in urban areas, many of them in middle-sized cities (50 000-120 000).

Three of the Swedish cities (Stockholm, Göteborg and Malmö) are relatively big towns, with specific traffic problems. The road space of these three metropolitan areas (corresponding to only 2% of the total road space of Sweden), has to cope with 25% of the total road traffic (*The Ecological City*, 1995, p 28).

3.2 Danish transport policy in the period 1987-1997

3.2.1 Introduction: transport policy before 1987

Danish transport policy in the decades preceding 1987 was fairly uncoordinated, according to the survey carried out at the request of the Danish Transport Council (*Dansk Transportpolitik - en oversigt*, 1993 - with a summary in English). Transport policy had long been a fragmented field composed of elements such as

1. investment policy
2. land-use and other physical planning
3. policies concerning licence fees and duties and
4. uncoordinated initiatives for the different transport modes

Reports on Danish transport policy and planning were, however, presented to Parliament at intervals by the Ministry of Public Works (see Kristiansen, 1995, p 97 for some examples).

Before 1987, Danish transport policy was thus very much concerned with the issue of investments in road infrastructure (note that the Danish Minister responsible for transport was, until the last years of 1980s, the head of the Ministry of Public Works). The interest in building a network of motorways has fluctuated over the years: in the thirties the first ideas (inspired by the German *Autostraden*) were presented by private firms. In the sixties a comprehensive plan describing the geographical structure of the network of motorways across the bigger Danish islands and the peninsula of Jutland, called "the big H", was developed by the Danish Road Directorate. In the seventies, this plan was modified, downsized and called "the little h" *(Trinvis udbygning af motorveje "i det lille h"*, 1976, see also Kristiansen, 1995, pp 59sqq).

A major change in the Danish transport policy took place in the late 80s and early 90s (*Dansk Transportpolitik - en oversigt*, p 10). This reflected a greater emphasis (after attempts in the 70s) on the necessity to integrate transport policy with environmental policy in the political debate towards the end of the 80s. At this time, Danish transport policy debate was also increasingly influenced by international issues, such as the coordination within the European Community (*op.cit.* p 10).

3.2.2 The Transport Action Plan of 1987

In March 1987, the Minister of Public Works (of the ruling Conservative-Centre coalition Government) presented an overview of Danish transport policy to *Folketinget*, the Danish Parliament (published in *Folketingstidende* 1986/87, col. 9290-9305). Here, *the goal of the current policy* was described as aiming at 'promotion of an efficient transport system for citizens and business' (col. 9290, my translation). Measures should, however, be taken to minimize a negative environmental impact and traffic injuries. Due consideration should also be given to 'energy and other societal aspects' of transport (col. 9291). In the case of individual mobility, the free choice of transport modes was to be respected. The population should be able 'as far as possible to use and profit from the advantages of the use of a private car' (col. 9292, my translation).

In the same year (1987), a Transport Action Plan was submitted to the Danish Parliament (*Trafikpolitisk handlingsplan*). To *promote the goal of efficiency* of the transport system, it was regarded necessary:

1 to realise the agreement from June 1986 between the Government and the Social Democratic Party to link the two biggest islands with the peninsula of Jutland by a rail and road bridge across the Great Belt (p 5)
2 to initiate discussions with the Swedish Government about a fixed link for rail and road across the strait between Denmark and Sweden (Øresund) (p 6)
3 to expand the motorways connecting the main centres of the country i.e. to finalize the "Big H" structure covering the different parts of the Danish land mass (pp 10sqq)
4 to make the railway more efficient for long distance transport (pp 21sqq)
5 to use various forms of Traffic Management and other measures in the Copenhagen area, where more roads were no solution (pp 15sq).

The main *measures* were, thus, investments in road and rail infrastructure. The *implementation* of the policy was to depend on close collaboration between the State, the counties (in Danish: *amt*) and the local municipalities.

Almost at the same time, the safety problem of transportation was dealt with by a parliamentary Commission. It presented an Action Plan in 1988 *(Færdselssikkerhedspolitisk handlingsplan)*. The *goals* of the Plan were to be realised in three steps aiming at a reduction in the number of killed and injured (p 10). The *measures* were orientated towards the transport users, the vehicles and the roads and their surroundings (pp 29sq). The Action Plan included ideas for local safety programmes (pp 71sqq) and for *the follow-up* of the Plan (pp 91sq). This Plan was supported by Parliament, but no budget was decided for its implementation.

3.2.3 The Transport Action Plan of 1990

After only three years, a more significant shift in Danish transport policy occurred. The reason behind this shift was that the Danish government had rapidly reacted to the publication of the Brundtland report *Our Common Future* (1987) by elaborating a kind of a national follow-up in 1988. Particular political attention should be paid to the energy and transport sectors.

Therefore, a Transport Action Plan for Environment and Development was presented in 1990, prepared by a cross-ministerial Commission under the direction of the Danish Ministry of Transport (previously Ministry of Public Works). The new plan (*Regeringens transporthandlingsplan før miljø og udvikling*), quoted below as 'Transport Action Plan of 1990', was submitted to Parliament in May 1990 and received broad political support in the debate on May 18th.

The basic *view of the problems* of the Danish transport system was inspired by the Brundtland Commission. The effects of transport on the environment were focused on and divided into three categories: global (the greenhouse effect), regional (vegetation damage, death of forests, acid rain and nitrogen deposition) and local (concentrations of toxic substances, noise, road accidents, insecurity, contamination of surface water and ground water, impact on nature, barrier effects, etc). The substances dealt with were CO_2, NO_x, SO_2, HC, CO together with lead and particles (pp 9sqq).

The volume of passenger transport was expected to increase substantially in passenger kilometres (by 40%) between 1988 and 2010 but only slightly (by 4%) between 2010 and 2030 as a result of an expected decline in population. The growth in freight transport was expected to be more impressive: it was estimated to increase in tonne kilometres by 55% between 1988 and 2010 and by 33% between 2010 and 2030. Transport was therefore expected to contribute substantially to the emissions of polluting substances in the future (pp 36sqq).

The strategic goal of the Transport Action Plan was to reduce the environmental problems caused by transport, both in the national interest and in accordance with international agreements. This goal was specified in a number of *objectives and quantitative targets*:

1 the energy consumption of the transport sector and the CO_2 emissions by this sector should be stabilized before the year 2005 and reduced by 25% in the period up to 2030
2 emissions of NO_x and HC should be reduced by at least 40% before the year 2000 and by 60% before the year 2010
3 emissions of particles should be halved in towns and cities up to the

year 2010
4   a reduction in noise levels in dwellings exposed to more than 55 dB to the extent 'that by 2010 not more than 100 000 dwellings are exposed to a noise level of more than 65 dB' (pp 29sqq).

Different ways of realising the objectives of the Plan were indicated together with the *policy instruments* to be used: A reduction of emissions from motor vehicles should be promoted by technical means as well as by an improvement in the energy efficiency of individual means of transport. The introduction of domestic standards and a higher level of taxes should therefore be considered. Furthermore, it was referred to the development of vehicle technology promoted at the international level and to future EC measures to limit CO_2 emissions. Denmark was to support European initiatives such as the introduction of compulsory standards for energy-efficiency in new cars, vehicle taxes that provide an incentive to use cars with better energy economy and a harmonization of fuel taxes at a high level (pp 179sqq; pp 183sqq).

A modal shift from car use to public transport and bicycles would improve the local environment substantially. The quality and price of public transport were regarded as key questions. In the case of local transport, better bus technology would be crucial to reach the environmental objectives of the Plan. In the case of regional and long-distance trips, the railway was regarded as already offering a good choice, and the electrification of certain railway lines was expected to improve the situation further (pp 186sqq). The Plan envisaged that Denmark would also be included in the European high-speed rail network (pp 130sqq).

It was indicated that the desired modal shift could be promoted by measures such as economic incentives, investments in improved systems for public transport, town planning aiming at a reduction of the need to travel and information campaigns for environmentally friendly modes of transport etc (pp 181sq).

The implementation process was mainly based on collaboration between the State and the municipal authorities. The Government would give economic support to stimulate new forms of public transport and new ideas about sustainable solutions to the transport problems of the individual cities (pp 187sqq). The individual ministers were made responsible for ensuring that a necessary follow-up took place (p 198).

Two years later, in 1992, the Ministry of the Environment discussed the future Danish transport system in its presentation of the national long-term planning in *Danmark på vej mod år 2018* (in translation: "Denmark on the road towards the year 2018"). The document emphasized the importance of increasing the efficiency in using the transport capacity of different vehicles and integrating the Danish transport system with the European system in an environmentally benign way.

The implementation of a comprehensive network of motorways and expressways and the bridges across the Great Belt and Øresund were regarded as important elements in the effort to achieve economic growth. A major transfer of transport from road to rail was estimated as difficult, as distances are, as a rule, relatively short in Denmark (part II, p 12). In densely urban areas, public transport should be given priority. In the report, no attempt was made to analyse the contradiction between the environmental objectives of the transport policy and the effects of the integration of the Danish road transport system in the European system.

3.2.4 The Traffic Plan of 1993

In 1992, the long-lived Conservative-Centre coalition Government was dismissed and a new Government under the guidance of the Social-Democrats was installed. This did not lead to any change in transport policy. However, the Danish Parliament decided that the new Government should present a comprehensive traffic plan covering the infrastructure investments up to the year 2005. For this reason, the Minister of Transport presented a Report on Danish Transport Policy to Parliament *(Trafik 2005: Trafikpolitisk redegørelse)* as well as a detailed Plan *(Trafik 2005: Problemstillinger, mål og strategier)*, both published in December 1993 (a summary in English is available).

The Traffic Plan of 1993 represents - in relation to the Transport Action Plan of 1990 - a step from policy to planning. The Report can be seen as the main political text and the Plan is a rather more detailed elaboration of the Report. The following analytical description is mainly based upon the Report (but both documents are also referred to below by 'Traffic Plan of 1993'). In the Report, the principles of the new government's transport policy were declared: the firm decision to fulfil the intentions of the Transport Action Plan of 1990 and to adapt the Danish transport policy to the principles of the Common Transport Policy of the European Union of December 1992, confirmed by the Council of Ministers in June 1993.

The main objectives of the policy were:

1 to develop a transport system which is sustainable in the sense that individual mobility can be realised in the future within the limits defined by natural resources and the environment (including climate, noise and safety) and
2 to strengthen the conditions for free competition (according to the Report pp 2sq).

The targets of the Transport Action Plan of 1990 concerning emissions of CO_2, NO_x and HC were repeated (in the Report pp 14sq). In a *vision*, the future conditions of transport in Denmark (around 2010?) were described in an attractive way (in the Plan, pp 105-109). Rapid technological development in combination with radically changed attitudes in the population were assumed to become the driving forces behind a successful creation of a sustainable Danish transport system.

To reach the goals of the Plan, *five elements of a strategy were indicated:*

1 to influence the volume of transport and its distribution on different modes of transport
2 to improve the alternatives to car use
3 to limit the problems of pollution
4 to reorientate the transport investments and
5 to strengthen planning and research in the field of transport (the Report, pp 2sq).

The main policy instruments and concrete measures for the implementation of this strategy were as follows: economic policy instruments should be used to influence the transport volumes and the composition of the car fleet. People should be stimulated to use public transport and/or bicycles instead of cars (the former by improving the quality of public transport), the capacity of different modes should be used more efficiently, the number of trips should be reduced by means of information technology, the use of cars in city centres should be reduced, the use of more energy-efficient and environmentally friendly modes of transport stimulated, the emission norms should be made more restrictive and increased use of alternative fuels should be studied (the Report, p 3 and the Plan, pp 10sqq).

A reorientation of road investments should be realised by giving more attention to aspects of safety and environment taking for granted, however, that road transport would continue to dominate in the future. The future road-net should be able to offer both citizens and business efficient, safe and environmentally friendly transport facilities.

In real terms: the motorway network (the "Big H") should be completed and the conditions for building a bridge across Fehmarn Belt to link the Danish islands to the continent should be analysed.

The Danish rail system should be modernized through continued electrification and through the introduction of high-speed trains to facilitate the integration of this Danish rail system with the European system (the Report pp 5sqq).

3.2.5 After 1993: evaluation of results and controversies about measures

The realisation of the Action Plan of 1990 and the Traffic Plan of 1993 was determined at the national level in the period 1993-1997 primarily by 1/ the directives of the European Union 2/ the annual national budget laws and 3/ national laws for particular projects or sectors.

The practical implementation of the Danish transport policy was, however, decentralized to a large extent, and took place mainly at the municipal level. In 1992, the government set aside a grant for the period 1992-1995 to stimulate the development and implementation of local action plans for traffic and environment in the municipalities. A preliminary evaluation of its impact was made in 1995 (*Evaluering af Trafik- og Miljøpuljen*) and a final evaluation is expected in 1998.

At the level of county (*amt*), there are one or two examples of conscious transport policy programmes. The most detailed one is *Transportpolitisk redegørelse* published by Vejle county (1997). The idea behind the programme of the county was to reduce the present unsustainable character of local traffic without jeopardizing the mobility and the life quality of the citizens. The programme was, however, more inspired by the Common Transport Policy of the EU (see below 5.2.2) and by the experience of local politicians and professionals than by the national transport action programmes (according to an interview in December 1997).

The results of the national policy for increased safety were evaluated in 1996 *(Status for den Færdselssikkerhetspolitiske handlingsplan af 1988)*. The targets of the safety plan of 1988 had been reached in the first three years of the period but, unfortunately, not in the years 1991-1995. A new Action Plan for Traffic Safety *(Hver olycke er én for meget. Regeringens handlingsplan for trafiksikkerhed)* was therefore presented by the Minister of Transport in 1997.

In early 1996, the Ministry of Environment and Energy presented a preliminary review of current Danish national planning: *Forslag til Landsplanredegørelse: Danmark og europæisk planpolitik*, in which the Danish transport system was briefly dealt with (*op.cit.* pp 40-49). Danish investments in road infrastructure were here seen within the framework of EU:s programme for Trans-European Networks (TEN). The conflict between the development of transport infrastructure and expected traffic growth, on the one hand, and the environment, on the other, was clearly articulated in the report. Already decided measures were regarded as being insufficient to stimulate a transition to less polluting and more energy-efficient modes of transport. More powerful measures were needed. Otherwise a policy for sustainable development would not be possible *op.*

cit. p 43). The Ministry of Environment and Energy had therefore already initiated a debate on the energy futures of Denmark in 1995 (by publishing a series of booklets under the common heading *Danmarks energifremtider*). Here, a number of possible measures were enumerated without indicating what kind of policy instruments should be used to reach the goal.

An evaluation of possible economic instruments was made by the Economic Council of the Government in spring 1996 (in a report entitled *Dansk økonomi - forår 1996* with an English summary). Various ways of internalizing these external costs of traffic were analysed:
- air pollution
- the greenhouse effect
- traffic accidents
- traffic-related noise and
- the use of road infrastructure.

The Council estimated that these external costs (the costs of congestion not included) corresponded approximately to 4% of GDP in early 1990s (p 171). To internalize these costs would require a doubling of the present price of fuel. Technical progress is however expected to reduce the external costs considerably. Furthermore, it would be inappropriate not the take the great regional variation into consideration. Fuel duties were therefore seen as imperfect instruments. More specific and direct measures were therefore recommended, such as introducing stricter technological standards, constructing safer roads and starting with road pricing (*op.cit.* pp 172sq).

The carbon dioxide problems constituted another case in the Council's view. In 2005, the carbon dioxide emissions from the transport sector would, given the present trends, exceed the 1988 level by about 20%. To stabilize the emissions of carbon dioxide from the transport sector at the 1988 level by 2005 (in accordance with the official target) would require an increase in fuel prices of around 66%. The Economic Council drew the conclusion that such a policy would incur 'excessive social costs' (*op.cit.* p 173) and therefore recommended a less strict target for the transport sector.

The Ministry of Transport, in its turn, had initiated a debate on the theme of transport, energy and CO_2 emissions in an Action Plan for the reduction of CO_2-emissions from the transport sector in spring 1996 *(Regeringens handlingsplan for reduktion af transportsektorens CO_2-udslip)*. This plan reflected the fact that the emissions of CO_2 from the Danish transport sector had increased by 7-11% (depending on different ways of estimating the increase) since 1988 (*op.cit.* p 8, foot-note 1), which was contrary to the target of stabilized emissions by 2005 at the 1988 level, a target confirmed by the Danish Parliament in 1996.

The Action Plan indicated a number of possible policy instruments to reach the target of stabilization by 2005, which meant a reduction of around 15% of the expected growth (assuming an moderate economic growth). EU:s initiatives (see below 5.5.3) were expected to lead to more energy-efficient vehicles, and the probable increase in car use following the drop in fuel costs per km was to be counteracted by a conscious price policy for petrol (p 21). The possibility of promoting the sales of energy-efficient vehicles by altering vehicle fees should also be considered as a possible measure (p 30) together with physical planning (pp 14-15). Measures should be taken to stimulate a modal shift to public transport and cycle transport (pp 16-19). The possibilities of a successive introduction of alternative fuels and engine technologies were regarded as promising, but only in the long-term perspective (pp 31-36). Information campaigns orientated both towards the general public and towards the business sector were looked upon as efficient instruments for the implementation of the new Action Plan (pp 36-40).

The Ministry of Transport also took the initiative to produce a study of the most cost-efficient measures to reach the target of stabilization by 2005 *(CO2-reduktioner i transportsektoren. Hovedrapport*, 1997). The results elaborated by a private consultant are presented without any assessment of the political feasibility of each measure. The consultant claimed that a 13% reduction could be achieved by using the following measures, at an annual social cost of between 290-590 million DKK:

1. the successive introduction of new standards of improved energy efficiency of new cars (4.4% per year) up to 2005 (in accordance with the programme of the European Commission)
2. a reduction of the registration fee of cars to compensate consumers for the increased costs of more energy-efficient cars
3. the introduction of a special environmental marking of energy efficient cars and
4. an increase in the price of petrol and diesel by 1.17 and 0.93 DKK respectively, up to 2005 in order to avoid the possibility that reduced kilometre costs of new cars would lead to more traffic.

3.2.6 The findings of the analysis

On the basis of the analytical description in the preceding sections, it is now possible to make the following statements
- that a coordinated transport policy is a late phenomenon in Denmark (the Transport Action Plan of 1987 being the first result)
- that the Danish transport policy strategies have gone through impor-

tant changes in the first half of the period 1987-1997
- that a significant shift in Danish transport policy was initiated, by means of a Transport Action Plan presented by the ruling Conservative-Centre Government in 1990, in which attempts were made to combine ideas of the role of transport for economic growth with environmental goals (the environmental impact should, however, no longer be 'minimized', as in 1987, but actually 'reduced')
- that the view of the transport problems became more complex in the Transport Action Plan of 1990, including the global, regional and local environmental impact
- that timetabled quantitative targets were formulated for the first time by the Transport Action Plan of 1990
- that the new transport policy of 1990 was confirmed and concretized by the new Social-Democrat Government in 1993 by means of a Traffic Plan (*Trafik 2005*), in which a more detailed interpretation of the concept of 'environmental sustainability' was presented
- that the environmental goals of the Transport Action Plan of 1990 were specified in more detail by the Traffic Plan of 1993 and concretised by a vision of a sustainable Danish transport system based upon technical development and radically changed attitudes in the population
- that the existence of conflicts between different transport policy goals was admitted, but the ways to reduce these conflicts were never analysed in the political documents of 1990 and 1993
- that a package of policy instruments and measures recommended by the Transport Action Plan of 1990 and the Traffic Plan of 1993 was intended to influence the technical standard of vehicles in use, to stimulate a shift to more energy-efficient and environmentally friendly transport modes (public transport and cycling) and, by means of economic instruments, to influence the transport volumes and the composition of the car fleet
- that the integration of Danish rail and road systems in the European transport system was regarded as important, requiring substantial investments in infrastructure
- that the implementation process was based on cooperation between the three levels of political administration in Denmark (national, regional and local) with the emphasis on the local level
- that it was the responsibility of the individual Ministers to evaluate the results of the policy
- that the period 1993-1997 was characterized by some evaluations of the results of the transport policies and by some controversies about adequate measures to be used in transport policy to reach its environmental goals.

3.3 Dutch transport policy in the period 1987-1997

3.3.1 Introduction: transport policy before 1987

The first coherent Dutch transport policy programme was elaborated in the late 1970s. A "First Transport Structure Plan" (*Structuurschema Verkeer en Vervoer* - abbreviated *SVV1*) was presented to the Dutch Parliament in 1977 and accepted by Parliament in the session of 1981.

Congestion was regarded as one of the most serious problems of the system, due to the ongoing "mobiliteitsexplosie" (*op.cit.* p 112). Car ownership figures were, however, still fairly low in the Netherlands (250 per 1000 inhabitants in 1975). The construction of more roads was thought of as an important remedy for the problems of congestion. An increased role of public transport was indicated as a means of reducing growth in car use.

At that time, the environment was perceived as a less important issue (Vleugel et al. 1990). The problems of the ozone layer were unknown and few people were aware of the problems of greenhouse gases. However, transport was seen as having a negative impact on 1/ 'het abiotisch milieu' 2/ 'het biotisch milieu' 3/ 'het cultuurlijk milieu' and 4/ 'het landschap' (*SVV1*, pp 146 sqq).

3.3.2 Initiating a new transport policy in 1988

After only five years (in 1986), the First Transport Structure Plan was no longer seen as adapted to the current conditions of Dutch transport. A new transport structure plan was therefore prepared by the coalition Government (consisting of Christian Democrats and right-wing Liberals) under Lubbers, and a draft for discussion was presented in November 1988: *Tweede Struktuurschema Verkeer en Vervoer: deel a beleidsvoornemen*, abbreviated *SVV2* (a German translation will be used here as a source). The draft included 1/ an analysis of the problems of the Dutch transport system, 2/ a preliminary formulation of a number of transport policy goals and targets 3/ a discussion of a number of concrete measures to reach the goals and targets and 4/ an analysis of how the infrastructural proposals would affect subsequent planning.

The main *problems of the transport system* were described as increasing congestion, particularly on the roads and, as a consequence of increasing use of cars (not least in connection with holidays and free time), reduced efficiency in public transport and in freight transport, increasing problems related to traffic injuries, to air quality, to the long-term energy provision (over-dependence on oil as an energy source) and to various threats to the biodiversity of flora and fauna and to the landscape (pp 9-15).

The *main goals of the strategy* were suggested to be:
- increased access
- increased efficiency in public transport
- improved environmental quality (pp 22sqq).

These goals should be achieved without using "unbalanced" *solutions* such as
- concentrating only on the upgrading of the infrastructure
- concentrating only on the use of economic policy instruments or
- using congestion as a conscious way of regulating traffic (pp 16sq).

A number of concrete *objectives* were presented (pp 22-29) and their economic and societal consequences discussed in detail (pp 30-94).

Stakeholders in transport, interest groups and organizations, as well as researchers, were invited to present their views of the draft (p 8). This invitation initiated a lively debate. Many actors tried to influence decision-making at this early stage. Particularly the idea of introducing road pricing was met by hard criticism. The Ministry of Transport and Public Works contributed to the debate by publishing a small booklet entitled *Rekening Rijden. Road Pricing in the Netherlands*. The final words of the text express doubts about the political feasibility of the idea: 'It is yet politically uncertain whether Road Pricing will actually be introduced in The Netherlands. What is certain is that we will have to restrict the use of the car to preserve quality of life and accessibility' (p 13).

The environmental problems of the transport sector became an important political issue in these years. The background of this was partly a report from the State Institute for Public Health and Environmental Protection (RIVM), in which the gravity of all the environmental problems was described. Another reason was that the commitment of the Dutch Government to environmental matters increased significantly. The First National Environmental Plan (*NEPP1*), entitled *To Choose or to Lose* in its English version, signed by four ministers (among them the minister of Transport and Public Works) was presented to the Dutch Parliament in May 1989 (Bressers and Plettenburg, 1997, pp 124sq). Here, the goals were set for environmental management for 2010 and for paving the way for sustainable development. Its implementation necessitated broad cooperation between authorities and target groups (*NEPP1*, p 171). The Plan also dealt with the serious problems of transport (pp 194-205).

The Environmental Plan of 1989 and the draft of Transport Plan of 1988 are closely linked as to policy, targets and measures. The environmental objectives related to transport are described by *NEPP1* in somewhat more definite terms than those of the draft of *SVV2* (pp 194sq):

- 'vehicles are to be used in traffic and transport which are as clean, quiet, economical and safe as possible and which are made of parts and material which are optimally usable for reuse'
- 'the choice of mode for passenger transport will result in the lowest possible energy consumption and the least possible pollution....'(this meant, given the anticipated technological development, a preference for public transport and bicycles)
- 'the locations where people live, work, shop and spend their leisure time will be coordinated in such a way that the need to travel is minimal'.

Measures suggested by *NEPP1* were expected to reduce car kilometres somewhat more than those suggested by *SVV2* (p 205).

In the final years of 1980s, transport policy thus became a comparatively controversial political issue in the Netherlands. This is illustrated by the fact that a proposal to curtail tax benefits for car commuters split the seven-year-old government in May 1989 (Bressers and Plettenburg, 1997, p124). This is probably the first example in Europe of a government fallen over an issue related to transport policy.

3.3.3 The Transport Structure Plan of 1990

In spring 1990, the new Dutch Government presented its bill on transport policy to the Dutch Parliament. The new transport structure plan (*SVV2*) was also published in an English version entitled *Second Transport Structure Plan (part d: Government decision)* from which I quote. The document, revised in relation to the draft after the public debate, exhibited 'many shifts of emphasis of a substantive nature' (p 4).

The text of the Plan was obviously inspired by the report of the Brundtland Commission. The concept of 'sustainable society' was defined as 'a society which meets the present generation's needs without jeopardizing future generations' ability to meet theirs' (p 8). In this document, a complete strategy (this term is used) for the future of the Dutch transport system was presented (from p 8). It was based on a view of the current problems of Dutch transportation. *The most pressing problems* of Dutch road passenger transport were now defined (pp 5-7) as
- congestion due to increased use of cars (reducing the efficiency of the road transport system)
- increasing number of traffic injuries
- environmental problems (reducing the possibilities of creating a good local environment and of attaining sustainable development in the country) and
- too much dependence on one single energy source (petroleum).

The strategy was further based upon a series of assumptions regarding the future by the year 2010: the population was expected to grow slowly, the size of the working population somewhat faster, the real income per worker would increase by about 65%. These factors would result in a substantial increase in car use, and a continuation of the policy of *SVV1* would lead to an increase in car km of about 70%. Time losses due to congestion would, in such a case, double and the costs associated with congestion increase fourfold.

The *general goal of the strategy* was therefore to strike 'a balance between individual freedom, accessibility and environmental amenity' (p 8). The existence of conflicts between these goals was openly admitted: 'We are thus faced with the challenge of finding intelligent and creative solutions to transport problems - solutions which will allow economic growth in the context of a sustainable society' (p 9). In short, accessibility should be favoured and mobility restrained.

The *main objectives* of the strategy were:
- to reduce the expected increase in car use, also in order to avoid unacceptable congestion,
- to lower the number of dead and injured in traffic accidents and
- to cut the emissions from the vehicles substantially.

This last objective was translated into a number of well-defined targets: Acidification should be halted through a reduction of the emissions of NOx and unburned hydrocarbons from road vehicles of 20% by 1995 (compared to the level of 1986) and of 75% by the year 2010. The risk of global warming necessitated a stabilisation of the emissions of CO_2 by 1995 at the level of 1989/90 and a reduction of 10% by 2010 (p 11).

The recommended *methods of reaching the objectives and targets* belonged to four categories:
- tackling the problems at their source (by the introduction of safe, clean and quiet vehicles, and by curbs placed on the expansion of infrastructure)
- limiting traffic volumes (p 15) by managing and restraining mobility (it was therefore necessary to raise the price of mobility as such)
- improving and favouring the alternatives to the private car: 'offering decent alternatives will not get enough people out of their cars unless negative incentives are also applied' (p 10)
- selective accessibility on the roads: 'In congested areas special measures will be taken to enable lorries, shared cars and buses to by-pass the jams' (pp 10sq).

In terms of *policy instruments and concrete measures*, a whole series of means should be used. More rigorous technical standards should be introduced to favour cleaner vehicles, and research should be supported in order to develop lighter and more energy-efficient vehicles, the spreading of which should be stimulated by means of financial and fiscal measures - a kind of push/pull strategy (pp 15sqq).

Urban planning should be used to discourage car use (p 32): 'The Government believes that urbanization must be limited and favours compact rather than sprawling cities' (p 40). The fragmentation of the country-side should be avoided and reduced (p 23). Curbs should be placed on the expansion of the infrastructure and priority should be given to improving capacity utilization, to widening of existing links and adding of extra links to eliminate bottle-necks and, lastly, to construction of missing links (pp 47-51). The Netherlands should be integrated with the European network of high-speed rail lines (p 40).

Pricing policies were regarded as one of the main instruments to reach the objectives and targets of the Plan. An internalization of the external costs of transport was seen as necessary: 'We have to recognize that we must pay for the comfort and convenience that the car provides, that social costs must be borne by those whose private actions give rise to them' (p 36). "Road pricing" was, however, rejected due to the hard opposition. The impact on low-income households was later considered as the important argument in this opposition (Rietveld, 1993, p 110). Instead, higher fuels taxes should be introduced together with a (conventional or electronic) toll system in and around the Randstad and a peak-hour surcharge (*SVV2*, pp 36-38).

In order to attain the environmental targets and to reduce congestion, the expected car expansion should be cut from an estimated 70% between 1986 and 2010 to 35% (p 12). A reduction from 70% to 50% could be achieved by immediate decisions and from 50% to 35% by future decisions (p 109). Alternatives to the private car, such as public transport (p 57) and cycling (pp 52sqq), should be favoured (p 10), in the case of public transport by means of substantial investments. Information campaigns should stimulate car-sharing (p 55). Campaigns to influence driver behaviour were included as well as speed limit policies (p 17).

The crucial part of all strategies is their *implementation*. In contrast to many other political documents, the Dutch Second Transport Structure Plan from 1990 includes an entire chapter entitled 'Implementation' (pp 114-121). In the Plan, it is said that '(t)he Ministry of Transport cannot do the job alone' (p 114). Instead '(t)he cooperation is needed of everyone involved in making decisions on transport: every individual, every firm, every local authority' (*ibid.*). Actions were needed at various levels: by the European Community, the Netherlands, the metropolitan regions, industry, social organizations and the public.

The roles of all these actors are explicitly specified. About industry, for instance, it is said:'Industry has a vital interest in high standards of accessibility and safe and efficient transport for its workers, but congestion due to the vast scale of car-borne commuting is making access more and more difficult... It is thus in industry's own interest to help reduce car-use for commuting purposes' (p 115). About social organizations, it is said: 'Social organizations - voluntary organizations, political parties and the like - help form the bridge between government and people. Their cooperation is essential in ensuring a broad base of public understanding and support for the often radical measures implied by a sustainable transport policy' (p 115). The authorities of metropolitan areas have to restrain car-use, particularly car-borne commuting, and to improve road safety (p 115). The role of the national government is to - establish emission standards, to enforce speed limits, to introduce a pricing policy, to improve accessibility on the trunk-road network, to invest in public transport and to regulate land-use planning (pp 114sq).

3.3.4 Successive evaluations and revisions of the policy in 1990-1997

The Dutch *Second Structure Plan* has become widely recognized as an impressive example of strategic thinking in transportation. The World Bank has therefore published a special version intended for transportation planners in Eastern Europe and in developing countries. Here, the principles of the Plan are described and motivated.

The Plan has now (spring 1998) been in operation for more than seven years. In order to monitor the implementation process, a specific project was defined as a part of the *SVV2*. The effects of the implementation of the Plan should be measured and the figures interpreted annually. The results and conclusions of this follow-up are published in annual reports entitled *Beleidseffectmeting Verkeer en Vervoer* (English summaries are available under the title of *Measuring the Impact of Transport Policy*). Here the changes in different indicators are recorded (in comparison with the basis year of 1986). The records include emissions of NOx by road traffic, emissions of CO_2 by road traffic, the number of deaths caused by traffic accidents, increases in car kilometres, etc.

The monitoring of the transport plan enables the Environment Ministry and the Transport Ministry to make annual revisions of the policy. Every year, an updated version of the Plan with concrete goals for the next five years is presented as an addendum to the budget of the Ministry (e.g. the 1993 version contains a *Medium Term Programme for Infrastructure and Transport 1994-1998*). Here, the results of the implementation of the policy are evaluated and analysed. New priorities for the following five year-period are presented and discussed. Finally, the major developments of traffic and transport for the last five years are described and the prospects for the year 2000 are mapped out, indicating to what extent they agree with the objectives laid down by *SVV2*.

A more comprehensive evaluation of the policy was carried out in 1993/94. The purpose was to find out whether the targets of *SVV2* could be reached under currently proposed policy measures and recent assumptions about socio-economic development (van der Waard and van der Hoorn, 1995).

The evaluators found that the Dutch population growth appeared to have been underestimated in 1990. A higher birth-rate together with a substantial legal and illegal immigration were regarded as the causes. Some of the investment programmes in the road and railway systems were facing financial problems due to budget deficiencies and increasing costs. The government's efforts to limit the growth of car use were compared to 'swimming against the tide' (*op.cit.* p 12).

It now appeared necessary to introduce more efficient pricing measures to reach the targets of the *SVV2*, although these measures probably could not be implemented before the year 2000. The targets for a reduction of the emissions would probably be met in the case of NOx from private cars, but not from lorries and vans. The targets for emissions of CO_2 would not be met.

The second National Environmental Policy Plan of 1994 (*NEPP2*), entitled *The Environment: Today's Touchstone*, also dealt with the environmental problems of transport in detail, such as climate change, acidification, eutrophication, disposal of waste, and resource dissipation (pp 139-151).

The results of environmental and transport policy in the years 1990-1994 were commented on as follows: 'Many measures have been taken by companies, the authorities and motorists to reduce the pollution caused by transport...Despite all these efforts, the environmental objectives of this sector will be difficult to realise' (p 20). An analytical passage on transport gives the reasons for the limited success: 'Public acceptance of some elements of policy is still inadequate. Problems in introducing road pricing illustrate this. This inadequate acceptance is related to 1/ the difficulty the government has in establishing a direct channel of communication with motorists and 2/ lack of awareness among motorists of the environmental effects of car use and related costs' (p 140).

The way out of this dilemma might be offered by the environmental organisations: 'Such organisations may be able to play an important role in gaining acceptance for policy and in directly influencing motorists' (p 141).

3.3.5 The findings of the analysis

On the basis of the analytical description in the preceding sections, it is now possible to make the following statements:
- that a first coherent transport policy (represented by the *First Transport Structure Plan*) had been formulated in the late 70s and accepted in 1981 by Parliament but it was already obsolete within five years
- that a significant shift in Dutch transport strategic thinking took place in the last years of the 80s, when a draft of a *Second Transport Structure Plan* was formulated
- that the draft of the new transport policy plan was exposed to a public debate, to which the stakeholders, representatives of many organizations as well as researchers were invited
- that the following debate increased the political temperature concerning transport in the Netherlands (one particular issue led to the fall of the Government in 1989)
- that transport policy had been already dealt with by the *National Environmental Policy Plan* of 1989, in which the environmental targets of transport policy were pushed somewhat further than in the *Second Transport Structure Plan*
- that the main principles and general goals of the new transport policy were accepted by Parliament in spring 1990
- that the perceived problems were 1/ rising costs of congestion, 2/ pollution becoming more and more serious and 3/ road accidents again increasing after years of improvement.
- that the main goal of the Plan - in the field of passenger transport - was to strike a balance between individual freedom, accessibility and environmental amenity (the conflict between these goals was openly admitted)
- that a sharp distinction was made between accessibility (which should be enhanced) and mobility (which should be constrained)
- that a potential clash was envisaged between measures to improve accessibility and the goals of a sustainable society
- that the general objectives of the Plan were 1/ a reduction of the expected increase in car mobility 2/ a reduction of the traffic injuries and 3/ a reduction of the environmental impact of transport
- that a number of timetabled quantitative environmental targets (concerning emissions of NO_x, HC and CO_2) were defined in order to achieve the third objective, also leading to mobility reduction targets
- that the main instruments to implement the new policy were stimulation of technical development (to favour the use of cleaner and more energy-efficient vehicles), improved physical planning (including support to public transport) to reduce the need of car use and pricing po-

licies to restrain mobility
- that the role of infrastructure investments as a solution to congestion problems was reduced in comparison with the *First Transport Structure Plan* of 1981
- that the implementation process necessitated the cooperation of a number of social actors
- that the implementation process in the period 1990-1997 was monitored by means of annual measurements and by more comprehensive evaluations and, finally,
- that annual revisions of the transport structure plan were carried out by the Ministry of the Environment and the Ministry of Transport.

3.4 Swedish transport policy in the period 1987-1997 (1998)

3.4.1 Introduction: transport policy before 1987

The first coherent national transport policy in Sweden was presented by a Social Democrat government in 1963 *(Regeringens proposition*, in English "Government bill", 1963:191) and accepted by a unanimous Parliament in December the same year. Earlier political decisions on transport and traffic had been less coordinated (for a survey see Sannerstedt, 1979, pp 2-7).

The new transport policy decision had been preceded by ten years of considerations and studies by an Investigative Commission. The aim of the policy was to provide the population in different parts of the country with safe and satisfactory transport facilities at a low *cost* (also reflecting the social costs of transport). Successive deregulation was intended to lead to more competition between different transport modes. Technical development should be stimulated (Sannerstedt, 1979; Wedin, 1982).

The decision on the policy had been unanimous, but its implementation gave rise to conflicts. The critics argued that public transport deteriorated, particularly in rural areas, that people without cars suffered from this development, and that the same development had negative effects both on safety and the environment. Despite the criticism, three political parties, the Social Democrats, the Centre Party and the conservative Moderate Coalition Party, continued to endorse the decision of 1963 until 1972, whereas the (Liberal) People's Party called for a reconsideration in 1971, and the Communists were against the policy all the time. In 1972 a new Commission was appointed to review the transport policy. It presented its report in 1978 (Sannerstedt, 1979, p 200).

On the basis of this report, a new Swedish national transport policy was launched by the ruling minority government of the People's Party in March 1979 (*Government bill* 1978/79:99). The objective of the 1979 transport policy was to provide citizens as well as business with satisfactory transport facilities at a low *social cost* within the limits defined by safety and the environment (pp 12 sqq). A combination of fees, taxes, investments and regulations was to achieve these objectives (p 14). Cooperation, not only competition, between different modes of transport was to be stimulated (p 16). Automobility as such was looked upon as something positive, as it gave the citizens a greater freedom of choice about where to live and where to work (p 8). At the same time, the increasing use of cars was producing certain problems in urban areas, such as reduced accessibility, irritating noise and polluted air (p 8). A special programme for promoting energy efficiency (this was the year after the second "energy crisis") was formulated (pp 171-187). It was based upon the widespread belief in the future scarcity of oil products. The programme included a strengthening of the role of public transport, stimulation of car pooling (pp 174sq), promotion of energy-efficient vehicles by levying a progressive fuel tax and means of stimulating the introduction of new car technology (pp 177sq). Some interest in the development of alternative fuels was also demonstrated (pp 182sqq).

3.4.2 The transport policy of 1988

Almost ten years later, another Swedish transport policy was presented by a Social Democrat government in January 1988 (*Government bill* no. 1987/88:50). It was based upon a number of expert reports (pp 10sq). The transport policies of 1963 and 1979 were evaluated and both regarded as partial failures (p 9).

The 1988 transport policy was based on a more complex *perception of the problems* of the transport sector in comparison with previous policies. This view included:
- the increasing negative environmental impact of all transport
- the inadequate up-grading of the road-net
- unsatisfactory transport facilities for certain groups
- regional imbalance in the transport structure
- the excessive number of traffic injuries and
- the economic crisis of the national railway system (p 10).

The environmental and energy problems were described in some detail (pp 51-54). Emissions of CO, NO_2, N_2O, HC, SO_2, and their effect on the environment and human health were discussed as well as the effects of ozone (at the ground level), particulate matter and noise. The problems of regional environmental effects such as acidification (p 26) and eutrophication (pp 53sqq) were emphasized. The problem of global warming, as a consequence of CO2 emissions, was *not* mentioned.

The *strategic goal* of the new policy was to create favourable conditions for 'a satisfactory, safe and environmentally friendly transport provision at the lowest possible socioeconomic cost' in the interest of citizens and business (p 22, my translation). The role of transport was said to be to maintain and develop the welfare of the citizens by using different resources as efficiently as possible. Five partial objectives of the policy were identified:
1 accessibility
2 efficient use of available resources
3 safety
4 environmental quality and efficient use of natural resources
5 regional balance (p 21).

The transport volumes were estimated to grow substantially, at least for the period until 2000 (pp 11sqq). Increased transport volumes were seen as a consequence of 'the internationalization of production' but also, and more important, a consequence of more trips made in people's leisure time. An attempt to limit this freedom of transport would have negative effects on the equal distribution of welfare (p 60). Automobility 'will remain an essential part of the future transport system' (p 161, my translation).

The environmental goals of the transport policy were also described in some detail. The emissions were to be reduced in the long run to the limits of human health and nature's tolerance (p 49). In the case of NOx, a general reduction of 30% was to be achieved by 1995 (with 1980 as the basis year), a reduction to which the transport sector should contribute. HC and CO had to be reduced by 50% during the same period (p 49). Apart from this, it was said that the air quality in urban areas had to be improved and the noise reduced. The energy use in motor vehicles was to be made more efficient, mainly through stimulation of technical development (pp 65-73). It was important to take advantage of the dynamism of "automobility" to adapt car use to the requirements of safety and environment (p 161).

The *policy instruments* indicated in the bill covered a whole range of measures. The different modes of transport were supposed both to cooperate and to compete. Decisions on transport facilities would be decentralized through deregulation (pp 30sqq). "Society" (i.e. the state, the counties and the municipalities) should, however, continue to keep the responsibility of maintaining and developing the transport infrastructure (pp 32sqq). The expansion of the road-net and the maintenance of the roads should be based upon true estimates of social costs. Favourable preconditions for public transport and environmentally friendly and energy-efficient transport should be created (pp 65sqq). Physical planning was seen as an important instrument in reducing the problems of traffic (p 60). Transport technology had to be stimulated in various ways (pp 65-68). The requirement that new cars should be equipped with catalytic converters was introduced in 1989. In the long run, cleaner vehicles were believed to be the principle solution to the pollution problem. In the meantime, people's behaviour was to be influenced by raising transport prices (p 30). Parliament passed the bill in spring 1988.

The particular problems of the three largest cities in Sweden (Stockholm, Göteborg and Malmö) were later studied by an Investigative Commission called "Storstadsutredningen" in 1990 (SOU 1990:16 with an English summary). The Commission indicated a number of measures to reduce the severe problems of the traffic in Stockholm, Göteborg and Malmö. Proposals were made to:
- upgrade and expand the public transport services
- construct main traffic routes that solve local environmental problems
- introduce car tolls and regional environmental fees
- restrict mileage deductions in metropolitan areas and increase fringe benefit taxation on free cars
- restrict the volume of heavy diesel-driven traffic in city centres
- increase the demands on noise levels for vehicles
- raise parking fines
- revise general regional and municipal planning.

These suggestions later resulted in three agreements between the national government and the local governments of Stockholm, Göteborg and Malmö (see below).

3.4.3 The changes made in 1988 transport policy in 1991-1994

During the last years with the Social Democrats in government, the economic recession that began in the early 90s became worse. Through a special bill (*Näringspolitik för tillväxt* 1990/91:87), the Government tried to stimulate economic activity in Sweden and increase Swedish competitiveness. One of the ideas was to initiate a huge investment programme for the transport infrastructure.

The same Government also presented an ambitious bill on environment policy (*Government bill no. 1990/91:90*). It was based on a comprehensive review of the state of the environment in Sweden and its problems (presented in a voluminous appendix). The objectives of the new policy were to
- protect the ozone layer
- reduce the effects on climate (through stabilization of CO_2)

- reduce the emissions of SOx and NOx and volatile organic compounds
- improve the local environment in urbanized areas
- to promote a responsible use of natural resources and
- to protect waters and seas from pollution.

Some timetabled targets were defined. Among the most important policy instruments were the use of economic instruments and the introduction of a new environmental code. Special measures were mentioned in the field of transport (pp 81-87; pp 300-372). The introduction of an environmental classification of motor vehicles was one of these instruments. This bill was passed by Parliament in spring 1991.

In the elections of September 1991, the Social Democrats were defeated by the opposition and a new Swedish Government was established: a Coalition consisting of the Moderate Coalition Party (whose leader became Prime Minister), the (Liberal) People's Party, the Christian Democrats and the Centre party. In January 1992, the new government presented its view on transport policy (*Government bill no. 1991/92: 100, appendix 7*). The position taken can be seen as a development of the Social Democrat transport policy of 1988. This bill was later followed by a bill treating the investments in infrastructure (see below).

When the new Government presented its bill on transport policy, transport activities in Sweden were no longer increasing at the same rate (in 1990, mileage decreased slightly). This change was interpreted as a result of increased VAT, of higher oil prices and, above all, of the contemporary weak economic development. In the medium term (to 2020), the traffic was, however, expected to continue to grow and the car was expected to remain the chief means of passenger transport (pp 3-4).

The *strategic transport policy goals* of the new Government were the same as those of 1988 (see 3.4.2) but the new Government laid more emphasis on the role of the transport sector in stimulating economic growth and in improving public welfare (pp 1-16).

More emphasis was also placed on *environmental goals* this time. global warming was now seen as a serious problem (p 9). In a short passage (pp 22-23), it is also said that one of the main tasks of the government is to carry out an environmental policy which *is compatible with sustainable development*. This is probably the first time that this concept is mentioned in any official documents on Swedish transport policy.

The main instruments for reaching the general objectives of the policy were deregulation and demonopolization. The new Swedish environmental policy meant, however, that each sector had to take responsibility for its environmental impact (p 9). Environment fees were introduced as a new policy instrument (p 22) and the standards for emissions were tightened (p 23). Particular measures were to be taken in the three larger cities (p 11 and pp 24sq). As regards passenger transport, the successful introduction of catalytic converters in Swedish cars was mentioned as a positive step (p 9). In order to reduce the negative environmental impact of transportation still further (p 18), more environmentally friendly vehicles and fuels were to be developed through international cooperation (p 10). In the railway sector, increased investments were to be made (p 14). Research was to be stimulated to develop transport systems adopted to the environment (p 12). The bill was passed by Parliament in June 1992.

The most important new initiative of the new Government was, however, the presentation of a bill on huge investments in road and railway infrastructure *(Government bill no. 1992/93:176)*. The aim of the in vestment policy was, as already indicated, not primarily transport-orientated but to stimulate economic activity and increase the welfare of the citizens. The objective of the plan was also to compensate for the geographical disadvantage of Sweden in the perspective of increasing European integration (p 4).

Substantial investments were also intended for the traffic problems of the three big cities, but this money would be partly generated by road fees *(Government bill no. 1992/93:100, appendix 7*, pp 156 sqq). Agreements were made for the Malmö area in June 1992, the Stockholm area in September 1992 and for the Göteborg area in June 1993. The implementation of these agreements, however, met with substantial problems and the agreements had to be revised later (in 1997-1998).

In December 1993, the Swedish Right-Centre coalition Government presented a "national strategy for sustainable development" *(Government bill no. 1993/94:111)*. In the spirit of *Agenda 21* agreed upon at the Earth Summit in Rio 1992, a strategy was outlined not only for reaching the goals of sustainable development in Sweden but also for Sweden's participation in the international efforts to achieve sustainable development on a global scale (p 1). Parliament approved the national strategy for sustainable development on the 24th of April 1994.

In the same year, the different governmental departments also began to adapt their proposals to the principles of the national plan. In the case of the Ministry of Energy and Environment, it underlined (in *the bill no. 1993/94:100 appendix 15)* that "the Precautionary Principle" should be applied in cases where scientific knowledge is insufficient for a final judgement (p 3).

The Ministry of Transport indicated its views of how to create 'a sustainable transport system' in Sweden in the *Government bill no. 1993/94:100 (appendix 7)*: 'Short-term and long-term environmental targets should be defined for all modes of transport. The targets should be formulated in such a way that they are compatible with environmentally sustainable development' (p 145, my translation). This bill was passed by Parliament (on the 16th of March 1994).

3.4.4 Elaborating a new national plan 1995-1997

In late December 1994, the Social Democrats, who again were in power (since September 1994), decided to entrust a new Investigative Commission ("*Kommunikationskommittén*") consisting of representatives of the political parties and some experts with the task of developing a new national plan for transport and communications in Sweden. The Commission was to elaborate principles for the creation of 'a transport system adapted to the environment, while promoting traffic safety, welfare, sustainable economic growth, regional balance and the competitive capacity of enterprise' (*directive number 1994:140*, my translation).

Some input into the work of the Commission had already come from a previous Commission on traffic and the climate (*SOU 1994:138* and *1995:96*) and was later offered by a working group under the guidance of the Swedish Environmental Protection Agency (SEPA). This group (called "*MaTs*" in Swedish) consisted of representatives of a number of governmental agencies and of the car and oil industry. It analysed the question of an adaptation of the transport system to the environment. Its results were presented in a final report entitled *Towards an Environmentally Sustainable Transport System* (1996).

The work of the new Commission resulted in three reports, two of them with substantial appendices (*SOU 1996:26, SOU 1996:165* and *1997:35*). The first report included an evaluation of the Swedish transport policy since 1988 and a discussion of the concept of sustainable development (with references to the Brundtland Commission, the Swedish Environmental Policy of 1991 and the final document of the Rio Summit in 1992), an overview of the environmental problems associated with Swedish transport (with more details in an appendix) and an analysis of different environmental goals.

The main concern of the report was, however, the development and maintenance of the infrastructure during the period 1998-2007. The Commission proposed a better coordination of infrastructure investments and transport policy: 'Infrastructure planning must agree with policy objectives for transport and the environment' (*SOU 1996:26*, p 23). It also suggested ways of increasing the political influence and control of traffic planning on national, regional and local levels (pp 151sqq). This proposal reflects a certain criticism of how investment decisions had been taken in the early 90s. The investments in the extension of the national highways were proposed to be reduced by more than half compared to the existing plan. Of the total investments, 60% was to be allocated to the railway and 40% to the road-net.

Based upon this report, a governmental bill on road and rail infrastructure was presented to Parliament in late 1996 (*bill no. 1996/97:53*). The Government modified the proposal of the Commission somewhat proposing an allocation of financial resources to road and rail on the principle of 50-50. The new bill was passed by Parliament in spring 1997.

The second report (*SOU 1996:165*) analysed the principles of using economic instruments in the road transport sector without taking a conclusive position. The final report of the Commission appeared in March 1997 *(SOU 1997:35)*. It contained, with its appendix, 1285 pages, including a summary in English. The report starts with a vision of the Swedish transport system in 2020. The vision is said to convey 'a picture of the road towards a long-term sustainable transport system and provides a platform for the proposals we make' (p 43). On Swedish roads, the growth both in the number of private cars and the number of traffic victims was expected to approach zero by 2020. By the same year, the emissions of NOx, SO2, HC and particles were expected to have reached levels that nature and human health can tolerate. The emissions of CO2 will, on the other hand, still remain at an unacceptable level (p 77sq).

The general goal of the new Swedish transport policy was suggested to be 'to offer citizens and business in all parts of the country a good, environmentally benign and safe transport supply which is social-economically efficient and sustainable in the long term' (p 43). The concept of 'sustainable development' was defined in some detail (p 98). The Commission rejected, explicitly, the idea that there are any inherent conflicts between the proposed transport policy goals and sustainable development (p 124).

To reach the environmental goals (the definition of which was based on the reports from the "*MaT's* group"), it was said to be necessary to define *timetabled targets* of reduced emissions from the transport sector to be reached within 25 years, while the long-term target for carbon dioxide was set to the year 2050 (p 45; p 104). Furthermore, it was proposed that the fossil fuel inputs in the transport sector should be reduced by increased energy efficiency and the introduction of bio-based fuels (pp 366sqq).

To reach the goals and attain the timetabled targets, a number of *policy instruments* were indicated by the Commission. A combination of economic instruments and regulatory devices was recommended (p 46). Some of these instruments had to do with technology. Sweden was to work within the EU to develop vehicle technology and harmonize standards (p 57; pp 61sq) but would be able to initiate the use of alternative fuels on a national basis (see above).

To reduce the need of transport, town planning was to be coordinated with the planning of infrastructure and traffic (p 64; pp 423sqq). The role of information technology in the future was seen as a way of adapting mobility in time and place rather than a method of reducing the transport need as such (pp 430sqq).

The main policy instrument recommended was, however, economic incentives. The external costs of traffic have to be internalised in order to 'influence individual and corporate transport choice and behaviour' (p 45), by introducing a higher carbon tax (to be increased by 0.1 Swedish crowns annually until 2020), by keeping the present differentiation in energy taxes on both petrol and diesel (according to the environmental performance of the fuels concerned) and by refraining from energy taxes on bio-based fuels for a long introductory period (p 47).

A strategy would also be devised to introduce road pricing in urban areas 'where this is justified by the external effects' (p 56). The time limit for this introduction in at least one urban area was proposed bo be not later than 2002 *(ibid.)*.

Finally, it was emphasized that it is essential for the authorities to use 'information as one of many instruments in pursuit of traffic policy objectives' (p 65).

The implementation of the new transport policy was proposed to be based on 'a developed system of intermodal follow-up and evaluation of transport policy aims, principles and measures' (p 59). The reason for this proposal was that, currently,'none of the transport authorities has the overriding aim of promoting an efficient, environmentally appropriate transport system' (p 59).

European cooperation in the field of transport (in terms of harmonized taxes and technical standards) was stressed as an important means of reaching the goals of the Swedish transport policy, particularly as 'the development of a long-term sustainable transport system calls for extensive international cooperation' (p 61).

When the Investigative Commission on a new transport policy presented its final report, its proposals were rejected outright by some important actors (see *Sammanställning av remissyttranden 1997)*.

Some of these actors (among them the Trade Union of Transport Workers, the Association of Automobile Manufacturers and Wholesalers and the Swedish Road Federation, a well-known lobbyist organisation) published extensive (and costly) advertisements in the newspapers in order to persuade the Government not to follow the proposals of the Commission.

3.4.5 The government bill on a new transport policy as of March 1998

In the beginning of March 1998, the Swedish Social Democrat Government presented its bill on a new transport policy *Transport policy for sustainable development* (*Government bill no. 1997/98:56*).

The bill did not include any *analysis of the problems* of the Swedish transport system in the late 90s. Rather the view of these problems was implicit. The use of the term 'sustainable' implied, however, that the present transport system was seen as unsustainable. The Government looked upon 'sustainable development' as a challenge to the whole of Swedish society. Its transport policy should be seen as an important part of the efforts to meet this challenge (p 11). Immediate action was seen as necessary to avoid intense conflicts in the future between a welfare state based on economic growth and the necessity to adapt the transport system to the ecological constraints (*ibid.*). Furthermore, some other changes in Swedish transport were identified: increased internationalization and the rapid development of information technology (p 12).

The bill was very explicit in describing *the goals of transport policy*. It distinguished between an overall goal, five partial objectives ("*delmål*") and some timetabled quantitative targets related to these partial objectives. 'The overall objective of transport policy is to offer citizens and business in all parts of the country a transport supply which is socio-economically efficient and sustainable in the long term' (p 16, my translation). This formulation was almost literally borrowed from the Commission (*SOU 1997:35*, p 43). The expression 'sustainable in the long term' was later defined as 'environmentally, economically, socially and culturally sustainable' (p 17, my translation). By 'environmentally sustainable' was meant (p 11):
- that the environment is protected
- that energy and other natural resources are used more efficiently and
- that the provision of energy and other natural resources is sustainable.

The five partial objectives were almost identical with those of the transport policy of 1988 (see 3.4.2), even if the wording was different:

1 an accessible transport system (the equitable aspects of transport policy will be followed by a special council, pp 71sq)
2 a high level of transport quality (by this expression was meant qualities such as regularity, security, flexibility and efficiency, pp 20sq).
3 increased safety
4 an environment not exposed to serious damage ("*en god miljö*") and
5 positive regional development.

The timetabled quantitative targets would be successively defined for each partial objective (e.g. for increased safety) so that they may be achieved by means of acceptable costs and sacrifices (p 16). They were are seen also as a basis for the monitoring of the transport policy (see below).

In the perspective of environmental sustainability, the targets for the partial goal related to the environment are of particular interest here. They were based on, but not identical with, the suggestions made by the Commission and the working group for a transport system adapted to the environment (*"MaTs"*) :

Table 3:1 Timetabled quantitative reductions of certain substances from the Swedish transport sector

Substance	Basis year	target	year
Carbon dioxide	1990	0%	2010
Nitrogen oxides	1995	-40%	2005
Sulphur	1995	-15%	2005
VOCs	1995	-60%	2005

Source: Government bill no. 1997/98:56, p 28

The principles of the transport policy were described at some length (pp 36sqq). The transport consumers' freedom of choice was initially emphasized. The cooperation between different transport modes was to be strengthened in order to facilitate the transition from one mode to another. At the same time, competition between different transport modes and transport producers was to be promoted. Decisions about transport production were to be decentralized. It was taken for granted that the role of the private car would remain the same in the reasonably near future (p 63).

The *principle policy instrument* was indicated to be socio-economically based taxes on transport. If it is not possible to reach the goals by this means, other policy instruments would be considered (p 38). Taxes on and fees for transport would be mainly based on variable costs and internalization of externalities (pp 42sqq). A long passage of the text was dedicated to a detailed discussion of the application of these principles (pp 148-163), which was expected to be difficult in several cases (pp 45sq).

A particular *strategy for an ecologically sustainable transport system* was also described (pp 72-77). A number of *concrete measures* concerning the structure of the transport system and concerning vehicles, fuels and infrastructure were indicated. The use of information technology and better coordination of urban planning and transport planning in order to promote the use of soft modes and public transport was mentioned (p 74) as well as the development of vehicle technology and improved fossil fuels, mainly within EU (pp 74sqq), and the adaptation of the building and maintenance of transport infrastructure to the environment (p 76). A particular programme for the introduction of biofuels was to be developed (pp 164sqq). The bill did not, however, include any proposals about increased Green taxes on energy and carbon dioxide in the transport sec-tor (p 152).

Concerning *the implementation of the policy*, the Government discussed the role of different actors in the bill (p 50) and introduced a new system for the follow-up of the implementation. Annual reports on the results of transport policy were to be presented to Parliament and monitory methods were to be developed (p 52).

3.4.6 The findings of the analysis

On the basis of the analytical description in the preceding part of the chapter, it is now possible to state
- that there exists a comparatively long tradition (since 1963) of coordinated transport policies in Sweden
- that new transport policies, as a rule, are prepared by Investigative Commissions
- that the transport policy of 1963 was followed by a revised transport policy in 1979
- that a certain shift in the view of environmental problems occurred in the Swedish transport policy of 1988 without mentioning global warming, however
- that the goals of the transport policy of 1988 included the idea of an environmentally friendly transport system
- that the transport policy of 1988 introduced a number of timetabled quantitative targets
- that the traffic problems of the three biggest cities in Sweden were subjected to special studies leading to agreements in the beginning of the 90s, the realization of which turned out to be very difficult and to necessitate revision
- that the idea of 'environmental sustainability' was accepted only step by step by the Swedish Government
- that the Government appointed, in late 1994, an Investigative Commission entrusted with the task of elaborating a New National Plan for transport and communications which should be able to

achieve an efficient, safe, equitable and sustainable transport system
- that the proposals of this Commission were presented in 1996 and 1997
- that the proposals included ambitious timetabled environmental targets and the idea of a successive increase the tax on CO_2.
- that the final report of the Commission provoked loud protests from organized economic interests in the field of transport
- that the Social Democrat Government presented its bill on a new Swedish "transport policy for a sustainable development" in March 1998
- that the Government based its the proposals on the suggestions of the Commission but modified some of the economic instruments (e.g. rejecting the idea of a successive increase in the tax on CO_2).

3.5 Conclusions

3.5.1 How did the transport policies change?

The objectives of this chapter were to answer the questions *how* and *why* transport policies have changed in Denmark, the Netherlands and Sweden in the period 1987-1997. The principle findings about how the national transport policies of these countries have changed were presented after the treatment of each country (see 3.2.6; 3.3.5 and 3.4.6) These empirical results can now be summarized in very general terms:

In the years 1987-1997, a number of important changes occurred in the national transport policies of Denmark, the Netherlands and Sweden. This becomes particularly obvious if the period 1987-1997 is compared to the years before 1987. Many of the changes are common to the three countries (the more important differences will be dealt with in the following chapter).

First, I claim that, since 1987, transport policy has become less fragmented than before, particularly in Denmark and in the Netherlands. Sweden has a somewhat longer tradition of coordinated transport policy making.

Secondly, I claim that the political perception of the problems of the transport systems has become more complex and better articulated in all three countries. For instance, more and more emphasis has been laid on the importance of environmental problems.

Thirdly, I claim that certain themes in transport policies have been more emphasized from around 1990 than during the preceding years: a renewal of the interest in road safety, in the role of the railway and, particularly in Denmark and Sweden, in road infrastructure investments.

The most impressive change is, however, the introduction of a new goal in transport policy: Environmental sustainability has been added to traditional policy goals such as efficiency, safety and equity.

Furthermore, it is reasonable to claim that the packages of policy instruments and suggested measures have become richer in their composition. Particularly, the internalization of the externalities of traffic has become a common issue. More interest than before has been focused on the implementation process.

Finally, however, I claim that the conflict between transport growth and sustainability is, as a rule, poorly analysed in the political texts. In some cases, this conflict is at least openly admitted.

3.5.2 Why did the transport policies change?

The question *why* the changes have occurred can now be addressed. The following analysis will be based on the theory of the cyclical character of transport policies presented in the introduction to this chapter. I will therefore first investigate to what extent some of the changes in the period 1987-1997 can be explained as traditional cyclical elements in transport policy. I think that att least three such elements can be identified.

Road safety became an important issue in the Danish transport policy in 1988 (3.2.2), in the same year in Swedish transport policy (3.4.2) and two years later in Dutch transport policy (3.3.3). Road safety is of course a permanent concern of road authorities but the political interest in safety questions varies in a significant way. The previous peak in interest belonged to the second half of the 60s (initiated by Ralph Nader's book *Unsafe at Any Speed*, 1965).

To some extent, the new interest may be attributed to the rising number of road traffic injuries due to increasing road traffic in the second half of the 80s. In Denmark, a rise in the number of killed occurred in 1985 after a long period of decreasing or stable numbers (*Færdssikkerhetspolitisk handlingsplan 1988*, p 18). In the Netherlands, an increase of around 10% in the number of roads deaths and injuries occurred in 1989 after years of improvement (*SVV2*, p 6). In Sweden, there was an in-creasing trend in the number of killed and injured from 1981-1988 (with the exception of the year 1987). Particularly, the number of killed and injured car drivers increased substantially, by 43 % between 1981 and 1988 (*SCB Trafikskador 1988*).

Another factor of importance was possibly the emergence of new advanced techniques concerning automatic speed control, warning systems and other safety applications of Road Transport Informatics. A technical development of this kind took place in the late 80s within the European programmes Prometheus and DRIVE. These new technologies were said to make it possible to choose a higher level of aspiration in safety matters. To put road safety on the political agenda again was therefore a way of preparing the market for new technologies.

A second cyclical element in the national transport policies in the three countries was a *renewed interest in upgrading the railway* system, initiated in Denmark 1987 (3.2.2), in the Netherlands 1990 (3.3.3) and Sweden in 1991 (3.4.3). This interest was partly concentrated on the introduc-tion of high-speed trains. I believe one has to go back to the 50s to find a similar interest in the development of the technical and organisational state of the railway.

The background of this renewal of interest was probably the common view that the road system, particularly in the perspective of European integration, was becoming overloaded in certain regions (as some airports) and that the railway offered less environmental impact per person-km in comparison with road and air transport. In the Danish case, the interest in the railway system was closely connected with the planned expansion of the entire transport infrastructure from late 1980s (see below). In the Swedish case, the role of lobbyists was probably important. An organization called "Rail Forum Sweden" was constituted in 1990 as an official lobby group, the role of which was to inspire a 'better use of the potential possibilities of the railway'. The expression is quoted from a book *Järnvägens andra revolution* (1995), written by a well-known Swedish industrialist, Curt Nicolin, who had been manager of the Swedish corporation ASEA. The idea of the "Scandinavian Link" (including also upgraded railway links), advocated by the regional offspring of the "European Round Table of Industrialists" (see below), played a role both in Denmark and Sweden,.

Increased interest in road infrastructure investments was also introduced as an important political issue in the years around 1990, in Denmark 1987, in Netherlands 1988-1990 and in Sweden 1988-1991.The investment rate had been fairly low during the 70s and 80s due to pressure from environmental organizations and from local opposition to new road building.

A number of factors contributed to the renewed interest in road infrastructure investment. In Sweden, the interest was very much due to the Swedish weak economic development. Investments in road infrastructure were believed to stimulate the national economic activities as a whole, a standpoint advocated by some economists and questioned by others (Dreborg and Jungmar, 1994). A similar view was expressed in the late 80s by the Thatcher government in the programme entitled *Roads to Prosperity* (1989). At the same time the upgrading of the Swedish road-net was seen as a necessary measure to compensate for the peripheral position of Swedish industry in relation the emerging Common European Market.

The attitudes to infrastructure investments in Denmark and the Netherlands were somewhat different. They are both important transit countries, close to the central parts of Europe. When road transport is increasing as a consequence of economic growth, their road infrastructure therefore easily comes into focus. In Denmark, in order to make transport more efficient and to integrate the country with the European transport system, huge investments were decided to expand the motorway system (to realise "the big H") and to establish fixed links across the straits surrounding its islands (including both road and railway links). In the Netherlands, infrastructure investments were rather seen as a means of reducing congestion problems by upgrading existing road capacity in various ways. At the same time, more roads were seen as disintegrating the landscape.

Another factor accounting for the renewed interest in road infrastructure around 1990 was certainly the activities of the "The European Round Table of Industrialists" (ERT). Its representatives used to meet with important officials and politicians in the 80s. A number of reports were also circulated to national decision-making bodies, to the press and the general public with titles such as *Missing Links* (1984), *Keeping Europe Mobile* (1988) and *The Need for Renewing Transport Infrastructure in Europe* (1989). These reports certainly played a role in building up pressure (Tengström et al. 1995, p 43).

The emergence of the EU programme for Trans European Networks (TEN) was the conclusive phase in this process. The main reason behind this programme was the belief that the integration of the European Union and the Internal Market required an upgraded road network. This idea was particularly pushed for by the "The International Road Federation" (IFR), consisting of a number of road-building companies which, in collaboration with two oil companies published a brochure in 1990 entitled *AIMSE. The motorway project for the Europe of tomorrow* (see Tengström et al. 1995, p 42). The main message of the brochure was that 'the road is needed more than any other transport system'.

Thus, three elements of the changed transport policies in Denmark, the Netherlands and Sweden can be explained by the theory of the cyclical character of changes in transport policy. Factors behind the changes have been economic cycles, technical innovations, underlying views in society and the pressure from various interest groups.

Doubtless, these cases could be elaborated further by using an institutional historical approach. Such an investigation is, however, beyond the scope of this study.

3.5.3 A new transport policy cycle initiated around 1990

The most important new element in the Danish, Dutch and Swedish transport policies in the 90s was, however, the introduction of a new goal: environmental sustainability.

The new development was announced by the Danish Transport Action Plan in 1990 and in the Netherlands by the Second Transport Structure Plan also in 1990 and somewhat later in Sweden, explicitly in connection with the setting up of an investigative Commission for a National Plan for Transport and Communications in 1994.

The main cause of this change in transport policy was evidently, in the theoretical perspective of le Clercq, the emergence of a new problem: the risk of global warming. In the theoretical perspective of Starkie, it may be said that global warming became a 'new issue' around 1990. The rising concern with the greenhouse effect had led to the formation of the Intergovernmental Panel on Climate Change (IPCC) in 1988. Its first report appeared in 1990. Although this report was very cautious in its statements, the risk of global warming was, from now on, added to previous environmental concerns (see chapter 2). The traditional environmental concerns also seem to have been given more political weight around 1990 than before as a consequence of the breakthrough of the problem of global warming. Therefore, a more complex and more alarming view of the environmental problems of the transport sector emerged at the level of national transport policy-making in the late 80s and early 90s. In the documents from before this period, environmental problems were regarded as more marginal phenomena. In the new situation, local problems (polluted air, noise) and regional problems (acidification and eutrophication) also seem to have been taken more seriously than before.

One factor that helped to highlight the greenhouse effect was probably the previous controversy on the depletion of stratospheric ozone ending up in the agreement of the 'Montreal Protocol' 1987 (on phasing out CFC-products and similar products). The expanding hole in the ozone layer had graphically illustrated how even small emissions of certain substances can disturb the function of the biosphere.

There are also some other indications that there occurred a general shift in the attitude of politicians to the problems of environment in the late 1980s. One instance is offered by the speech given by Mrs Thatcher, the British Conservative Prime Minister of those days, to the Royal Society in September 1988. This speech is generally considered as a 'watershed in British political culture towards environmental issues' (Liniado, 1996, p 87, note 14 where he refers to Grow-White, 1993).

The general character of these new insights among policy makers was later commented on by the President of the International Social Science Council, Luis Ramallo, at a conference on Human Dimensions of Global Change in September 1995. He described the new situation as 'a fourth revolution in the history of mankind': After the Copernican, Darwinian and Freudian revolutions, '(p)erhaps we are facing a fourth revolution in the most profound sense. A revolution that comes from the fact that we are aware for the first time of two factors: limitation, scarcity, precariousnes of our living, and secondly, total interdependence of the earth system' (*Global Change, Local Challenge* I, p 5).

In short, I believe that the emergence of the problem of global warming is to be seen as the main factor initiating a new cycle of transport policy in the three countries around 1990 together with the publication of the report of the Brundtland Commission in 1987. The dynamics of the social reconstruction of the picture of the problems of the transport sector are, however, still obscure. It is reasonable to believe that new scientific findings played an important role in the process of change. The role of the media was, however, also important (on their role in the ozone case, see Nolin, 1995). What they chose to focus on and in what perspective they presented the scientific findings can be assumed to have had a substantial impact on the process. The role of pressure from different environmental organizations was probably also of great importance (cf Jamison et al. 1990). To clarify the dynamism behind the social construction of the new view of the problems of transport and how it affects the social representations of these problems in different social groups and institutions requires, however, a particular investigation which is also beyond the scope of this study.

3.5.4 The first stages of the new cycle of transport policy

A cycle in transport policy can be analysed in terms of different stages. The following analysis of the new cycle is based upon Starkie's theoretical perspective. In the view of Starkie, a transport policy cycle is typically composed of five stages:

1 the pre-problem stage
2 alarming discovery and euphoric enthusiasm
3 realising the cost of significant progress
4 gradual decline of interest and
5 the post-problem stage.

I think that *the pre-problem stage* is clearly visible in the Danish transport policy of 1987 as well as in the Swedish transport policy of

1988. There are still no signs of a radically changed perception of the problems of the transport sector. The same applies to the First Dutch Transport Structure Plan, approved by the Dutch Parliament in 1981.

The alarming discovery of the global warming problem is, on the other hand, easily datable to the years around 1990. The following *euphoric enthusiasm* was very much associated with interest in the concept of 'sustainable development', successfully propagated by the Brundtland Commission in 1987. An ethos of global solidarity influenced policy debates at that time in international fora, also probably a consequence of the end of the Cold War, a process which occurred in the years 1989-1991.

The formulation of the new goal in transport policy was therefore logically based upon the concept of 'sustainability'. Direct references to the Brundtland report *Our Common future* (1987) were openly made in Danish and Dutch documents on transport policies, though this report itself, in fact, mentioned the transportation sector very rarely (see Tengström 1993, p 33). The Danish Transport Action Plan of 1990 used the expression 'policy for sustainable transport' (p 173), the Dutch Second Transport Structure Plan of 1990 talks about 'transport in a sustainable society' (p 8) and the Swedish Ministry of Transport used the expression 'a transport system sustainable in the long term' in the government bill no. 1993/94:100 (*appendix* 7). The long-term sustainability of the current transport systems was thus no longer taken for granted. The new goal of transport policy was therefore to create good preconditions for the development of sustainable transport systems.

The third stage of the transport cycle is described by Starkie as a period when *the costs of significant progress are realised*. I believe that the development of Danish, Dutch and Swedish transport policies in the period between 1993-1997 represents that stage. To corroborate this claim, a number of facts already mentioned above can be referred to.

In the Danish transport policy debate between 1993 and 1997, the focus was partly on the economic and social costs of a consequent implementation of the new policy. The target of stabilized emissions of carbon dioxide from the transport sector at the 1988 level by 2005 seemed to be difficult to reach and the discussion concerned the possible size of associated social costs.

In the Netherlands, a similar situation prevails. According to the evaluation of the Dutch transport policy carried out in 1993/94, the introduction of pricing measures to limit the traffic volumes seemed unrealistic before the year 2000. The political costs were seen to be too high.

In the Swedish case, the proposals of the special Commission on a new National Plan for Transport and Communications were sharply criticised by organized economic interests. In its bill of March 1998, the Government mitigated, in a significant way, the use of economic instruments, which had been suggested by the Commission.

3.5.5 The future of the new transport policy cycle

Following Starkie's theoretical perspective on the normal development of a new transport cycle, one should expect, for the next few years, a period of *gradual decline of interest* in the problem of global warming and in the question of the sustainability of the transport systems leading to a *post-problem* stage. Such a development is, in my view, far from improbable. If the new cycle is concluded around 2005, it is, on the other hand, far from improbable that a second cyclic period with its focus on sustainability will be initiated around 2010, possibly stimulated by a new wave of environmental concern.

My interest here is, however, not to make predictions. In the final chapter of this study, I shall return to the question of transport policy for the near future and do it from a point of view characterized more by prescription than prediction.

4 Differences Between Danish, Dutch and Swedish Transport Policies

4.1 Introduction

4.1.1 The aims, focus and research questions of the chapter

The principle aim of this chapter is to identify, describe and explain significant differences between the transport policies of Denmark, the Netherlands and Sweden in the period 1987-1997, focusing on the issue of environmental sustainability.

Two basic research questions are to be answered:
- in what respects are there any differences between the transport policies of the three countries in relation to environmental sustainability?
- how can these differences, if any, be explained?

The aim of the third question is to assess, in a comparative perspective, the political capacity of the three countries to confront the new problems of transport:
- which country seems to have developed the most comprehensive capacity to deal with the new problem of reducing the unsustainability of the present transport systems?

In order to address these research questions, I will, in the following comparative analysis, deal with 1/ the *content* of the policies, 2/ the *processes* of transport policy-making and 3/ the current development of *ecological modernization capacities*.

The analysis of the content will be structured in accordance with my previous categorisation: 1/ the policy-makers' perceptions of problems 2/ their formulation of goals 3/ their selection of intermediate objectives, policy instruments and concrete measures and 4/ their expressed views of the implementation and evaluation of the policy.

The analysis of the policy-making will be based on the analytical description of the changes in transport policies (see chapter 1) and, with regard to explanations, on a number of different factors (see 4.1.2).

The analysis of the current development of the societal capacity to deal with the problem of the present unsustainable character of the national transport systems will be based on the concept of 'ecological modernization capacity' (EMC) used, among others, by the German political scientist, Martin Jänicke (Jänicke, 1990). This capacity is assumed to consist of four variables: economic performance, consensus ability, innovation capability, and strategic proficiency. The societal capacity to deal with *environmental* problems in general has been studied in some empirical studies based on cases taken from different countries (Jänicke and Weidner, 1995; Christiansen, 1996a; Jänicke and Weidner, 1997). No empirical study of the ecological modernization capacity in relation to the problems of transport and environment has, however, appeared so far. I will, therefore, discuss some points of departure for such a study below (4.6.1).

It is my hypothesis that the differences between the transport policies of the three countries will turn out to be fairly unimportant. As we have seen in the previous chapter, there are impressive similarities between the three countries as to the changes in their transport policies in the period 1987-1997. Another reason for my hypothesis is that it is a well-known fact that differences in transport policy within the same European region are less pronounced than differences between transport policies of European countries situated at a certain distance from each other (Jones et al. pp 172sq).

4.1.2 The theoretical basis of the comparative analysis

Comparative analyses can be carried out in various ways. They are often based upon case studies. A great number of case-orientated comparative methods are in present use (for a survey, see Ragin, 1987, pp 35-52).

No serious comparative studies of national transport *policies* have been carried out (to my knowledge). A comparative study of national transport *planning* was recently presented by Gary Haq in a publication entitled *Towards Sustainable Transport Planning: A Comparison between Britain and the Netherlands* (1997). Here, the author also deals, to some extent, with the national policies of the two countries.

If differences between national transport policies have been observed in previous studies, they have usually been associated with various sets of factors such as dissimilarities in geographical preconditions for transport and different political and cultural patterns (Jones et al. 1993). National characteristics, international ideological currents and historical heritage are also used as explanatory factors (Bjørnland, 1993, p 89).

As the present study focuses on the environmental aspects of transport policies, the following comparative analysis can also profit from the theoretical experience gained in comparative studies of *environmental* policies (defined above in 1.3.1). However, the comparative study of environmental policies is also at an early stage. Political science has not yet acquired 'an adequate understanding and interpretation of the dynamics of the political process aimed at formulating and implementing environmental policies' (Lundqvist, 1996a, p 13). However, this new research field has already produced quite a few interesting approaches and theoretical achievements.

An interesting example is offered by a recent international comparative study of environmental policies in a number of countries, entitled *Successful Environmental Policy* (Jänicke and Weidner, 1995). The focus of this study is on the outcomes (not on processes or institutions) of environmental policies in 12 OECD countries (most of them European). The editors have selected 24 cases, all described as "success stories", i e 'outstanding environmental improvements in a comparative perspective' *(op.cit.* p 11).

In their introduction, the editors identify five different categories of factors influencing the outcome of the policies:
- *structures* such as socio-economic factors, institutional framework conditions and cultural preconditions
- *situations* such as socio-economic contexts, the development of conflicts and the exploitation of unpredictable advantages
- *actors* such as organizations, coalitions of interests and stakeholders (being opponents or proponents of different elements of transport policy)
- *strategies* conceived as the purposive application of instruments over time requiring a 'strategic capacity' of the policy actors in terms of planned and coordinated action and, finally,
- *time* seen as an indispensable dimension of analysis *(op. cit.* p 16).

I will make use of these categories in my own analysis after having made some modifications (the focus of this chapter being the content of policies and policy processes, not outcomes).

A second example of an interesting comparative study is entitled *Governing the Environment: Politics, Policy and Organization in the Nordic countries* (Christiansen, 1996a). It is based on case studies of the four Nordic countries, Denmark, Finland, Norway and Sweden. In the introductory chapter, the Swedish political scientist L.J. Lundqvist indicates that this study is focusing on the *content* of the policy (i.e. goals, policy instruments, etc) and on the *capacity* of the political systems to deal with environmental problems. The explanation of differences between the four Nordic countries is based on national patterns of *policy processes* and *policy organization*.

The basic hypothesis of the mentioned study was that observed differences in environmental policies can be explained by 'national differences in political and administrative structure and culture' (*op.cit.* p 14). Secondly, the question was raised, 'which conclusions can be drawn about the national systems' political capacity in dealing with 'new' policy problems' if identified policy differences reflect political differences (*op.cit.* pp 14sq)? The answer to this research question was based on a theoretical approach developed by Jänike (Jänicke, 1990).

In another recent book, entitled *National Environmental Policies: A Comparative Study of Capacity-Building* (Jänicke and Weidner, 1997), Jænicke and others offer empirical analyses of capacity-building in very different societies such as Japan, Korea, Chile, China, Nigeria, Russia, United States, Germany but also in Denmark, the Netherlands and Sweden. I will make use of the empirical results of this study.

Two older studies are also of interest in this context. One of them is a sociological approach to the study of Green activism in Denmark, the Netherlands, and Sweden. This publication is entitled *The Making of the New Environmental Consciousness. A Comparative Study of the Environmental Movements in Sweden, Denmark and the Netherlands* (Jamison et al. 1990). The authors of this comparative study arrived at the conclusion that there are some significant differences between the environmental movements in these three countries:

> The environmentalist knowledge interests formed differently in Sweden, Denmark, and the Netherlands, producing distinct 'movements' in each of these countries. Subject to similar international influences and propagating a common environmentalist message, the new environmentalism as it emerged in Western Europe took on different national colourations (*op.cit.* p 198).

I will also make use of the results of this study in analysing the role of Green actors in the political process.

The other study is an early example of a comparative study of policy-making processes based upon the cases of USA and Sweden. It was published as early as 1980 by the Swedish political scientist L.J. Lundqvist. It is entitled *The Hare and the Tortoise: Clean Air Policies in the United States and Sweden* (Lundqvist, 1980) and can be seen as a minor classic in the field. Lundqvist distinguished between two different political processes concerning the environment: a process of bargaining with the stakeholders and interest groups, on the one hand, which results in a slow but result-orientated process (called "the Tortoise", with Sweden as the typical example) and a more dramatic process leading to the formulation of symbolic goals out of reach of present policy instruments. This process was described as having a quick start but weak tenacity (called "the Hare"), with USA as the typical example.

At the outset of his comparative study, Lundqvist derived the following two propositions from earlier studies of the same kind:

> 1 The more open and conflict-oriented the political system, the more immediate and substantial the response to problems of environmental quality but the less substantial and successful the implementation of adopted policy alternatives.
> 2 The more closed and consensus-oriented the political system, the slower and more incremental the response to problems of environmental quality and the more deliberate and successful the implementation of adopted policy alternatives (*op.cit.* p 34).

Summarizing his results, Lundqvist found, however, that only the first part of the two propositions turned out to be true in these particular cases. The US response to the problems of increasing degradation of air quality was certainly more rapid than the Swedish one. Policy implementation, being "a different game" than policy making, exhibited, however, the surprise. The right of US citizens to appeal to the court created favourable conditions for the implementation of 1970 Clean Air Act Amendments (*op.cit.* pp 195sq). The difference between the two procedures was therefore less pronounced than expected. The view of the difference suggested by the Greek fable was all but conclusive.

In my own analysis, I intend to use the following factors in explaining identified differences in the content of transport policies and in transport policy making processes:

1 The geographical context: the structure of the land surface and population density patterns are seen as important factors. There are substantial differences between the three countries in these respects (see above, 3.1.3).

2 The situational context such as socio-economic contexts (for instance, economic recessions), the development of conflicts and the exploitation of unpredictable advantages.

3 The structural and cultural context: such as socio-economic factors, institutional framework conditions and political culture.

4 The actor-orientated context: such as organizations, coalitions of interests and stakeholders (being opponents or proponents of different elements of transport policy).

5 The strategical context: conceived as the purposeful application of

instruments over time requiring a 'strategic capacity' of the policy actors in terms of planned and coordinated action .

The presentation of the empirical arguments in the following sections will make it inevitable to repeat some of the basic facts already mentioned in chapter 3.

4.2 The transition to a more alarming view of the environmental problems of transport

4.2.1 Some differences in the transition

The issue of global warming together with some other factors initiated, according to my interpretation, a new cycle in transport policy around 1990 in Denmark and the Netherlands and, somewhat later, in Sweden (see above, 3.5.3). The new cycle began with a political reconstruction of the picture of the problems of the transport sector. This reconstruction not only included the risks of global warming but it also contained a reinterpretation of the local and regional environmental problems, which now were taken more seriously than before. As to the *content* of the new perception of the environmental impact of transport, there was no significant difference between the three countries.

However, the transition to the new, more alarming view of the problems associated with transportation exhibited a significant difference between Denmark and the Netherlands, on the one hand, and Sweden on the other. The Danes and the Dutch responded to the new situation significantly more rapidly than the Swedes, as far as transport policy was concerned.

In 1988, the Danish Conservative-Centre coalition Government published a document which was the first national follow-up of the report of the Brundtland Commission. In this document, a national strategy for the environment and development was presented indicating energy and transport as two societal sectors particularly crucial to the implementation of the strategy. These sectors therefore became the subject of intensified studies. After these studies had been completed, the first *Transport Action Plan for Environment and Development* was published in 1990 by the same Government. It clearly described the new and more alarming view of the environmental problems of the transport sector.

Also in the year 1988, the Dutch coalition Government, consisting of Christian Democrats and right-wing Liberals, described the new picture of the problems of the transport sector in "Part A" of the Second Transport Structure Plan (*Tweede Struktuurschema Verkeer en Vervoer: deel a: beleidsvoornemen"*). Here, the problems of acidification (of soils and vegetation) and of global warming, leading among other things to rising sea levels, were strongly emphasized (p 11). After two years, a definite transport plan (called "Part D") based on this perception of the problems was accepted by the Dutch Parliament in spring 1990.

In Sweden, the new transport policy of 1988 presented by the Social Democratic government did not mention the greenhouse effect at all. Nor had the report of the Brundtland Commission any visible impact on Swedish transport policy-making at this time. However, the still ruling Social Democrats presented, in 1991, a bill on *environmental* policy describing the environmental threats in much more serious terms than before, including the risks of a climate change.

After the elections in September 1991, the new Swedish Conservative-Centre Government documented (in spring 1992) its support of the transport policy of 1988. The text included, however, a more alarming view of the problems of greenhouse gases and of the problems of acidification, eutrophication, photochemical oxidants and air pollution (see 3.4.3). However, the final step in the process toward a more alarming view of the environmental problems of transportation was not taken until March 1998, when the Social Democratic Government presented its bill on a new Transport Policy entitled *Transport Policy for Sustainable Development* (governmental bill 1997/98:56). The bill did not contain any detailed discussion of the environmental problems of transport but subscribed to the view generally accepted at the Rio Earth Summit of 1992. The Government also stressed the risk of serious conflicts between welfare and economic growth, on the one hand, and the necessity of creating a transport system which is compatible with the ecological constraints, on the other (*op.cit.* p 11).

Thus, there are some significant differences between the three countries as to the way their policy-makers responded to the emergence of a new view of the environmental problems of the transport sector. How can these differences be explained?

4.2.2 Explanations of identified differences

The comparatively slow Swedish response to the new picture of environmental problems related to transport is, in my view, primarily explained by the Swedish administrative and political culture: by 1988, Sweden had developed a long tradition in transport policy-making, particularly in comparison with Denmark but also with the Netherlands. New transport policies were preceded by long periods of studies and considerations (extending over quite a few years). The role of such Investigative Commissions, including not only representatives of the political parties in Parliament but also affected interests and specialists from administrative agencies, is to produce more knowledge about the issue in question, to promote political consensus, to reduce conflict with organized interests and to offer the government the possibility of controlling the formulation of new policies. This institution has been regarded as the Swedish model of capacity-building (Lundqvist, 1997, p 61).

I believe that another explanatory factor is to be found in the internal debate of the Social Democrats in the late 80s. In its bill on environmental policy of March 1988, the Social Democratic government emphasized, at the rhetorical level, the necessity of respecting the limits of nature by means of new lifestyles and new patterns of consumption (as a concession to the Green opposition within the party), but, in reality, there was no deviation from the traditional attitude of the majority. This was based on the view that environmental problems of production and transport could and should be solved by means of technical development (Anshelm, 1995, pp 120-124).

The Dutch political background was quite different. In the late 1980s, its Government was inspired to increase its commitment to environmental objectives, not only by the report of the Brundtland Commission (1987) but also by the Minister of the Environment personally (Bressers and Plettenburg, 1997, pp 124sq) and by alarming reports of RIVM, the National Institute of Public Health and Environmental Protection (*op. cit.* pp 121sq). The Government immediately initiated a public debate on transport policy, where both the general public and the NGOs were confronted with new aspects of the environmental problems of transportation. This process was characterised by open conflict in contrast to the conflict-reducing strategies typical of Denmark and Sweden. In 1990, the *Second Transport Structure Plan* was accepted by the Dutch Parliament after some modifications, initiated by the public debate (see above, 3.3.3). This Plan is still (1998) in operation.

The rapid reaction of Dutch opinion to the risks of climate change may also, to some extent at least, be seen in a geographical context. The emerging threat of a climate change caused by an increased greenhouse effect could lead to higher sea levels. In the Dutch original, it was phrased in the following way: 'het 'broeikaseffekt', met gevolgen voor het klimaat en het niveau van de zeespiegel' *Tweede Struktuurschema Verkeer en Vervoer: deel a*, p 11). This threat certainly had a particular impact on people living in a country, of which one half was already below the present sea level.

The political situation in Denmark differed from that in Sweden and in the Netherlands. Since the 1970s, Danish environmental policy had 'mobilized environmental groups, business organizations, and political parties, as well as individual politicians building a political platform on the environment as a political problem, but the political and administrative responses were shaped within the traditions of cooperation and consensus so characteristic of Danish political life' (Christiansen 1996b, p 89). The existence of a Green majority in Parliament was probably the decisive factor in the treatment of environmental issues (see below, 4.3.1).

The contemporary Danish political situation can therefore be regarded as one of the key factors underlying the rapid Danish transition to a more alarming view of the environmental problems of transportation. In my view, a certain role was also played by the fact that, in contrast to Sweden, transport policy had not yet become institutionalized practice in Denmark (see above, 2.2.6).

The role of Green movements in the three countries may also have contributed to the differences in the transition. These movements have very different characteristics. Danish environmentalism has been associated by some scientists with 'the populist 'grass-roots' tradition of Danish political culture' (Jamison et al. 1990, p 192).

In the Netherlands, on the other hand, they found that Green movements were more professional and usually mobilized voters by means of expert-orientated and "legalistic" arguments *(op.cit.* p 187).

Environmental organizations in Sweden, finally, were regarded by the same authors as more "technocratic" and the Swedish attitude to environmental problems as being mainly pragmatic and utilitarian (*op. cit.* p 188).

It is thus reasonable to assume that the populist character of the Danish Green movement may have helped to prepare the political ground for the early Danish acceptance of a new view of the environmental problems of transport (cf below, 4.3.4).

To summarize: The differences identified between Danish, Dutch and Swedish political responses to the new and more alarming view of the environmental problems of the transport sector can primarily be ascribed to differences in political and administrative culture and, in the Danish case, the prevailing political situation. Secondly, the differences may be associated with the role of the Green actors in the Danish case, and with geographical factors in the Dutch case.

4.3 The introduction and formulation of environmental sustainability as a political goal

4.3.1 Political processes leading to the formulation of the goal of environmental sustainability

The beginning of the new cycle in transport policy was, above all, marked by the introduction and formulation of a new goal in transport policy called "sustainability". This concept was, as we also have seen in chapter 3, either taken in the narrow sense of 'environmental sustainability' (as in the case of Denmark and the Netherlands) or in the broader sense of 'environmental, economic, social and cultural sustainability' (as in the Swedish case). The new goal was added to the traditional goals in transport policy, such as efficiency, safety and equity.

Were there any differences in the policy-making processes leading to the introduction and formulation of the new goal in the three countries? How was the goal of sustainability defined, if defined at all? Were there any conflicts between the new goal and the traditional goals of transport policy being identified and discussed? How can the differences in these aspects, if any, be explained?

The Dutch process of introducing and formulating a new goal in transport policy was inspired by the report of the Brundtland Commission. Almost immediately after its publication in 1987, the Dutch government designated "sustainable development" as the general guideline for its overall policy (Bressers and Plettenburg, 1997, pp 125sq). As we have already seen, the preparation of a transport policy for a sustainable society began in 1988 with the publication of the so-called "Part A", a draft of a new national *Transport Structure Plan* (see above 4.2.1). This document aroused great interest in the Netherlands: 'No policy proposals have ever elicited such a massive response. Local authorities, industry and large numbers of social organizations and advisory bodies have expressed support for and criticism of aspects of Part A' (quoted from Part D: p 5). Many of these actors 'sought to bring maximum in-fluence to bear on decision-making at an early stage' (*ibid.*). The Dutch Government found that 'there is every reason to set out a more ambitious programme than was felt necessary in 1988' (*ibid.*). The setting of environmental targets in transport policy was very much influenced by the *First National Environmental Plan* in 1989.

The Danish *Transport Action Plan* of 1990 was not preceded by a similar procedure, but the existence of a Green majority in Parliament and Green lobbyism seems to have been of importance (see above 4.2.2). The Ministry of Environment may also have played an inspiring role as in the Netherlands, even if 'policies (are) decided upon and implemented according to the dominating tradition with the ministry in question' (Christiansen, 1996b, p 93). Some studies carried out by transport consultants represented a first step towards a Danish expert culture in transport policy (personal information).

The political process resulted in the following formulation in the *Transport Action Plan* of 1990: 'it is necessary to guarantee that the future development of the transport sector corresponds to sustainable development' (p 9, my translation). In my view, the new Action Plan therefore represents a new step in Danish transport policy. However, remarkably enough, the *Traffic Plan* of 1993 presented by the new Government, dominated by Social Democrats, was still described by the Minister responsible as 'a first step towards a new orientation of (Danish) transport policy' (the Plan, p 3, my translation).

The Swedish case again exhibits a different policy-making procedure. The first indication of the emergence of a new goal in transport policy was made in a bill on road and railway infrastructure investments in 1993. Here, it was said that Sweden had to develop *a long-term sustainable transport system* in accordance with the agreements at the Rio conference in 1992 (*government bill 1992/93:176*). In the same year, the Minister of Transport indicated that a *'long-term sustainable transport system'* should be created in Sweden (see above 3.4.3). A similar view was repeated when, in 1994, an Investigative Commission was entrusted by the Government with the task of preparing a future decision on a new Swedish transport policy (*directive as of December 22, 1994*).

In the beginning of the English summary of the final report of the Commission, *Ny kurs i trafikpolitiken* or in English "A new course in traffic policy" (*SOU 1997:35*), it was stated that '(a) transport system of the future must be economically, socially, culturally and ecologically sustainable' (p 43). To reach the goal of environmental sustainability, the Commission proposed ambitious quantitative environmental targets and a successive increase in the CO_2 tax 'to influence individual and corporate transport choice and behaviour' (above 3.4.4). The entire proposal of the Commission provoked, however, a strong reaction and heavy criticism from important actors when they were invited to comment on the report of the Commission, according to the Swedish tradition of transmitting the report of an investigative Commission to a number of institutions, authorities and organized interests (see *Sammanställning av remissyttranden*, 1997).

When the Swedish Government, at last, presented its bill on a new transport policy to Parliament in March 1998, the overall goal of Swedish transport policy was indicated being to achieve a transport system which is environmentally, economically, culturally and socially sustainable and which is efficient in terms of societal economy (p 17).

This overall goal was translated into a number of partial objectives: 1/ a transport system accessible to all 2/ high quality of transport (in terms of reliability, regularity and security) 3/ safe traffic 4/ an environment without severe problems (=*"god miljö"*) and 5/ positive regional development (p 18). Most of the partial objectives were, in their turn, provided with timetabled targets (for instance, for reduced road injuries and reduced emissions of pollutants).

There are, thus, some significant differences (as to inspiration, procedure and public participation) between Denmark, the Netherlands and Sweden in the policy-making processes leading to the introduction and formulation of sustainability as a new goal in transport policy.

The question of how 'environmental sustainability' was defined now requires particular attention.

4.3.2 The definition of 'environmental sustainability'

The Danish Transport Action Plan of 1990, launched by a Conservative-Centre government, emphasized that the development in the field of transport had to be compatible with sustainable development (see above). The definition of this concept was, in its turn, taken from the Brundtland Commission ('development that meets the needs of the present without compromising the possibilities of future generations to meet their own needs'). The content of the concept of 'environmental sustainability' was slightly better defined through the claim that the Danish patterns of consumption have to be compatible with the global ecological framework.

The new Danish government in 1993, dominated by Social Democrats, emphasized that the transport system should be transformed in a way which permitted 'the necessary mobility within the limits set by the consideration of resource use and environment impact (such as energy, climate, polluted air, traffic injuries and noise)' (quoted from *Trafik 2005: Problemstillninger, mål og strategier* p 10, my translation).

Thus, to achieve environmentally sustainable transport (*"bæredygtig transport"*), one should pay attention to the level of mobility that was said to be 'necessary' (how 'necessary' should be defined in its turn seemed to be an open question).

In the Dutch *Second Transport Structure Plan* of 1990, a sustainable society was defined in the terms of the Brundtland Commission as 'a society which meets the present generation's needs without jeopardizing future generation's ability to meet theirs' (p 8). The implication of this was that it is necessary to 'build a transport system which does not shift the burden of environmental problems onto future generations' (*ibid.*).

This meant, in real terms, setting 'limits on the external effects of our transport system - on air pollution, on energy consumption, on noise nuisance, on the number of victims, on the impact on wildlife and the countryside, on the erosion of the quality of urban life, on the consumption of space' (*ibid.*).

In the final report of the Swedish Investigative Commission on a new National Plan for the Transport and Communications (*SOU* 1997:35), it was initially emphasized that '(a) transport system of the future must contribute to economic and social development without depleting natural resources, destroying environment or ruining human health' (*op.cit.* p 43). Somewhat later, the following definition of 'environmental sustainability' was used: 'The requirements of long-term sustainability in the transport sector means that transport operations shall not be a cause of human health deteriorating in any respect, and that emissions, noise, intrusion or other negative effects of transport operations shall not cause serious damage to nature or the cultural heritage' (*op.cit.* p 44). A number of more detailed criteria for sustainable development were also presented by the Commission (*op.cit.* p 98).

The governmental bill of March 1998 included definitions of what is meant by 'environmental sustainability', 'economical sustainability', 'social sustainability', and finally, 'cultural sustainability' (p 11). Environmental sustainability presupposes, according to the Government, that three intermediate political objectives can be reached: 1/ that the environment is protected, 2/ that energy and other natural resources are used more efficiently than today and 3/ that the country will have a sustainable supply of energy and other natural resources.

There are, thus, only some minor differences in the definition of the concept of 'environmental sustainability' in the three countries.

4.3.3 The treatment of the conflict between different goals

The introduction of a new political goal may give rise to conflict between this goal and the traditional ones (see my discussion of this topic in 1.2.4). In the basic political documents on Danish, Dutch and Swedish transport policy in the 90s, there are, however, few examples of discussions of any conflict between environmental sustainability and other goals of transport policy.

In the Danish *Transport Action Plan* of 1990, it was only briefly said that the aim of Danish transport policy was to promote 'an efficient transport system for citizens and industry minimizing the negative impact of transport on the environment and safety' (p 173, my translation). Here, the priority was thus given to efficiency. The Danish *Traf-*

fic Plan of 1993 was somewhat more explicit in dealing with conflicts between different goals. It ends with a vision of a possible future of the Danish transport system, where the problems of today have been solved or, at least, reduced in a significant way.

Here, it is taken for granted that it will be possible to eliminate the conflict between the goal of environmental sustainability and other goals in transport policy in the future if better technology is developed and if people change their attitudes and behaviour.

In the Dutch *Second Transport Structure Plan*, it was first briefly said that it was necessary to strike 'a balance between individual freedom, accessibility and environmental amenity' (p 8). It was later, however, also emphasized that 'measures to improve accessibility can clash with the goal of a (n/ environmentally, my comment) sustainable society' (p 9).

It was therefore established from the very beginning that 'the notion of the sustainable society places limits on the extent to which the transport can be allowed to serve narrow economic goals' (p 9). Here, there is a weak indication that the goal of environmental sustainability is perceived as more important than that of accessibility.

The Swedish Investigative Commission on a new National Plan for Transport and Communications claimed that there was no inherent conflict between the proposed goals in transport policy and sustainable development (p 124). This view was later criticized by quite a few of the institutions among which the proposal was circulated for comments (see *Sammanställning av remissyttranden* 1997, p 3).

In the bill of March 1998, the Swedish Government followed the Commission and claimed that there was no inherent conflict between the main goals of its new transport policy but admitted that there might be, in the short term, some minor conflict between various partial objectives (pp 17sq), an attitude which was immediately criticized in an editorial in *Dagens Nyheter*, one of the leading newspapers in Sweden (1998-03-07).

To summarize: there are some differences in the way the political documents deal with the potential conflict between environmental sustainability and other goals of transport policy.

The Dutch way is to admit the conflict openly without analysing the possibilities of handling the conflict in any detail, the official Swedish attitude is to deny the existence of an inherent conflict, and the Danish attitude is to hope that the conflict can be resolved by technical development and changes in values and behaviour.

4.3.4 Explanations of identified differences

Some disparity was identified regarding the policy-making process and the way the conflict between the new goals and traditional goals was being handled, whereas there were no significant differences in defining 'environmental sustainability'. I believe that the differences in the national policy processes can again be largely explained by differences in political culture and by some historical factors.

It is well-known that the Brundtland report (1987) played an important role in the Danish debate on environmental policy in the late 80s (Andersen, 1997, pp 168sqq). There was also an ongoing process of integrating environmental policies into other policy sectors. The Ministry of Transport was, however, at the same time more concerned with 'its traditional task of expanding the motorway network' than with environmental policy questions (*op.cit.* p 169). The parliamentary situation nevertheless favoured the integration of environmental and transport issues.

The Danish parliamentary situation towards the end of the 1980s during the successive governments of the Conservative Prime Minister Poul Schlyter has been characterized as 'chaotic and abrupt' where environmental issues were concerned. This circumstance gave 'not only the opposition, but also environmental interest organizations and public institutions solid platforms for affecting the environmental policy agenda' (Christiansen, 1996b, p 90). In Parliament, the Social Democrats and two Left parties were able to form a Green majority with the Radical Liberals most of the period 1982-1993 (Andersen, 1997, p 165).

The case of water environment planning in early 1987 has been taken as an obvious example of this situation in a scientific analysis (Andersen and Hansen, 1991). The authors refer to the fact that there was a green wave in the country at that time (*op.cit.* p 69) and to the existence of the Green majority in Parliament (*op.cit.* pp 59sq). The media played a central role in the entire process (*op.cit.* pp 76sq), and so did the Danish Association for the Protection of Nature (*op.cit.* pp 78sqq). The government was therefore exposed to intensive pressure to take a very ambitious decision. The entire process from initiation to decision about the water environment can be described in terms of a change from result-orientated bargaining to the politics of symbols (*op.cit.* p 132). This interpretation was based on Lundqvist's policy model "The Hare and the Tortoise" (see above, 4.1.2). Danish environmental policy was thus seen as having moved from the principle of the "tortoise" to the principle of the "hare" in the second half of the 80s. This means that goals and targets were defined that could not be reached, given the available policy instruments.

I believe that the Danish *Transport Action Plan* of 1990, which introduced the goal of sustainability into Danish transport policy, representing a very rapid reaction to the report of the Brundtland Commission and rapid acceptance of the new and more alarming view of the environmental problems of transport, can be understood in the specific Danish political and historical context. It is true that the Green majority in Parliament had disappeared for a while in 1988, when the Radical Liberals were included in the Government (Christiansen, 1996b, p 37), but it was soon reestablished and persisted until the Social Democrats took over in 1993 (Andersen, 1997, pp 165sq). Another circumstance of importance is the role of the Danish Green movement. It exerted a strong influence throughout the 1980s. The Danish government's early repudiation of nuclear energy in the beginning of the 1980s and the passaging of the world's most stringent legislation regulating the release of genetically manipulated organisms have been mentioned as examples of the success of the Green movement (Jamison et al. 1990, p 192). I believe that the *Transport Action Plan* of 1990 should be added to these examples.

This feature of Danish political life becomes particularly evident in a comparison with the Swedish policy-making process. In the beginning of the 80s, Sweden was regarded as the archetype of a "Tortoise" in environmental matters. This situation seems to have remained the same in the late 80s with the Social Democrats still in government. Sweden did not abandon its traditional way of reacting to new environmental problems, by means of more or less technocratic measures, nor its tradition of preparing a new transport policy, by means of an Investigative Commission and inviting various actors to comment on the reports of this Commission. This procedure resulted in a time lag of eight years. The introduction of environmental sustainability as a new goal in transport policy was therefore a slow, step-by-step process. One factor of importance was that Sweden was hit much harder than Denmark and the Netherlands by the economic recession in early 90s. Environmental problems of traffic growth closely associated with economic growth did not appear to be particularly urgent during most of the early 90s. Furthermore the fact that the car industry plays an important role in the Swedish economy (in contrast to in Denmark and the Netherlands) might have contributed to a hesitant attitude to a new and far-reaching environmental goal in transport policy. Another feature of importance is that an official reaction to the report of the Brundtland Commission was never presented. The agreement at the Rio Earth Summit in 1992 was instead used as the international point of reference, a fact which may be interpreted as an expression of Swedish political formalism.

When the Investigative Commission on a new transport policy published its report *A New Course in Traffic Policy* in the second half of 1997, the entire proposal was rejected by important actors as a basis for a new transport policy (see *Sammanställning av remissvar*, 1997). The publication led to an open conflict with these actors. Some of them (the Trade Union of Transport Workers, the Association of Automobile Manufacturers and Wholesalers and the Swedish Road Federation) financed extensive advertisements in the newspapers, claiming that 'the Swedish government does not make decisions on a very slight foundation' (my translation). This means that these organized economic interests argued for the conservation of the principle of the "Tortoise". One of the advertisements was addressed to the Minister of the Environment claiming that 'we know that you know that the environmental problems are global and that Sweden as a small country cannot solve them by itself' (in *Dagens Nyheter* 1997-11-07, my translation).

The Dutch way of policy-making in connection with formulating the *Second Transport Structure Plan* of 1990 was again different from the Danish and the Swedish way. When the Dutch Government initiated a process of public debate and open conflict about a preliminary draft of a Transport Plan (Part A) in 1988, the Dutch 'pragmatic tradition of accepting differences in opinion' (Jamison et al. 1990, p 186) appeared to come into play. The acceptance of open conflicts may have increased the legitimacy of its present transport policy. Another consequence of a high level of conflict is the fact that the Netherlands is probably the only country in Europe which has witnessed a governmental crisis following a proposal in transport policy (see 3.3.2).

Differences in political and administrative culture and the different historical settings are thus of importance in explaining the differences identified concerning the political processes resulting in the formulation of the goal of environmental sustainability and the way the conflict between this goal and other goals of transport policy was treated in Denmark, the Netherlands and Sweden.

Different attitudes to conflicts between the Dutch political culture, on the one hand, and the Danish and Swedish political culture, on the other, also seem to explain the differences observed in dealing with incompatible goals in transport policy. The Scandinavian way of building consensus by means of a strategy of avoidance seems to be different from the Dutch way of admitting and accepting conflicts as important steps towards consensus. I will describe this in more detail below (4.6.3).

The internal debate within the Swedish Social Democratic Party illustrates what happens when conflicts between different political goals are denied or not made explicit. A Swedish scholar, J. Anshelm, has shown, in a study entitled *Socialdemokraterna och miljöfrågan*, 1995 (in translation "The Social Democrats and the Environmental Issue"), that the leading group of this party has tried to integrate the handling of environmental problems within their party's traditional view of its historical role in societal change: to compensate the problems of an expanding capitalist market economy with socially, and now also environmentally, responsible policies (Anshelm, 1995, pp 176-180).

According to this view, there is no fundamental conflict (in Sweden) between economic growth and environmental sustainability. This general view is, however, exposed again and again, to internal controversies when concrete projects are on the agenda. The decision of the Swedish Social Democratic Government to make an agreement with the Danish Government about the construction of a bridge across Öresund is cited by Anselm as an example of an issue that brought this inherent but suppressed controversy within the party to the surface (*ibid.* pp 145sqq).

4.4 The selection of intermediate objectives, policy instruments and concrete measures

4.4.1 Introduction

The implementation of environmental sustainability as a new goal in transport policy necessitate the selection of intermediate objectives, adequate policy instruments and efficient concrete measures.

Political documents are seldom structured in a logical way, but I believe that four intermediate objectives associated with the goal of environmental sustainability can be identified in the Danish, Dutch and Swedish texts. These objectives were

- to influence the traffic volume and/or the distribution among different transport modes
- to influence the level and/or the composition of the energy consumption
- to influence the technical standard of the fleet of vehicles
- to influence the environmental adaptation of new infrastructure.

In the following, I will first find out what the texts say about the intermediate objectives, one after another, and analyse the selection of policy instruments and concrete measures intended to attain these objectives. Differences in objectives and policy instruments will be explained step by step. In the final part of this section, I will summarize the results of my findings.

4.4.2 To influence the traffic volumes and the distribution among different transport modes

Historically, traffic volumes have increased with economic growth. In a policy for sustainable transport, it seems therefore necessary to decouple this interrelationship, as the growth of traffic tends to counteract other measures aiming at sustainability. However, the documents show little sign of such an intention.

The Danish *Transport Action Plan* of 1990 included an estimate that Danish passenger traffic would grow rapidly to 2010 but after that very slowly between 2010 and 2030 (see 3.2.3). In *Traffik 2005* from 1993, a certain political will to influence the estimated increase was indicated: 'It is the position of the Government that the traffic increase has to be influenced in such a way that this increase and its environmental consequences will be totally less than expected otherwise' (the *Report*, p 2, my translation). In the Dutch *Second Transport Structure Plan* of 1990, a clear political will was demonstrated to limit the increase in individual mobility and to halve the increase in car use estimated at 70% in the period 1986-2010. The reason was primarily to mitigate the environmental impact of car use but also to reduce the problems of congestion which were becoming very serious: 'The simple need to ensure accessibility in major urban areas forces us to restrain the increase in road traffic, but we want to go a step further by, where possible, calling a halt to the growth in travelling distances, including by public transport' (*SVV2*, p 9, on the quantity of the reduction see p 12). The Swedish Commission on a new transport policy estimated in its report (*SOU 1997:35*) that the growth in car use would continue and level out not earlier than around 2020 (p 71). A certain political interest in limiting traffic increase in the metropolitan areas had been acknowledged around 1990 (see above, 3.4.2). The Swedish Minister of the Environment had also indicated in 1994 that transport increase had to be restrained in the Union for the sake of the environment (see below, 5.3.4). However, no such intention was included in the government bill of March 1998.

There are, in principle, five policy instruments that can be used to influence passenger transport growth in terms of motor vehicle kilometres: 1/ physical planning to reduce the need to travel, 2/ the promotion of a modal shift from car use to public transport and cycling (car users being more mobile than others) 3/ the application of economic instruments to restrain the growth of transport volumes 4/ the promotion of information technology as a substitute for physical travel and 5/ an increase in the load factor of vehicles. The three countries differ somewhat in their selection among these policy instruments and concrete measures.

Concerning *physical planning*, the Dutch *Second Transport Structure Plan* of 1990 emphasized the necessity 'to ensure that location policy assists in the management of mobility' (p 29). The ultimate aim of the Dutch use of the physical planning instrument is to favour 'compact rather than sprawling cities' (p 40). In the Danish *Transport Action Plan* of 1990, it was said rather vaguely that 'a target-oriented planning initiative concerned with the land-use and transport planning' should be promoted (English version of the Transport *Action Plan,* p 12). This idea was elaborated further in the *Traffic Plan* of 1993 (the *Plan*, p 13). The Swedish Government laid emphasis on the integration of workplaces, services and dwelling-houses in its bill of March 1998 (*the bill 1997/1998: 56*, p 74).

The promotion of a *modal shift* (from private cars to public transport) has been indicated as an an intermediate objective as well as an adequate measure in Danish and Swedish transport policies, but public transport is regarded as complementary to car transport rather than as a real alternative (see above 3.2.3 and 3.4.2). The Dutch *Second Transport Structure Plan* of 1990 was more outspoken concerning modal shift as a policy instrument: 'The aim is to offer a real alternative to the private car with a view to improving the quality of life, protecting the environment and enhancing road safety' (p 40).

As to the *economic instruments*, there is a well-known historical difference in taxing car ownership between Sweden, on the one hand, and Denmark and Netherlands, on the other. Vehicle taxes were much higher in Denmark and Holland than in Sweden in 1990, the acquisition tax being highest in Denmark and the annual ownership tax highest in Holland (Schipper, 1995). The result of this policy is that these two countries had car fleets consisting of smaller vehicles than in Sweden in the first half of the 90s as well as fewer cars per capita than in Sweden. Now, there seems to be a general tendency to go from a tax regime based on heavy annual vehicle taxes to taxes on the use of the vehicles. The Swedish government has indicated a will to pursue this policy but has also pointed out the practical problems associated with such a shift in its bill of 1998 (*the bill 1997/1998:56*, pp 41sqq).

The interest in introducing "road pricing" has to be seen in this context. The Dutch have been most outspoken here, seing it primarily as a way of controlling car mobility. In Plan A of 1988, road pricing had been advocated as the most convenient economic instrument, but there was 'significant political and public opposition to the proposal' (*SVV2*, p 36). While the focus on road pricing remains in the Netherlands (1998), there has been somewhat less political interest in introducing this instrument in Denmark and Sweden.

To stimulate the use of *information technology* is sometimes regarded as a measure to reduce mobility. Politicians in Denmark, the Netherlands and Sweden have so far, for various reasons (technical, economic, questions of integrity etc), been somewhat hesitant about the widespread introduction of this new technology. So far, it has only had a minor effect on traffic volumes.

There are, thus, some differences in the political interest in reaching the objective of influencing transport growth. The Dutch interest in influencing traffic volumes, particularly car use, is certainly associated, to a large extent at least, with the geographical context. This densely populated country is already contending with difficult congestion problems and the Dutch Government therefore has a particular incentive to promote restrictions on passenger car mobility.

A cultural factor may, however, be at work here if we may believe the results of a recent German study. H.-P. Kleebinder (1995) has categorized the sociocultural role of the mobility by car in some European countries (including the Netherlands and Sweden but not Denmark). In Italy, for instance, he finds evidence for a strong emotional attitude to the car and its use. In the Netherlands, he identifies a more neutral attitude to the car. In every-day life, the car represents only one of several alternatives for transport (*op.cit.* p 221). It plays a major role for leisure activities. In Sweden, on the other hand, he finds a more calculating attitude to mobility by car: it is a question of (what he regards as) rational transport functions (*op.cit.* p 216), a finding that may astonish a native Swede. However, the Swedish car also serves as a '*Fluchtmittel in die Natur*' (*op.cit.* p 216). Kleebinder concludes that the role of the car in the Swedish transport system can therefore not so easily be limited by political means as in the Netherlands (*op.cit.* p 215). However, there is reason to believe that the psychological barriers to car restraint are at work everywhere (Diekstra and Kroon, 1997).

The historical difference between Danish and Dutch car tax regimes, on the one hand, and the Swedish one, on the other, has traditionally been explained by the role of the car industry in Swedish economy and politics compared to that in Denmark and Holland, two countries without an important domestic car industry (Schipper, 1995).

4.4.3 To influence the level and composition of energy consumption

In a transport policy aiming at environmental sustainability, a self-evident objective is to influence the energy consumption, particularly when it is based almost exclusively on fossil fuels. Current trends are, however, working against the possibility of cutting the energy consumption: increasing transport volumes, increasing congestion and many consumers' preferences for more powerful cars.

The Danish *Transport Action Plan* of 1990 mentioned the objective of influencing the energy consumption in terms of stabilization in the short term and in terms of a reduction in the long term (pp 173sq). In the *Traffic Plan* of 1993, the same objective was repeated (the *Report* pp14sq). The Dutch *Second Transport Structure Plan* of 1990 was more explicit than the Danish Plans: '(c)utting consumption of fossil fuels is also (apart from the necessity to reduce the risk of global warming, my comment) desirable with a view to making sensible use of finite energy resources and reducing our dependence on imported oil' (p 16). Since the oilcrises in the 1970s, Swedish transport policies (for instance those of 1979 and of 1988) have revealed an interest in increasing energy efficiency. The recent Commission on a new National Plan for the Transport and Communications has, however, not only suggested that energy efficiency should be promoted and that 'fossil fuel imputs in the transport sector will have to be heavily reduced' (*SOU 1997:35*, p 60), but also that the successive introduction of bio-based fuels should be supported (*op.cit.* pp 60sq) and that the transport system should be based on renewables in the long run (*op.cit.* p 113). The government bill of 1998 followed this suggestion, stressed the importance of using more environmentally friendly fossil fuels in the short and medium term (*the bill 1997/ 1998:56*, pp 74sqq) and included a programme for the production and distribution of biogas and incentives to speed up the introduction of motor alcohols based on biomass (pp 164sqq).

In selecting policy instruments and measures for reaching the objective of increased energy efficiency, the Dutch *Second Transport Structure Plan* of 1990 was comparatively more detailed (pp 16sq). It mentioned not only the setting of standards for more fuel-efficient cars and the use of fiscal and financial but also the promotion of changed driving habits (such as speed reduction), if necessary enforced by means of technical devices. The Plan also recommended a reversal of the current trends towards heavier and more powerful cars and considered, finally, various ways of restraining car use as a way to reduce energy use as well as environmental impact. The Plan therefore envisaged a switch from charges associated with the ownership of a car to charges associated with its use (pp 36sqq). However, such a shift from fixed to variable costs necessitated some harmonization of taxes within the EC community. 'In the meantime the Government has decided to increase petrol duty by eight cents a litre from November 1990' (p 37).

The Danish *Transport Action Plan* of 1990 regarded vehicle taxes as an efficient instrument to provide incentives to use cars with greater energy economy, as there were great differences in the energy efficiency among large sections of the current stock. A future harmonization in EC of fuel taxes at a high level was seen as a complementary instrument (English version of the *Transport Action Plan* pp 7sq).

The only significant difference in the national policies to influence the level and composition of energy consumption is the present Swedish interest in introducing biofuels. Lobbying by potential producers in Sweden may partly explain this.

4.4.4 To influence the technical standard of the fleet of vehicles

It is more or less self-evident nowadays that there is a political will to influence the technical standard of the domestic fleet of vehicles not only for the sake of safety but also for the sake of the environment. Political declarations on these lines are numerous.

The most efficient policy instrument in this area is *technology forcing*. This policy instrument can, however, only by used by very strong political actors, such as the Federal Government of the USA and, possibly, the EU. The Swedish government, for instance, is unable to exert any strong pressure on the SAAB and Volvo corporations to optimize car technology, as these enterprises operate on a worldwide market, while Denmark and the Netherlands, being without own strong car industries, are only able to cooperate with other political actors at the international level (for instance, at the EU level).

The Danish *Transport Action Plan* of 1990 therefore maintains that '(i)t is important that the Danish authorities should press for the development of more energy- and environmentally-efficient methods of transport. In order to be effective, however, this must take place at an international level, within the framework of the EC for example' (quoted from the English version of the *Transport Action Plan*, p 11). The Swedish government bill of March 1998 mentioned the development of new vehicle technology within the European Union (*the bill 1997/1998:56*, pp 74sq). What happens at the European level will be treated in the following chapter.

The possibility of influencing the *spreading of best available technology* (BAT) is, however, a political instrument that is also available for politicians in minor countries. This instrument is frequently used, and there are no differences between the three countries in this respect. One particular way of stimulating the spreading of the best available technology is to define technical standards for new vehicles. Such rules are, however, nowadays more and more harmonized within the European Community in order to avoid setting up new barriers to the free trade (see the following chapter).

The introduction and use of cleaner and safer technologies may also be influenced by means of various taxes and other economic incentives. This possibility is stressed by the Dutch *Second Transport Structure Plan* of 1990 (pp 36sqq). Similar views are also expressed in Danish and Swedish transport policy documents. Another method used in Sweden is to introduce an environmental classification of vehicles or fuels by which the tax may be adapted to the technical standard of the vehicle or fuel. A third method used in Sweden is the introduction of "environmental zones" in the biggest cities in 1997, where only vehicles of a certain technical standard are permitted. A fourth method used in Denmark is scrapping subsidies as a way of getting rid of unclean and unsafe vehicles more rapidly than without subsidies.

There are, thus, some differences between the three countries in stimulating the spreading of best available vehicle technology but no differences at all in their inability to influence the automobile industry. Here, they all are interested in European cooperation.

4.4.5 To influence the environmental adaptation of new infrastructure

Political decisions about investments in roads, rails, tunnels and bridges have a strong impact on the efficiency and equity (accessibility) of the transport system but, to some extent, also on its safety and on the environment. The adaptation of the building and maintenance of transport infrastructure to the environment is, however, often recommended.

The usefulness of infrastructural investments in attaining environmental targets (apart from in areas with very heavy traffic) is, however, very marginal. This was one of the main ideas put forward by the Swedish Commission on a National Plan for the Transport and Communications (*SOU 1996:26*, pp 103sqq). Expanded road and rail infrastructure may increase the unsustainability of the transport system.

In Denmark, by tradition, transport policy has been concerned very much with investments in infrastructure for road transport. In the Netherlands, the situation for investments in roads is somewhat different as a consequence of the high population density of the country. The Dutch *Second Transport Structure Plan* of 1990 indicated the necessity of imposing certain restraints on infrastructural development in order to avoid a further fragmentation of the countryside (p 23). In the Swedish transport policy in the first half of the 90s, there was a kind of competition between the two main blocks in Swedish politics, both arguing for increased investments in road building as a way of reviving the Swedish economy. The investigative Commission entrusted with the task of preparing a new National Plan for Transport and Communications suggested, however, a substantial reduction of the investment plans (by about

50%), emphasizing the importance of making strict social cost evaluations of each road project. This reduction was explicitly motivated with the Precautionary Principle (*SOU 1996:26*, p 105).

The difference between Denmark and the Netherlands in infrastructure investment policy is certainly to a large extent explained by geographical factors. Motorways and bridges are believed to reduce fragmentation in Denmark, whereas investments in road infrastructure are seen to increase the fragmentation of the Dutch land area. The Swedish case is somewhat different. Road investments were here believed by many to increase economic growth (Dreborg and Jungmar, 1994). This belief seemed to lose some ground towards the end of the 90s. The main argument for road investments in Sweden is now rather the necessity to compensate for the peripheral geographical position of the country. Again, the geographical factor plays a role.

Concerning the application of Environmental Impact Assessment (EIA), there are small differences between the three countries. The methods used vary somewhat. The Swedish way is to use formalized EIAs that are, in practice, *ex ante* evaluations (Vägverket: *Miljökonsekvensbeskrivning för vägar. Handbok 1995)*. The Danish method has been less formal and incremental: what is learnt by experience in one project is applied in the next project (Transport Council: *Miljøvurdering af transportprojekter - et casestudie* 1994). The Netherlands like Sweden uses the formalized EIA process resulting in an Environmental Impact Statement (EIS), but, in contrast to many other countries, the Dutch EIA system also includes a compulsory *ex post* evaluation. The aim of this evaluation is to control the actual environmental impact and to inform about the quality of the predictions (Arts, 1994).

Thus, there are certain differences between the Danish and Swedish infrastructure policies, on the one hand, and the Dutch, one on the other. The Dutch policy represents a reconsideration of the effects of infrastructure investments. The explanation of this difference is clearly associated with geographical factors. In the case of EIA, the Dutch method is somewhat more refined.

4.4.6 A summing up of identified differences and suggested explanations

Summing up these observations, it is reasonable to claim that the number of identified significant differences as to the selection of policy instruments and concrete measures is remarkably small and the identified differences are hardly surprising. The explanations of the identified differences that have been suggested are associated more with geographical than with other factors.

Concerning attempts to influence transport volumes: The use of physical planning as a means to restrain mobility is more pronounced in the Dutch case than in the Danish and Swedish ones. The main explanation is to be found in the geographical structure of the Netherlands. Here, land use policies have a long tradition. Several policy instruments are used not only to promote sustainability but also to reduce congestion.

The differences in the view of modal shift as an instrument for influencing transport volumes are more evident. The Dutch policy is not outspoken pro-car.

The official view of public transport as *a real alternative* to the private car, and not as a complement to the car, can be seen both as a consequence of population density and as an effect of a well-developed environmental policy.

Concerning the attempts to influence the energy consumption: There are no significant differences regarding the attempts to increase the energy-efficiency of transport even if the Dutch effort to influence driving behaviour is more pronounced.

However, the Swedish Government recently presented a programme for the introduction of non-fossil fuels. The difference between the Swedish transport policy and the Danish and Dutch policies in this respect is probably due to pressures from potential producers of biofuels in Sweden.

Concerning attempts to influence the technical standard of the fleet of vehicles: There are no differences between the three countries as to their inability to use the instrument of technology forcing.

Some differences between the three countries in their will to promote the spreading of best available vehicle technology (BAT) have been identified. It is difficult to trace the origin of these differences.

Concerning the attempts to influence the environmental adaptation of the infrastructure: In the 1990s, the Netherlands has followed a more restrictive policy than Denmark and Sweden towards expanding its road infrastructure. The explanation is the geographical structure of the country: a very densely populated land area which is threatened by fragmentation if the road infrastructure is expanded further.

The instrument of Environmental Impact Assessment (EIA) has been applied with varying methods in the three countries but witout any treat success.

4.5 Implementation and evaluation

4.5.1 Some differences in implementing strategies

The final part of a transport policy strategy deals with how to implement the policy and how to evaluate the implementation. This part of the strategy is particularly vital if a goal such as environmental sustainability is to be realized. Concerning the implementation and evaluation of transport policies, it is easy to identify significant differences between the three countries.

The Danish *Transport Action Plan* of 1990 was very brief on questions of implementation and evaluation (p 198). The government intended to cooperate with local governments and with organizations (not specified) to fulfil its policy. The Danish way of implementation is, therefore, very decentralized. In order to stimulate and support this decentralized implementation, a particular fund was created in 1992 for the realization of local traffic and environment plans. The use of this money is being evaluated at present (spring 1998). Reports on the implementation of the plan were to be published.

The Danish Department for Environment and Energy contributed a report in 1995 (*Natur- og miljøpolitisk redegørelse* 1995). Here, several targets of Danish transport policy were here expected to be attained by means of already decided measures, apart from the target for the emissions of carbon dioxide. An estimate of the impact of transport policy on the development of the energy consumption in Denmark was made by the Energy Board in 1995 (*Danmarks energifremtider*, pp 90-97). Here, too, the emissions of carbon dioxide were regarded as the main problem, as other emissions were expected to be reduced by around 50% in the next 10-15 years (p 93).

The Ministry of Transport reports annually to the Danish Parliament but published a more comprehensive report in 1997 to stimulate public debate (*Trafikredegørelse*, 1997). The increasing importance of the cooperation within the European Union was stressed, particularly concerning the creation of an efficient and environmentally sustainable transport system in the Union (*op.cit.* p 9).

The Dutch *Transport Action Plan* of 1990 contained a much more detailed description of the implementation and evaluation process than the Danish one. It included an entire chapter (pp 114-121) on this part of the strategy (see above, 3.3.4). To monitor the process, annual measurements of the effects of the policy were to be made, interpreted and published in reports entitled *Beleidseffectmeting Verkeer en Vervoer*. This way of monitoring the transport plan was intended to enable the Ministry to make annual revisions of the policy. This evaluation was to be a responsibility shared between the Ministry of the Environment and the Ministry of Transport. Thus, the Dutch implementation and evaluation process is much more centralised than the Danish one. In 1993, it was claimed by the *Second National Environmental Policy Plan* that the chief obstacle to achieving the environmental objectives of the transport policy was inadequate public acceptance of some important elements of the policy (pp 139sq): 'the difficulty the government has in establishing a direct channel of communication with the motorists' and 'lack of awareness among motorists of environmental effects of car use' (p 140). The Ministry of Transport carried out another evaluation of the transport policy (v. der Waard and v. der Hoorn, 1995). The purpose was to find out whether the targets of the Transport Plan of 1990 could be reached by the year 2000 or 2010 with currently proposed policy measures and under recent assumptions about socio-economic development. The government's effort to limit the growth of car mobility in the long-term was here compared to "swimming against the tide" (*op.cit.* p 12). Therefore, the introduction of road pricing measures appeared to be the only way of reaching the targets of the Plan of 1990. This could, however, not to be implemented before the year 2000. The targets for a reduction of the emissions would probably be met in the case of NOx from private cars, but not from lorries and vans. The targets for emissions of carbon dioxide would not be met at all.

The implementation of Swedish transport policies is also traditionally centralized (Lundqvist, 1997, pp 49sqq). However, the Swedish way of implementing environmental policies has changed somewhat since the middle of the 1980s. Supervisory and control activities have been, to a large extent, *decentralized* to regional and local authorities. At the same time, environmental responsibilities have been *integrated* into all sectors of society (Lundqvist, 1996b, pp 322sq). The government bill of March 1998 analysed the different roles of some important actors in the implementation of the new transport (*the bill 1997/1998:56*, pp 50sq).

Swedish transport policies have traditionally been evaluated in connection with the preparation of a new transport policy. The transport policies of 1963 and of 1979 were, for instance, evaluated before the decision of 1988 (see above, 3.4.2). In 1994, the Investigative Commission for a new Swedish National Plan for Transport and Communications was given the task of evaluating the transport policy initiated and implemented by the Social Democrat Government in the period 1988-1991. No systematic method of evaluation had been developed in Swedish transport policy. The final report of the Commission therefore stated: 'A developed system of *intermodal follow-up* and evaluation of transport policy aims, principles and measures is lacking at present and we therefore propose that SIKA (the Swedish Insitute for Communication Analysis) be tasked with reporting regularly to the Government on progress in achieving the aims of transport policy, and with presenting a concise causal analysis of such development' (*SOU 1997:35*, p 59). In the bill of 1998, the Government introduced a new procedure promising annual reports on the implementation of the new transport policy to be presented to Parliament, and it also followed the suggestion to develop better methods of monitoring the implementation process (*the bill 1997/ 1998:56*, pp 52sqq).

4.5.2 Explanations of identified differences

There are, thus, some significant differences between Denmark, the Netherlands and Sweden concerning the principles and methods of implementation and evaluation. The differences have much to do with different administrative cultures reflecting different historical experience.

The decentralized administrative structure of Danish political organization is regarded as 'a core trait of Danish environmental policy' (Christiansen, 1996b, pp 91). Historically, this can be traced to the constitutional conflicts in the late 19th century between the Danish farmers struggling for independence and local self-governance and the ruling bourgeoisie in Copenhagen (Andersen, 1997, p 160). This profound scepticism towards central rule has resulted in a political and administrative culture emphasizing public control and responsibility at the local level. Central regulations therefore mainly take the form of guidelines rather than of binding directives. The implementation of political decisions take place at county and local levels and is 'strongly backed by effective lobbying from the two associations organizing municipalities and counties' (Christiansen, 1996b, p 91). Systematic evaluations are, on the other hand, a new and not yet institutionalized phenomenon in Danish transport policy.

The Dutch and Swedish way of implementation is much more centralized but with different characteristica. The Netherlands has a long centralized planning tradition. Not least the system of canals and the defence against inundation have required centralised administration and control (4.6.2). The Swedish administrative structure was originally created in the 17th century when the country mobilized its military strength to play a role on the Central European scene. The present trend to decentralize and integrate the responsibility in environmental matters is creating new problems. The authorities within the transport sector are sometimes unable (or unwilling?) to take this responsibility. The Swedish National Road Administration cannot do very much to reduce, for instance, the emissions of CO_2 from road transport (Eriksson, 1997).

The systematic evaluation typical of Dutch transport policy has no corresponding tradition in Denmark or Sweden (yet). Again, the administrative culture of the Netherlands is the most probable explanation of this difference. After all, there also seems to be a difference in the political will: the Dutch principles of implementation and evaluation seem to indicate more of a strategy-orientation than the Danish and Swedish transport policies. What I mean by this statement will be clarified in the following section of this chapter. The actual results of the transport policies of the three countries aiming at a reduction of the unsustainable character of present transport systems will, on the other hand, be evaluated in the last chapter but one.

4.6 The emergence of ecological modernization capacities in national transport policies: some differences and their explanation

4.6.1 The building-up of ecological modernization capacity in national transport policies

Modern societies are confronted with environmental problems of unprecedented seriousness. There is therefore an increasing scientific interest in studying current political responses to this situation (for instance, Jænicke and Weidner, 1995, Christiansen, 1996a, Jänicke and Weidner, 1997). As an analytical instrument, the concept of 'ecological modernisation capacity' (EMC) has been used by several researchers (Jänicke 1990, Andersen, 1994, Lundqvist, 1996a). I am going to make use of the concept of EMC as an analytical tool without taking part in the scientific discourse on the character of ecological or environmental modernization (for instance, Christoff, 1996, Hajer, 1997 and Mol, 1996).

On the basis of the preceding comparative analysis of the transport policies of Denmark, the Netherlands and Sweden, with the focus on environmental sustainability, I intend to compare the three countries' ecological modernization capacities in the field of passenger transport, thereby addressing the third research question of this chapter: *which country seems to have developed the most comprehensive capacity to deal with the new problem of reducing the unsustainability of the present transport systems?* The following is thus an evaluation of *policy-making processes.* The *outcome* of the processes will, as already indicated, be assessed in the last chapter but one.

In my analysis, I will make use of the four elements of the analytical concept of EMC that were mentioned above (4.1.1) and do it in the following order: economic performance, strategic proficiency, innovation capability, consensus ability.

First of all, it is self-evident that EMC requires a certain degree of *economic performance*. Both the amount of GDP/capita and the average percentage of economic growth are of importance in this context. A high GDP/capita makes it possible to adapt industrial production to what the environment demands and leads in many cases to what is called "dematerialisation" of the consumption (less energy and material is used for each unit of GDP). Furthermore, in a situation of economic growth, it is easier to allocate resources to the implementation of environment policy (e.g. to finance subsidies to enhance the spreading of best available technology).

In the field of transport, economic growth tends to accelerate the conversion of the fleet of vehicles and makes it viable to adapt the motor technology to what the environment demands (for instance, by means of catalytic converters) and to a higher degree of energy efficiency. At the same time, however, a higher GDP/capita leads to a higher level of mobility and a higher level of car use. The main result is increased 'unsustainability in urban travel', as has been demonstrated by a British transport researcher, T. May: In an urbanized area, economic growth generates more trips, more dispersed land use, longer trips, higher car ownership, less public transport use, less walking/cycling and the final result is increased energy use, increased pollution, and increased losses of greenfield sites (May, 1993, p 235).

The economic performance of Denmark, the Netherlands, and Sweden in the period between 1987-1997 has developed unequally. Sweden was more seriously hit by the economic recession around 1992. It has been losing its previous position in the league of welfare states. The public budget has gone through a period of serious cut-backs (1994-1997) which has also influenced the allocation of resources to environmental measures. The economic performance of Denmark and the Netherlands appears to be more impressive in the period 1987-1997 (see 6.2.1).

It is evident, however, that the market forces will not be able, by themselves, to create a national ecological modernization capacity, at least not in the field of transport. *Strategic proficiency* generated by the political system is required. The EMC related to the transport sector is mainly a political capacity.

Strategic proficiency consists of 1/ the environmental policy-making capacity of the political system and 2/ the implementation capacity in the field of environmental policy (compare Lundqvist, 1996a, p 23). I will apply this distinction in the following comparative analysis.

The policy-making capacity is (according to Lundqvist) based upon in what way and how quickly the perceived environmental problems are integrated in the political debate and transformed into authoritative decisions. I would add another feature: the ability to articulate the strategy in explicit terms. The implementation capacity refers, in its turn, to the ability of implementing organizations to take actions which lead to the achievement of the main policy objectives.

In the comparative perspective, *the political responses* of both Denmark and the Netherlands to a more alarming view of the environmental problems of transport were very rapid (already in 1988) and led to authoritative decisions in both countries in 1990. The Swedish response was much more hesitant and the proposal for a new transport policy compatible with "sustainable development" was not presented until March 1998, resulting in a time lag of eight years.

The Dutch response to the new and alarming view of the problems was, in its turn, much more advanced than the Danish one. The strategic proficiency of the *Second Transport Structure Plan* of 1990 was characterized by the following features: the conflict between environment and accessibility was admitted, the strategy was divided into five steps and each step based on policy categories consisting of a number of policy areas each of these provided with a target scenario. The Swedish transport policy of 1998 was also fairly well structured and worked out. It distinguished between an overall goal, which was translated into partial objectives that were provided with timetabled quantitative targets (see above 3.4.5).

The principles and methods of *implementation* were also very well developed in the Dutch *Second Transport Structure Plan* of 1990. The difficulty of the task is openly admitted: 'The goal of a sustainable society with a transport system geared to its needs will not be easy to achieve; on the contrary, it will require unprecedented endeavours' (p 114). Therefore, it is stated that 'every individual, every firm, every local authority will have to take responsibility for their part in the task of achieving a sustainable society' and that 'action will be needed at various levels: the European Community, the Netherlands, the metropolitan regions, rural areas, industry, social organizations and the public' (*ibid.*). The procedure is then described exhaustively (pp 114-121).

There is no corresponding analysis of the implementation process in Danish policy documents, while the Swedish government bill of March 1998 included a two-page discussion of the role of some important actors in the implementation process (*the bill 1997/1998:56*, pp 50sqq). The Dutch way of *evaluating the results* of the implementation can, without any doubt, also be seen as superior to the Danish and Swedish ways (see above, 4.5.1). This judgement refers to the principles and methods, not to the actual results of the implementation (to be assessed below). Thus, in terms of strategic proficiency, the Dutch approach is superior to the Danish and Swedish counterparts.

The third element of EMC is the *innovation capability* of the political system. Lundqvist's interpretation of the concept refers to the ability to gain an understanding of the causes of the environmental problems, their scope, complexity, resource requirements, and social consequences. Furthermore, the relations between policy-makers, on the one hand, and scientists, environmental bureaucrats and interest groups, on the other, have an impact on what he calls "the institutional perceptivity" (Lundqvist, 1996a, p 23). I would, however, argue that innovation capability is also based on 1/ the ability to develop well-defined intermediate objectives in order to reach the overall goals of transport policy, 2/ the ability to identify new policy instruments and new concrete possibilities for obtaining the intermediate objectives and timetabled targets of the policy and 3/ the ability to develop new principles and methods of implementation.

Comparing the innovation capability of Denmark, the Netherlands and Sweden in the field of the environmental problems of transportation, it appears that the Dutch *institutional perceptivity* in the late 1980s was clearly superior to the Swedish one and somewhat superior to the Danish one. The Dutch political system integrated the environmental problems of transportation in the public political debate in a way that has no correspondence in the Danish or the Swedish political process. In the case of Denmark, the new perception of the problems of transport seems to have contributed to the establishment of transport policy as an independent and no longer fragmented policy area.

Innovation capability in terms of being able *to develop intermediate objectives and of adopting new political tools* to carry out a transport policy aiming at environmental sustainability is not so impressive in any of the three countries. The Dutch intention to reduce the expected growth in car use is an innovative element in the formulation of the intermediate objectives of transport policy, but the strong Dutch interest in introducing road pricing has not yet (1998) resulted in anything concrete. The Danish idea of scrapping subsidies as a way of getting rid of unclean and unsafe vehicles more rapidly than without subsidies was used with modest success *(Skrotningspræmien: Effekter for miljø og bilpark, 1995)*. The Swedish use of environmental classification of vehicles and fuels and the introduction of environmental zones in urban areas are, on the other hand, in operation. A recent evaluation indicates that at least the classification of fuels has been compratively successful (Erlandsson and Laveskog, 1997). Thus, concerning innovation capability, the differences between the three countries are not so impressive.

The final element of EMC is the *consensus ability*. Here the two Scandinavian countries seem, *a prima vista*, to be outstanding as a consequence of their tradition of consensus-building in politics (compare

Lundquist's judgement in 1996a, p 23, where he talks about 'consensus - a much revered feature in the Nordic political culture'). There are, however, certain differences between the two Scandinavian countries in the way consensus-building takes place. In the Danish case, new proposals are subjected to an informal procedure where the proposals are discussed in preparatory committees during which organized interests are consulted (Andersen, 1997, p 167). The corresponding procedure in Sweden is much more formalized. Investigative Commissions with representatives of the different political parties are entrusted with the task of preparing a proposal. The aim of this is to try to build consensus around a certain issue before the proposal is discussed in Parliament. Organized interests have often been represented on these Commissions. Other actors are entitled to comment on the report of the Commission before the Minister presents the government's bill in Parliament. The relation between controllers and polluters in Sweden has been characterized by cooperation and consensus on the objectives and methods (Lundqvist, 1997, p 48).

I am, however, somewhat sceptical about the positive notion of Scandinavian consensus-building. I believe that this way of building a consensus is very much based on a strategy of avoiding open conflicts. The emerging result is therefore often a superficial kind of consensus. Very difficult problems may be overlooked or ignored. The Dutch acceptance of open conflicts during a period of public debate, after which authoritative policy decisions are made, is perhaps a much more satisfying way of building consensus. Particularly concerning implementation strategies, the Dutch policy has striven to initiate constructive debates between the authorities and the target groups (Bressers and Plettenburg, 1997, p 116). This way of handling conflicts is, however, only successful when the realization of the environmental objectives is regarded as necessary by the participants involved (*op.cit.* p 128).

What conclusions can be drawn about the capacity-building in Denmark, the Netherlands and Sweden where traffic and environment are concerned? I do not hesitate to claim that the most outstanding ecological modernization capacity of the three is to be found at present in the Netherlands. The rapid political response to new elements in the view of the environmental problems of transportation, the integration of these problems into the public debate, the carefully elaborated strategy to meet the problems, certain innovative thinking in setting objectives, in selecting policy instruments, in implementing and evaluating the policy are some of the arguments for this judgement.

The actual outcome of the ecological modernization capacities in the field of transport in Denmark, the Netherlands, and Sweden is, as was indicated above, quite another story, and it will be assessed in chapter 6.

4.6.2 Explanations of differences in capacity building

Looking for explanations of the different national abilities to develop EMC in the field of transport, one immediately associates the differences with the political cultures in the three countries.

In Sweden the traditionally technocratic attitude to environmental problems is probably of importance. This attitude is a barrier to more dramatic changes in the perception of the problems and to more radical solutions: since it is thought that environmental problems can in principle be solved by introducing best available technology (supported by economic and legal instruments) and by means of (the international) technical development. The attitude of the leading group of the Social Democratic Party (very often in government) is also of importance. The historical mission of the party has been, according to the dominant view, to compensate the capitalist market forces with socially responsible policies and is now to compensate the same market forces with environmentally responsible policies as well. Therefore, in the view of the leading group, there is no fundamental conflict between economic growth and sustainability (see above, 4.3.4).

The Danish political culture is less technocratic than the Swedish one and more populistic in the field of environmental policy. Therefore, there are no such barriers to more radical political decisions concerning the environment (for instance, to refrain from nuclear power) as in Sweden but, in the field of transport policy, there is a weak tradition of professional analysis which reduces the possibilities of developing an ecological modernization. It is further difficult to believe that the decentralized way of implementing transport policies is conducive to the establishment of strategic proficiency.

The Dutch ability to develop EMS in the field of transport, impressive in comparison with the Danish and Swedish performance, has to be seen against a background of several factors. First, the Netherlands is known internationally for its strategic ability in comparison with many other European countries and sometimes compared with Japan in this respect (Jänicke and Weidner, 1995, pp17sq). Since the decolonisation period, careful land use planning has been of vital importance in this densely populated country, for instance, in order to balance different interests (de Jongh, 1996, p 4). The present ambition to influence not only the technical standard of vehicles and the development of infrastructure but also the daily behaviour of the transport users (cf the definition of transport policy above, 1.1.1) is impressive.

Secondly, its strategic proficiency in transport policy seems to have some connection with the long Dutch tradition of handling the problems generated by the neighbourhood of the North Sea. Since the Middle-Ages the fight against floods from the sea has created a tradition of common action (de Jongh, 1996, p 3). The use of the system of canals for various purposes has fostered cooperation and interaction between different actors. It is worth noticing that the Minister of Transport is also Minister of the *Waterstaat*.

Thirdly, I believe that the Dutch acceptance of a higher level of conflict regarding transport policy issues has also played a significant role. Green organizations are efficient and professional (Jamison et al. 1990, p 187) but Transport Business and Car Business are, on the other hand, strong lobby organizations with good contacts with certain political parties and the media. Open conflict is, however, sometimes favourable for the articulation of the different elements of a problem or a strategy.

The methods of consensus building are also of importance. The consensus-building process has been described in the following way by de Jongh, former deputy director-general for the Environment in the Dutch Department of Environment and the one who inspired the integrated environmental planning policy. Referring to the ideas of Richard Rorty, he claims that

> (i)n the consensus building process, scientific information is of crucial importance...(it) always consists of an amount of uncertainty; this should not be hidden away from policy makers but should play an explicit role in the design of policies. The constant monitoring of costs, emissions and environmental qualities is a way to deal with uncertainties: contingency plans are another way to answer uncertainties in a sensible way.

de Jongh also emphasizes the importance of the interaction between Green organizations and other organized interests in the process: 'The direct contact between environmental groups and adversaries from the public and private sectors can be an important management tool to change adversaries into stakeholders' (de Jongh, 1996, p 53). I believe that this attitude to consensus building has a strong bearing on the creation of EMC.

4.7 Conclusions

At the outset of this part of the inquiry, I presented the hypothesis that there were only fairly unimportant differences to be found between Danish, Dutch and Swedish transport policies in the period 1987-1997. The reason for this view was that, in the previous chapter, a number of striking similarities had been found regarding the changes of transport policies. However, the hypothesis turned out to be unfounded to some extent, as a limited number of significant differences were actually identified. After all, no major surprise appeared. In the introductory section, some possible explanatory factors were described based upon recent comparative studies of *environmental* policies.

A first significant difference was observed in the transition to a new and more alarming view of the environmental problems of the transport sector. Denmark and the Netherlands made this transition much more rapidly than Sweden. This difference between Sweden, on the one hand, and Denmark and the Netherlands, on the other, was related, primarily, to different political and administrative cultures, secondly, to the role of Green organizations in Denmark, and to geography in the case of the Netherlands (a country already partly below the present sea level is more exposed than others to the greenhouse effect).

There were also some significant differences, this time between all three countries, in the national policy-making processes leading to the introduction and formulation of environmental sustainability as a new goal in transport policy. The differences arose from how the new policy was initiated, elaborated and made acceptable to different interests. The definition of environmental sustainability was, on the other hand, almost the same in the three countries. In contrast, there were certain differences between the three countries in dealing with the inherent conflict between the goal of environmental sustainability and the traditional goals in transport policy. This conflict was openly admitted and de-scribed in Dutch political documents but more or less overlooked or de-nied in the Danish and Swedish ones.

The identified differences in policy formulation have their immediate background in differences in political and administrative cultures. At the same time, however, the economic recession in Sweden seems to have played a certain role. The varying importance of certain actor groups (car industry, transport interests, Green organizations) should not be underestimated as explanatory factors.

The selection of intermediate objectives, policy instruments and measures to attain the new goal did not exhibit any significant differences. The only major exception to this general rule was the Dutch political will to restrain the increase in transport volumes and to develop real alternatives to the private car as well as their attitude to road infrastructure investments. The main background of these few differences is to be found in the geographical structure of the Netherlands (a densely populated area).

Concerning the implementation and evaluation of transport policy, there were again significant differences between all three countries. First, the Dutch way of implementing and evaluating the results is much more refined than the Danish and Swedish counterparts. Second, the Danish way of implementing is much more decentralized than the Dutch one. This decentralization has deep historical roots. Implementation of transport policy in Sweden has become somewhat more decentralized since the middle of 1980s. The differences in implementing and evaluating are largely due to traditional differences in the way the three countries have been administered.

The final evaluation of the 'ecological modernization capacity' of the three countries in the field of transport resulted in the conclusion that the Dutch transport policy appeared to be superior to the Danish and Swedish transport policies in terms of strategic proficiency, to some extent, also in its innovation capacity and, finally, in its way of consensus building. The background to this fact was found in the Dutch tradition of handling the problems generated by the neighbourhood of the North Sea. The use of the system of canals for various purposes has also fostered far-reaching cooperation at the national level.

5 The European Dimension

5.1 Introduction

5.1.1 The objective, focus and limitations of the chapter

The basic objective of this chapter is to integrate the main theme of the study, three cases of national transport policies, into a European context by making an explorative study of the relation between national and European transport policies.

The relevance of the two preceding chapters in a European perspective is associated with the idea that the variety of current national transport policies constitutes a kind of 'pragmatic experimental laboratory' (an idea put forward by Jones et al. 1993, pp 167 sq). The existence of such a "laboratory" may stimulate the development of transport policies in Europe.

At the same time, however, it is of importance to study how the national policies are influenced by European transport policies. The main objective of this part of the inquiry is therefore to investigate *how* the national policies are related to European transport policies. But what do we mean by 'European transport policies'?

First of all, the expression may refer, rather vaguely, to some common features in national European transport policies compared with, for instance, American and Asian transport policies. Orfeuil and Bovy claim, for instance, that 'European transport patterns are different from those of the North-American and the Japanese' and take the view that the main differences in mobility may be explained by geography, culture and 'the domestic economic context' (Orfeuil and Bovy, 1993). I believe, however, that the differences between European and American mobility patterns also reflect some differences in transport policies, for instance stronger political support for public transport in Europe. As a first approximation, therefore, 'European transport policies' may refer to more or less historically determined and to more or less spontaneous common features in European transport policies and practices.

Secondly, there is a growing tendency to strive consciously for the harmonization of transport policies in Europe, at first within the framework of the European Conference of Ministers of Transport (ECMT) and, since the late 80s, within the European Union. Harmonization has so far mainly been associated with common traffic rules, taxation regimes, vehicle standards and deregulation policies.

In the future, the problems of congestion in densely populated areas and the environmentally unsustainable character of the current European transport system will probably increase the need to harmonize the national transport policies. This need has also to do with the fact that unintentional negative consequences of a national transport system may spill over to other countries. Emissions from traffic (together with emissions from other sources) are both "exported" from and "imported" to an individual country. Some European countries are net exporters, others are net importers. In 1985, Denmark was, for instance, a net exporter of NOx, exporting 80 000 tons and receiving 18 300 tons (*Danmark på vej mod år 2018*, 1, p 22). Pollution also has a negative impact on the "commons" of the European region such as the North Sea and the Baltic Sea (Tengström, 1994).

Attempts to harmonize transport policies in Europe may, *a priori*, be seen as new restrictions on, as well as new opportunities for, national policies. A strong common European transport policy may constitute a barrier to a free choice of national policy options. Such a European policy may, on the other hand, be seen as a necessary condition for reaching important national transport policy goals. But, in the second case, if the main agreements are to be made at the European level, it is justifiable to ask what remains of national transport policy-making?

The focus of the chapter is therefore on the question: *how and to what extent has the situation of the national policy-makers been influenced by the development of a common European transport policy, particularly when it comes to the creation of environmentally sustainable transport systems?* For obvious reasons, the discussion of this question will be limited to the three North-European countries which are the principle object of the present investigation. A comparison with other European countries would have been of great interest but is beyond the scope of the present inquiry.

Studies of the relation between national transport policies and European transport policies are, according to my present knowledge, a new field of research (see next paragraph). The inquiry has therefore to be explorative rather than purely analytical.

5.1.2 Previous studies

There are comparatively few previous studies of interest in connection with the objectives of this chapter. Those that are of interest belong to two groups 1/ studies of European transport policies and 2/ studies of the

the relation between national and European transport policies.

The first group consists of quite a few publications. Here are some of them: The history and present situation of the European Conference of Ministers of Transport is presented in the book *The European Conference of Ministers of Transport 1953-1993* (1993). The early history of the transport policy of EC is treated, for instance, by J.Erdmenger in *Vers une politique des transport pour l'Europe* (1984 but cited in an updated version in Swedish of 1986). M. Schinas and J.-A. Vinois have dealt with the historical development of the transport policy of EC up to 1993 in an article entitled *"Transport Policy"* (1993). There is a Danish survey of the emergence of the present Common Transport Policy (*EF's Transportpolitik - en oversigt*), initiated by the Danish Transport Council (1993). The article entitled '*Transport Policy: the European Laboratory*' (Jones et al. 1993) has already been referred to.

Current problems of European transport and transport policies are treated in an anthology entitled *Transport in a Unified Europe: Policies and Challenges* (Banister and Berechman, 1993). One of the articles (Dugonjic, Himanen, Nijkamp and Padjen, 1993) deals with the question of environmental sustainability. In another anthology, Holzinger presents a success story in transport and environment in an article entitled '*A Surprising Success in EC Environmental Policy: The Small Car Exhaust Emission Directive of 1989*' (1995). The attempts to solve the problems of transport and environment in Europe have been treated in a chapter entitled *"The European dilemma"* in a recent British study, *Towards Sustainable Planning* (Haq, 1997). The same theme was treated by myself and two collaborators in *Sustainable Mobility in Europe and the Role of the Automobile* (Tengström et al. 1995).

The second category of scientific literature consists of very few studies (to my knowledge). Bjørnland has compared the development of transport and transport policies in EEC with corresponding developments in Norway and Sweden before the latter country entered the European Community (Bjørnland, 1993). In a minor study in Swedish, the relation between environmental policies in the Nordic countries and the European Union is considered (Bergdahl, 1996). In his analysis, the author includes the environmental problems of the transport sector.

5.1.3 The disposition of the chapter

As a background to the main part of the chapter, a survey of the history of the European Conference of Ministers of Transport and of the transport policy of the European Community (Union) will follow upon this introduction. Thereafter, a study will be presented of how the role of the

146 Towards Environmental Sustainability?

Common Transport Policy (CTP) of EEC (EU) is described in Danish, Dutch and Swedish transport policy documents. To approach the key question of the chapter, i.e. how and to what extent has the situation of the national policy-makers been influenced by the development of a common European transport policy in their attempts to reduce the present unsustainable character of the national transport systems, the policy-making within the Union will be analysed. The results of this analysis will be tested by discussing some current, concrete transport and environmental issues. The chapter will end with a final summary and some conclusions.

5.2 Towards a harmonization of European transport policies

Two political institutions have played important roles in the attempts to coordinate European transport policies: the European Conference of Ministers of Transport (ECMT) and the Commission of the EC (EU). Before entering upon a discussion of the main issue of this chapter, it might be convenient to contrast the role of ECMT and the role of EC (EU) in establishing a harmonized European transport policy.

5.2.1 Towards a Pan-European Transport Policy - the role of the ECMT

The European Conference of Ministers of Transport was founded in 1953. The number of members of ECMT has been growing since its beginning. In the middle of the 90s, the Council of the Conference comprised the Ministers of Transport of no less than 30 European countries. At their meetings, the ministers of ECMT make *recommendations* about different issues, such as general lines of transport policy, infrastructural needs, road safety and traffic regulations, protection of the environment, application of new technologies, etc (*The European Conference of Ministers of Transport 1953-1993: Past, Present and Future*, 1993).

With the increasing importance of the EEC, the role of ECMT is no longer regarded to be the same as before. The Conference may currently be of more interest to non-members of the European Union than to the members of this union. The ECMT's perspective on European traffic is therefore not necessarily identical with that of EEC (*op.cit.* p 33). A meeting of the ECMT on Crete in March 1994 resulted in a declaration calling for a 'pan-European transport policy'. In May 1996, an Action Programme for 1996-1999 was adopted by ECMT regarding the integration of new countries in Central and Eastern Europe into the West-European transport systems. The future role of ECMT will partly depend on how the expansion of the European Union proceeds.

However, the role of ECMT should not be underestimated. The secretariat of ECMT (located in Paris) cooperates very closely with the OECD and initiates studies affecting policy-making at the European level as well as at the national level. Round Tables and Symposia organized by ECMT result in conclusions that are sometimes transformed into proposals for policy decisions submitted to the Ministers. Their decisions have certainly had an impact on national transport policies (although, as far as I know, no study has been made of this impact). The effects of Round Tables and Symposia have probably been limited.

The question of 'environmental sustainability', the key issue of this study, has been dealt with by the ECMT in the last few years. An early resolution, No. 66, *On Transport and Environment* (1989), states 'that the impacts of transport on human health and the environment must be limited to levels which human beings and nature can cope with in the long run'. A series of detailed recommendations follows which are the result of a special ECMT ministerial session (documented in a report entitled *Transport Policy and the Environment* 1990).

In 1992, a seminar on the theme 'Transport Policy and Global Warming' (a report carrying the same title was published in 1993) was a direct response to the Ministers' demand to include the dangers posed by global warming in the concerns of ECMT. The conclusions of this scientific seminar comprised statements such as 'current trends are clearly inconsistent with the Rio aspirations', 'new technology can improve matters, but there is no complete technological fix immediately available' and 'progress to a viable view of the problems appears to be hindered by the fact that transport ministers have not usually taken the initiative in formulating a sector policy for transport and the environment, and are not believed by others to be taking the matter sufficiently seriously'.

However, in collaboration with the OECD Group on Urban Affairs, ECMT set up a Project Group on Urban Travel and Sustainable Development in 1993. Its final report, entitled *Urban Transport and Sustainable Development* (1995), delineates some strategic ideas for urban policies to be applied in the 1990s and beyond: 1/ to reduce the need to travel 2/ to reduce the absolute levels of car use and road freight in urban areas 3/ to favour more energy-efficient modes for both passenger travel and freight 4/ to reduce noise and vehicle emissions at source 5/ to encourage more efficient road use 6/ to reduce casualties 7/ to improve the attractiveness of cities for residents, workers, shoppers and visitors (*op. cit.* pp 133sq). The main conclusion of the project group was that 'lifestyles and technology of western countries and the direction of development in the rest of the world will have to change. The logical place in which to start promoting such changes is in cities' (*op. cit.* p 30). The group also claimed that current policy instruments are inadequate for reaching the new objective (*op. cit.* p 147).

In April 1994, the conclusions and recommendations of the project group were accepted by the Committee of Deputies, the task of which is to prepare the work of the meeting of the ministers. Despite this, there is still not enough agreement on a pan-European strategy for solving the problems of urban transport (Short, 1996, p 14).

5.2.2 Towards a Common Transport Policy of the EU - the role of the Commission

In the history of the European Union, the idea of a Common Transport Policy (CTP) goes back to the Treaty of Rome, signed in 1957. The aim of this agreement was, among many other things, to guarantee freedom to provide transport services in the Community.

The application of this principle was, however, slow and long delayed by national interests, which became apparent in meetings of the Council of Ministers. In 1982, the Commission and the European Parliament therefore submitted the case to the EC Court of Justice, which decided in 1985 that 1/ the Council of Ministers had violated the Treaty of Rome by its passivity in transport matters and 2/ that from now on all transport of people and goods should be free for any company within the community (Erdmenger, 1986).

In the period 1985-1993, transport policy became more important within EC than before, partly as a result of the rapid growth of EC transport and of increasing pressure on transport infrastructure and the environment. During the preparations for the establishment of the Internal Market, deregulation of transport was speeded up. The political focus was on the increase in the cost-efficiency of transport, which was expected to contribute to the global economic competitiveness of the EC. At the same time, however, EC transport policy was influenced by the new and alarming view of the environmental impact of the transport sector (*EF's Transportpolitik - en oversigt*, 1993). In the Maastricht Treaty (agreed upon in 1992), the environmental aspect of economic growth was therefore strongly emphasized. The transport system should not only become efficient and of a high quality. It should also be adapted to the constraints of the environment. The keyword of the day was 'sustainable development'.

At the time when the Maastricht Treaty was signed, the Commission had already initiated a debate on the problem of transport and environment by issuing a Green Paper on *The Impact of Transport on the Envi-*

ronment (*COM/92/46*) in February 1992. On the basis of the discussions of this Paper, the Commission presented in December 1992 a White Paper entitled *The Future Development of the Common Transport Policy: a Global Approach to the Construction of a Community Framework for Sustainable Mobility* (*COM/92/494*). This was approved by the Council of Ministers in June 1993.

The new Common Transport Policy (CTP) is pursued by the Commission by means of annual five-year Action Plans (the last one available refers to the period 1995-2000). This document (*COM/95/302*) contains detailed plans for three areas 1/ improvement of quality (refers to the development of the transport system, to environment and safety) 2/ the internal market (refers to access to and structure of the market, to costs and fees, and to the social dimension of the market 3/ the external dimension (refers to the relation to the world outside EU).

In the first period of the new Common Transport Policy, the question of an upgrading of the road-net of the Union has been very much in focus. Such an upgrading was seen as a way of integrating the different parts of the Union and as a way of stimulating economic growth within the Union. Already in the Maastricht Treaty, the principles of the development of Trans-European Networks (not only for all kinds of transport but also for energy and telecommunications) had been agreed upon (article 129b-d). A Master Plan for the road network in the Union was presented in 1993. More detailed plans were drawn up in 1993-1996 and a concrete programme (up to 2010) for the upgrading of the road, rail, inland waterways, sea and air transport networks in the Union was accepted by the Council in July 1996.

Furthermore, the Commission has, by means of other Green Papers, also invited discussions on particularly difficult issues related to the Common Transport Policy. One paper was entitled *The Citizens' Network - fulfilling the potential of public passenger transport in Europe* (*COM/95/601*). The aim of this paper was to involve the citizens of the European Union directly in the debates on the problems and solutions of European transport. The background of this initiative was the fact that 40% of the households in the Union do not have access to a car and the fact that the costs of congestion on the roads of the Union have been estimated at about 120 billion ecus annually, which 'is four times more than is spent on public passenger transport across the EU' (p 4).

The title of the second Green Paper was *Towards Fair and Efficient Pricing in Transport* (*COM/95/691*). The aim of this Paper was to stimulate the member states to introduce efficient pricing of the transport costs. The reason is the size of the total external costs of transportation in the Union. These costs (congestion, accidents, air pollution and noise) are estimated at 250 billion ecus per year.

In 1996, the problems of the railway system in the Union were treated in a White Paper, entitled *A Strategy for Revitalising the Community's Railways*. The difficulty of the railways in competing with other transport modes had inspired the initiative. The ideas of the Paper were approved by the Ministers of Transport in December 1996.

5.2.3 A first summing up

In brief, there are clear tendencies in the 1990s to harmonize transport policies in Europe, mostly within the present European Union but also, albeit to a lesser degree, at the pan-European level. Informal and spontaneous forces, as well as more formal political agreements, are working along the same lines.

During the last few years, the interest of the Commission has been focused on the development of the Trans-European Networks, on the future role of public transport and on the possibility of internalizing the external costs of transport. The ability and political will of the Council of Ministers will, however, determine the outcome of the policy-making.

5.3 The role of the Common Transport Policy in national policies

5.3.1 Introduction

The Common Transport Policy of the European Union can be assumed to be of greater importance than the recommendations of the European Conference of Ministers of Transport for Denmark, the Netherlands and Sweden, all being members of the European Union (the Netherlands from 1957, Denmark from 1972 and Sweden from 1995). It is therefore of interest to study how the Common Transport Policy of EU (CTP) is looked upon in the national transport policy documents of the three countries. Therefore, I intend to scrutinize some important political texts to see what they say about the relation between national transport policies and CTP (with reference to environmental sustainability).

In my interpretation of these texts, I intend to focus on three aspects: 1/ Are there frequent references in the national transport policy documents to the harmonization of transport policies in Europe? 2/ Is the Common Transport Policy of EU regarded as imposing restrictions on or as creating new opportunities for policies aiming at reaching the goal of environmental sustainability? 3/ Are there any references to the role of European cooperation in handling the inherent conflict between economic growth and environmentally sustainable transport?

5.3.2 Denmark and the Common Transport Policy of EU

In the Danish *Transport Action Plan* of 1990, the role of a harmonized European transport policy was looked upon rather as a factor restricting national decision-making than as a new opportunity. It was explicitly stated: 'The efforts of the EEC to harmonize economic duties and fees lay down comparatively narrow boundaries for the member states to change the duties and fees in the transport sector' (p 181, my translation). In the same document, the EC was, however, called upon to take new initiatives 'to harmonize fuel taxes at a high level, campaigns, etc to encourage energy-friendly motoring, environmental labelling, and efforts to make all public authorities pay heed to the environment when procuring new transport equipment' (p 13 of the English summary). It was also emphasized that 'Danish authorities should press for the development of more energy- and environmentally-efficient methods of transport within the framework of the EC' (the English summary, p 11).

When the EC White Paper of December 1992 on a Common Transport Policy aiming at sustainable mobility had been approved by the Council of Ministers in June 1993, the Danish attitude to the CTP became more positive. It was emphasized in the Danish Traffic Plan of 1993 that Denmark was interested in playing an active role in the creation of a sustainable European transport policy: 'An increasing part of national traffic policy is shaped within the framework of EC cooperation. The Council of Ministers has agreed to the principles laid down in the White Paper of the EC Commission on a Common Transport Policy... Denmark is playing a constructive and active role in the efforts to establish the future sustainable European transport policy' (the *Report*, p 3, my translation). This statement refers, in concrete terms, to the construction of Trans-European Networks and to the harmonization of taxes and fees related to infrastructure and external costs.

Three years later, in the *Action Plan for the Reduction of Emissions of CO_2* (1996), presented by the Ministry of Transport, the EU initiative in December 1995 (see below) to force the European car industry to produce more energy-efficient cars was looked upon as promising (p 15). The Danish government was said to be interested in supporting this initiative (p 29).

In *Forslag til Landplanredogørelse*, presented by the Ministry of the Environment and Energy (January 1996), another Danish step towards more active participation in European planning policy was announced. It was said in the text (p 12) that other countries such as the Netherlands, Germany and France have been much more active in the planning discussions. It was now the intention of the Danish Government to increase the Danish participation in this process (*ibid.*). The Danish road and rail

152 Towards Environmental Sustainability?

infrastructure was therefore described in the perspective of the contemporary EU planning for Trans-European Networks.

5.3.3 The Netherlands and the Common Transport Policy of EU

In the Dutch *Second Transport Structure Plan* of 1990, references to European transport policy were more frequent than in the contemporary Danish *Transport Action Plan*. The Netherlands was said to have been the driving force (more than Denmark, as it seems) in the attempts to establish a common European transport policy both within ECMT and EU (p 83). The reason indicated was that the effectiveness of the Dutch national transport policy must be regarded as being dependent on the adoption of parallel policies elsewhere in Europe, particularly in the neighbourhood (*ibid.*).

In the Plan of 1990, the Netherlands was said to owe 'its wealth in significant measure to its position on major European transport arteries' (p 9). The future of its position was therefore connected with the European transport networks: 'If the Community's logistical system falters this will have a direct adverse impact on the competitive position of our entire production system' (p 7).

The necessity of common European actions in a number of policy areas was noted by the Plan (p 83). These areas were specified in a comprehensive list (p 114). Some of these requirements are related to passenger transport on land:
- the setting of emission standards, maximum speeds, safety requirements and technical measures affecting driving behaviour and speed
- pricing policies aiming at harmonized duties, taxes and tolls
- agreements on the establishment of high-speed (railway) lines.

In several passages of the Dutch *Second Transport Structure Plan*, the necessity to harmonize taxes and technical standards was emphasized. If the real cost of transport was to be passed to the user, this necessitated a 'framework of fiscal harmonization in the European Community' (p 9). Restraining traffic growth requires likewise an extension of the system of tolls 'into a more comprehensive pricing mechanism' and would be achieved 'by working in the European context for a sharp increase in fuel taxes' (p 106).

The Dutch Plan applauded (p 15) the EC introduction of US standards of 1983 on emissions from motor vehicles (see below) by January the 1st 1993 (p 15) but deplored the absence of a common EC levy aimed at restraining car use (p 17). The absence of EC regulations relating to both technical requirements and road-users' behaviour to increase road safety was also regretted (pp 21sq). A shift from fixed to variable costs of car use was regarded as being 'best done in a European framework' but such a framework was not in sight (p 37). To set stricter noise-emission standards within the European Community, 'the Netherlands is pressing in Brussels for these to be based on the most recent technical advances' (p 18).

In the case of expanded road and rail infrastructure, the Dutch transport policy of 1990 has, as we have seen above, become less expansion-orientated than before in the case of road infrastructure. Instead, the integration of the Netherlands into the European railway network of high-speed lines was emphasized as an important policy objective (p 39). In order to compete with the air lines, existing rail lines would be upgraded and new lines constructed forming high-grade links with the European network (p 42).

In dealing with the conflict between transport growth and environmental sustainability, the Plan regards the role of both EU and ECMT as being very important for the attainment of the goals of the Dutch national transport policy. Otherwise, environmental gains in the Netherlands 'can be cancelled out by unlimited emissions in other countries' (p 83). The Dutch view of the conflict between transport and environment was summarized in a fairly strong sentence: 'What matters is that the balance between mobility and environment, between accessibility and quality of life, should appear on the European agenda and that the policies of the European Community and of the individual states should reinforce rather than undermine one another' (p 83).

5.3.4 Sweden and the Common Transport Policy of EU

In dealing with the Swedish case, it should be remembered that Sweden was not a member state before 1st of January 1995. Before the Referendum on Swedish membership in the Union in November 1994, the Swedish minister of the environment initiated a public debate on a future Swedish policy within the EU on environmental issues by publishing a booklet on these questions (*Det svenska miljöarbetet i EU* - Ds 1994:-126). The transport system was there indicated as the most troublesome aspect of the current environmental problems (p 6). According to the report, the long-term objective of the environmental policy of EU should therefore be to create a sustainable transport system fully adapted to the environment. One of the targets on the road to this goal should be to reduce the amount of transport.

The influence of the transport policy of EC on Swedish (and Norwegian) transport policies before Sweden's membership of the Union has been studied by Bjørnland for the period up to 1993 (Bjørnland, 1993).

His conclusions are of interest here, even if he focuses on freight transport. He claims that 'Sweden is more true to the spirit of EC transport policy than the EC Member States themselves' (p 81). He exemplifies with four areas: infrastructure investments (Sweden developed a very ambitious programme in the early 90s for connecting the Swedish road system to the European networks), liberalization of transport markets ('Sweden is probably far ahead of the rest of Europe', p 83), technical harmonization ('being a member of the EEA Sweden will have to import cars that pollute more than the existing norms in Sweden allow', p 87) and fiscal policy ('The Scandinavian countries are among the very few countries in Europe implementing a policy aiming at including external effects...in the prices paid...Sweden is implementing this policy more effectively than Norway', p 91).

That membership of the European Union does not necessarily lead to a stricter environmental policy in the field of transport has been stressed by The World Bank in its study entitled *Sustainable Transport* (1996). A concrete example was taken from Sweden: 'Good taxes do not necessarily survive. The Swedish kilometre tax on diesel vehicles, which made it possible to capture the combined effects of differences in axle weights and distances traveled using the same instrument, was replaced by a flat tax on diesel early in 1994, ostensibly to conform with existing European Union tax structures' (*op.cit.* pp 100sq, foot-note 1).

After the admission to the European Community, there have been some important references to European transport policy in Swedish political documents. In the brief of the Government (*1994:140*) to the Commission entrusted with the task of preparing a new National Plan for Transport and Communications, it was said that the Commission should present proposals as to how Sweden could contribute to the Common Transport Policy (CTP) within the framework of the European Union, and how Sweden could work for the creation of an European transport system adapted to the environment, when establishing the Trans-European Networks.

In an informal PM (dated 96-10-21) distributed to the members of the investigative Commission, different alternatives were proposed for the internal discussion: should Sweden work for a far-reaching harmonization of economic instruments or should the country defend its freedom of action as much as possible? This question illustrates the dilemma of the member states of the European Union.

In the final report of the Commission, it was explicitly said that '(t)he development of a long-term sustainable transport system calls for extensive international cooperation. We must actively participate in that cooperation and influence the common European transport policy. In order to succeed in this, we need to develop a strategy for our Euro-

pean work in this sector, based on the traffic policy aims we propose' (*SOU 1997:35*, p 61). Priority should be given to a limited number of questions, among which are the following:
- harmonized provisions concerning road use charges and road taxes, applying to all road traffic within the EU
- further harmonization of technical standards, including active participation in research, development and demonstration
- the possibility of facilitating large-scale introduction of bio-based fuels with the aid of differentiated rates of taxation and
- wider scope for using economic instruments to introduce, respectively cleaner and safer technology in road vehicles (*op.cit.* pp 61sq).

In the annual debate about Swedish activities within the Union held by Parliament's Subcommission on Foreign affaires (*Utrikesutskottet*), it was stressed in 1996 that 'Sweden has supported measures intended to create sustainable development within the transport sector' (*UU 25 1995/96*, p 5, my translation). In the debate in the following year, 1997, it was emphasized that 'attempts to refer, in the name of subsidiarity, questions that are best dealt with at the community level to the national level should be rejected (*UU 13 1996/97*. p 15, my translation). In the bill on a new transport policy (*the bill 1997/98:56*), presented by the Swedish Government in March 1998, it was first stated that the Commission had not analysed the impact of the European Union on Swedish transport policy (p 55). The Government pointed to the new possibilities of acting within the Union, but emphasized, at the same time, the fact that membership of the Union must be seen as an external framework setting restrictions on national transport policy (p 56). The bill enumerated a number of issues to be dealt with at the level of the European Union, such as fair rules for competition and the development of North-South corri-dors on the Continent (pp 57-60). One of these issues addressed the question how to increase traffic safety and reduce environmental impact in the Union. The Commission should, according to the Swedish Government, develop an integrated programme for measures in the field of transport and environment and increase the control that common rules are applied in all member states (p 59).

5.3.5 A second summing up

In Danish, Dutch and Swedish documents on transport policy during the 1990s, there are quite of few references to the role of EU in harmonizing taxes and other conditions of transport.

In 1990, the Danes saw the role of EEC in national transport policy as restrictive rather than as offering new opportunities, but the Danish attitude was nevertheless, 'to press for the development of more energy- and environmentally-efficient methods of transport' within the framework of the Union. After the Common Transport Policy of EU had been approved in 1993, the Danish attitude appeared to be more positive about the possibilities of harmonization in order to promote the creation of sustainable transport systems in the Union. Issues of importance in the context were harmonization of taxes, common planning of infrastructure and the promotion of energy-efficient and environmentally friendly car technology.

The Netherlands has a longer tradition than Denmark of exerting pressure in Brussels. In the Dutch texts of 1990, there are several suggestions for necessary harmonization, not only of taxes and other duties, but also of technical standards (concerning safety, noise and environment). There is also a strong interest in developing high-speed railway lines at the European level in order to reduce the pressure on air traffic in the Netherlands. The Dutch regret, however, the absence of a common policy to restrain car use (in order to reduce congestion). They believe that both EU and ECMT need to play a more active role in handling the conflict between economic growth and the long-term environmental sustainability.

Before and after it became of member of EU, Sweden seems to have been interested in adapting its national rules to the transport rules of EEC in a scrupulous way (not always leading to the preservation of environmentally friendly rules). During the preparations of the new Swedish Transport Policy of 1998, however, it was informally discussed whether Sweden should work for far-reaching harmonization of economic instruments or defend its own freedom of action. The final proposal of the Commission recommended the harmonization of taxes and technical standards but also common measures of facilitating an increased use of bio-based fuels. In the annual debates on foreign policy in 1996 and 1997, it was emphasized that Sweden should support the creation of sustainable transport systems in the Union and reject attempts to refer to the principle of subsidiarity in this context. The government bill of March 1998 foresaw an active Swedish policy in the Union in connection with a number of concrete issues, among them the question of increased traffic safety and reduced environmental impact.

Summarizing these observations, it is motivated to state
- that references to European harmonization of transport policies are frequent in Danish, Dutch and Swedish political documents
- that CTP is regarded as the main political framework
- that CTP is regarded both as imposing restrictions on and creating opportunities for policies aiming at reaching the goal of environ-

mental sustainability
- that there are few references to the conflict between economic growth and environmentally sustainable transport.

5.4 The Common Transport Policy: role and implementation

5.4.1 Introduction

Given the results of the preceding analysis, it is now possible to approach the key question of the chapter:
How and to what extent has the situation of the national policy-makers been influenced by the development of a common European transport policy when it comes to the creation of environmentally sustainable transport systems in the Union?

To do so, it is necessary to look closer at the policy-making in the Union and at the implementation of its transport policy, with particular emphasis on the question of the conflict between economic growth and environmental sustainability.

5.4.2 The conflict between economic growth and environmental sustainability

The conflict between economic growth and environmental sustainability within the emerging internal market of EC prompted an early study. In the late 1980s, a special committee was entrusted with the task of analysing the conflict. It produced a report in 1989, which was entitled: *1992. The Environmental Dimension. Task Force Report on the Environment and the Internal Market.*

The deregulation of the Internal Market was expected by the Task Force to lead, among many other things, to less expensive cars and less expensive fuels which, in turn, would result in increased traffic volumes and in an intensified environmental impact. The Task Force claimed that the whole idea behind the Internal Market would be at risk unless the serious conflict between economic growth and the environment was solved.

However, when the EC Commission launched its proposal for a Common Transport Policy in December 1992, it was concerned, primarily, with increasing congestion in the Union. The reason was the fact that growth in GDP leads to 'disproportionately higher growth of transport activity'. The volume of passenger road traffic in the Community had increased, in terms of vehicle-km, by about 3.7 % annually in the EEC countries during the period 1970-1990, while economic growth in the Community had averaged 2.6% in real terms in the same period (§ 10 and § 26). The number of cars was estimated to increase by 25-30 % during the period 1990-2010 (§ 26). As '(t)he present traffic situation in many city centres and conurbations is one of complete saturation or close to it' (§ 77), the future situation was looked upon as an obstacle to the overall economic development of the European Community (§ 75).

The Commission also admitted the existence of a conflict between transport and the environment, describing the serious problems associated with the transport sector's energy consumption, its operational pollution, its land-intrusion, etc (§§ 20sq). The Commission regarded the current amount of emissions from the transport sector as a serious problem and also mentioned global warming as a future threat (§ 22; § 149). The Commission drew the conclusion from these premises that there was a risk that the development of the transport sector was 'unsustainable in the medium to long term due to its broad environmental impact' (§ 28). Setting the goals of the new policy, the Commission described the fundamental objectives in the transport field as follows: it is important to create 'transport systems that will provide services efficiently, safely and under the best possible environmental and social conditions' (§ 57). It also referred to the concept of 'sustainable development' and claimed that, from now on, environment protection should be integrated 'into the definition and implementation of other Community policies including transport' (§ 36). The approach of CTP was 'summarised as the pursuit of *sustainable mobility*' (§ 40).

At the same time, the idea of sustainability was also the basic concept of the *Fifth Environmental Action Programme* of the Union (COM /92/ 23), proposed by the Commission in 1992 and accepted by the Council of Ministers in 1993. Its title was *Towards Sustainable Development*. Being a part of the Community's preparations for the Earth Summit in Rio de Janeiro in 1992, it contained a strategy which stated how to meet environmental challenges. This strategy was based on six principles:
- environmental considerations are to be integrated into all policy areas
- more effort should be put into developing means (policy instruments), especially economic means
- partnership and shared responsibility of efforts to be orchestrated more strongly
- changing of attitudes and patterns of consumption and production
- new law enforcement measures to be introduced and
- a wider international environmental scope to be employed.

Five policy sectors were indicated as particularly important for further evaluation, among them transport (together with agriculture, energy, production industry, tourism).

There are several indications that the Commission has a political will to acknowledge its awareness of the inherent and unsolved conflict between economic growth and environmental sustainability. In a document entitled *Economic Growth and the Environment: Some Implications for Economic Policy Making* (COM/94/465), the relation between economic growth and the environment was regarded as being "crucial":

> 'Prosperity, or well-being in a broad sense, does not exclusively depend on economic welfare as conventionally measured, but also on the clean air we breath and the health of the natural environment upon which we rely for many services. We used to take these for granted. Now, as our development becomes more intensive, pressures on the environment are becoming increasingly strong. Therefore, policies should aim at development patterns that respect the environment and can be sustained over time' (p 1).

In the same paper, the Commission says that it has 'tentatively analysed the consequences of the principle of *environmentally* (the italics are mine) sustainable development for economic and fiscal policy making and wishes to present some first conclusions for discussion in this Communication' (p 1). The main conclusion of the Commission is that one should rely on market-based instruments but adjust them by means of environmental taxes. There is, however, a need to 'integrate environmental objectives in all sectors of society' (p 19). Therefore, 'relevant policy makers will have to define, in collaboration with the social partners and other public authorities, cost effective environmental policies for those areas for which they carry the main responsibility' (p 19).

5.4.3 The character of the decision-making in the Union

It is well known that decisions within the Union are preceded by complex procedures. The Commission is the only institution that has the right to make proposals. According to the Maastricht Treaty, the majority of the members of the European Parliament are, however, able to ask the Commission to submit a proposal.

The Commission prepares a future decision by emitting "communications" to the Council of Ministers and to the European Parliament. In these, they present a preliminary version of a proposal. They may also initiate a wider debate on an issue by publishing a "Green Paper".

The final version of a proposal takes the form of a "White Paper". This is submitted to the Parliament and to the Council for decisions. The decisions of the Ministers are prepared by the Committee of Permanent Representatives (COREPER). A decision in the Council of Ministers has, in many cases, to be unanimous.

The final decisions of the Council of Ministers are of different kinds. The most important ones are Regulations (their content is immediately applicable in all member states) and Directives (these have to be transformed into national legislation). Other kinds are Recommendations and Conclusions. In certain cases (for instance, budget decisions), the European Parliament has the right to adopt Regulations and Directives in cooperation with and on equal footing with the Council. If there is disagreement between the Council and the Parliament, a Conciliation Committee is entrusted with the task of finding a compromise.

With these principles in mind, it is now time to see how policy-making within the Union functions. It is well known that, according to the Maastricht Treaty, this is based upon the Principle of Subsidiarity. This principle determines what is within the competence of the European Union and what should be handled at the national level (where again the question of subsidiarity may be raised with reference to counties and municipalities).

5.4.4 The role of the Principle of Subsidiarity

The Principle of Subsidiarity was introduced into the political life of the European Community in 1992 by the *Treaty of Maastricht* (article 3b). The idea was borrowed from another complex organization - the Roman Catholic Church. In the organizational life of the EU, it means that the Community has to make political arrangements only when current objectives of the EU are more easily attained at the Community level than at the national level (for a more detailed analysis of this rule, see, for instance, Sahibzada, 1994).

The application of the Principle of Subsidiarity is not based on well-defined criteria and is particularly complex when there are policy issues at stake for which the responsibility is shared between different political levels. Environment is such a concern, being common to several levels (Bergdahl, 1996, p 2). The rules for decision-making in the field of environmental policy are described in Article 130s of the Maastricht Treaty. All decisions taken by a member state on environment policy have to be compatible with the Treaty. This refers particularly to the idea that environmental laws must not be used as obstacles to fair competition within the Internal Market. This rule represents a clear restriction on national decision-making. New national environmental laws and regulations have to be submitted to the Commission for approval. If they are disapproved, the member states have the right to submit the case to the European Court, the decision of which is conclusive. The freedom of action of the individual national government is therefore circumscribed by these rules (*op.cit.* pp 10sqq).

The influence of the Commission itself is, on the other hand, also weak in relation to the Council of Minister, a rule which does not always benefit environment policy, particularly when it is question of transport and environment. The application of the Principle of Subsidiarity has therefore been questioned in the case of transport and environment by high representatives of the Commission. The previous EC Director General for Transport, Mr Coleman, declared in a speech in September 1992 that he had some doubts about the efficiency of the Principle of Subsidiarity in the case of transport and environment (Tengström, 1993, p 74). His colleague, the Italian EU Commissioner responsible for the environment, Ripa de Meana, made an even stronger statement in an interview in July 1992 when he returned to Rome to become Minister of the Environment. He claimed that it would be a catastrophe for the environmental policy if the control of the environmental standards was left to the Member States (Bjørnland, 1993, p 22).

5.4.5 The problems of the implementation processes

Policy-making is one thing, the implementing of a policy is another. This truism is exemplified by the outcome of the *Fifth Environmental Action Programme* of 1993. In a report on its implementation which became official on January 10th 1996 (COM/95/624), the transport sector was identified as the most difficult problem in the implementation of the action plan. The principle of sustainable development was said to be particularly difficult to apply in this sector. The political attempts to internalize the external environmental costs of transport have failed not-withstanding the efforts of the Union and its member states to realize this principle.

The role of different social actors are crucial to understanding the background of these problems. In a previous study, made in collaboration with two colleagues, I have analysed their role in the development and implementation of decisions on transport matters in the Union (Tengström et al.1995.).

Quite a number of these collective actors were identified. Many of them are important actors in European economic life. Others are influential non-governmental organizations. They are not only able to influence future decision by means of lobbying but some of them also have the power to influence the implementation of the decisions in various ways. The most important actors are:
- Association des Constructeurs Européens d'Automobiles (ACEA)

- Organisation Internationale des Constructeurs d'Automobiles (OICA)
- The European Petroleum Industry Association (EUROPIA)
- The International Road Federation (IFR)
- The European Road Transport Telematics Implementation Coordination Organisation (ERTICO)
- The European Round Table of Industrialists (ERT)
- La Federation Internationale de l'Automobile/Alliance Internationale de Tourisme (FIA/AIT)
- The European Federation for Transport and Environment (T&E)
- "Friends of the Earth - Europe".

This list is far from exhaustive (railway and air transport organizations are, for instance, not included in the list). Many other actors, particularly at the national level, can also be supposed to play a role.

We found that the actors identified had very different views of the problems of the transport systems and of what should be done about the problems. In a theoretical perspective, these differences can easily be associated with the socio-psychological theory of 'social representations' (presented above in 1.2.2). This theory says that people create their views of different phenomena by means of communication in order to understand and master the world, and that their representations are shaped through omissions, additions and perversion in a way that satisfies the needs and interests of a certain group.

A recent example of a social representation of European transport that deviates strongly from the one presented by OECD, ECMT and the European Union is offered by a book entitled *Transport in Europe* (Gerondeau, 1997). Its author is President of the Union Routière de France and can be associated with the European "road lobby". He claims that there are a number of ideas in circulation in Europe which can be 'disproved by an objective analysis of the facts' and mentions, for instance, the ideas that

- roads create traffic
- congestion can only get worse
- road traffic is a major contributor to the greenhouse effect
- road traffic does not pay its true cost
- transport policy is influenced by a powerful "road lobby" (p xxxiv).

These ideas are, according to Gerondeau, 'unfortunately sometimes backed up by unreliable 'expert' reports. The result is that even the most official organisations, the Organisation for Economic Cooperation and Development (OECD), the European Conference of Ministers of Transport (ECMT) and the European Union itself are misled and often come to mistaken conclusions' (p xliii).

Despite such differences of opinion (based partly on cognitive disagreement), it can be assumed that the creation of efficient, safe and sustainable transport systems in Europe is a genuine interest to most of the actors. In our study, we draw, therefore, the conclusion that the failure of the implementation of the common policy for "sustainable mobility" should, to some extent, be seen as an *interaction failure* (a concept that we coined in connection with our analysis). We suggested that a way out of the dilemma could be to intensify the controversies about how to create efficient, safe, equitable and sustainable transport systems in the Union.

Our idea of the role of the interaction failure was quoted in the summary of the highlights of the conference *"Towards Sustainable Transportation"*, held in Vancouver in March 1996 (p 54). And so was the idea of removing this barrier to sustainability through the medium of intensified controversies about sustainable mobility, perhaps mediated by networks of actors that are to become 'social carriers of sustainable mobility objectives' with the European Commission taking the initiative in building the network (Tengström et al. 1995, p 44).

5.4.6 A third summing up

The conditions for a harmonized European policy (within the framework of the Union) aiming at a substantial reduction of the present unsustainable character of the national transport systems do not seem to be favourable (cf Jones et al. 1993, p 179 and Bergdahl, 1996, p 19). Certainly, the conflict between economic growth and environmental sustainability is openly admitted by the Commission, the only institution authorized to make proposals, but the Commission has not been able, in the case of transport policy, to analyse the conflict in order to identify political alternatives based on clear priorities.

The Commission's approach to transport and environment has therefore been characterized as "schizophrenic" (Haq, 1997, p 54). The reason indicated was that the idea of a single European market is 'based on free movement and encourages mobility, which, if undertaken by one of the main forms of transport such as road, is in the long term unsustainable' (*op.cit.* p 55).

Furthermore, the Principle of Subsidiarity seems to be an inadequate principle in relation to transport and environment. This is indicated by the reaction of two previous commissioners. The required unanimous decisions of the Council of Ministers are often difficult to reach. The implementation of decisions actually arrived at is, finally, made difficult by influential actors who are unwilling or unable to cooperate in order to promote the creation of sustainable transport systems in Europe. Some of these actors are, at the same time, probably able to influence by means of lobbying) both the composition of the political agenda of the Union and the decisions made by the Council of Ministers.

Finally, it is somewhat unclear in political texts what is to be sustained. The goal of CTP is said to be 'sustainable mobility'. It can be questioned whether an activity such as traffic or mobility can be made 'sustainable'. It is rather the transport system, consisting of vehicles, infrastructure and a constant energy supply, which can be made sustainable.

5.5 Recent issues concerning transport and the environment

5.5.1 Introduction

The validity of the conclusions drawn in the preceding paragraph will now be tested by means of a discussion of some transport and environment issues treated by EU in the last few years. I will begin by mentioning a success story to show that important decisions on environmental matters *are* possible within EU.

The last year of the 1980s witnessed the emergence of the *Small Car Directive* of 1989 in making catalytic converters mandatory in the whole EC area from January 1st 1993. This decision has been called "The 1989 miracle" (Holzinger, 1995).

The *Small Car Directive* showed that it was possible to take decisions in EC that were more than 'lowest common denominator' decisions. Environmentalist actors among EC member states (Denmark and the Netherlands were among them) and two of the EC institutions (the Parliament and a strong Commissioner) were able to overcome the resistance of some car-producing EC member states (Holzinger, 1995).

In a global context, this success was not so impressive, however. Decisions to limit the emissions from cars had already been taken in the United States in 1983 and in Japan even earlier, in 1976.

The question is now (1998) to what extent it has been possible to continue on this road of success. In order to answer this question, a number of concrete examples of current transport and environment issues will be reviewed. The critical discussion of selected issues is possible to follow in publications such as *Environment Watch, T&E Bulletin* and *Acid News*.

5.5.2 The harmonization of national CO_2 taxes

The emissions of CO_2 are a growing concern of EU, particularly after the agreements in Rio (1992) and, recently, in Kyoto (1997). The contribution of the transport sector to the total emissions of CO_2 from the member states is substantial. They correspond, according to Eurostat, to 26% of the total emissions (the cars are responsible for about half of these 26%). The Commission expects the emissions from traffic to increase substantially up to 2010 (COM /95/682). This estimate is questioned by ACEA (*ACEA, Newsletter* 46, 1997).

The Commission has, against this background, initiated a discussion about the possibility of introducing a harmonized CO_2 tax in the member states. This initiative led to a long and complex chain of events.

The idea of a financial neutral tax on energy use and CO_2 emissions was originally launched by the Environment Commissioner Ripa de Meana in 1991 (*T&E Bulletin,* 46, 1996). The proposal for a common CO_2 tax met resistance particularly from the United Kingdom and was finally stopped by a British veto in 1994 (*T&E Bulletin,* 32, 1994). When the negotiations continued in 1995, they collapsed due to German resistance. This country insisted, supported by Austria and Sweden, that an agreement on voluntary taxes should be followed by an introduction after four years of a mandatory harmonized CO_2/energy tax in the entire Union (*Environment Watch: Western Europe* 4:22, 1995).

The Dutch Minister of the Environment tried, however, to break the deadlock in the negotiations on a voluntary CO_2 tax by inviting those member states which were assumed to be in favour of such a tax, i.e. Belgium, Netherlands, Luxembourg, Austria, Denmark, Sweden, Finland and (on the condition indicated above) Germany to prepare a common action. Most of these countries already had, at that time, some form of energy/CO_2 tax (*Environment Watch: Western Europe* 4:21, 1995). The initiative led nowhere, as several member states (UK, Ireland, Spain, Portugal and Greece) were uninterested in or hostile to the introduction of such an agreement (*Acid News* 2, April 1996). Germany therefore declared in 1996 that it would, as the first country in the Union, introduce from 1997 a system of annual taxes for cars differentiated according to emissions (*T&E Bulletin,* 49, 1996).

Thus, after more than six years, no final decision on a harmonized tax was in sight. Much of the real influence on the outcome of this issue was exerted by the Economic/Financial Council (Ecofin), where the links to transport and environment problems are weak. However, in March 1996, Ecofin asked the Commission to draw up a new proposal for an energy/CO_2 tax. It remains to be seen whether any breakthrough will occur in the last years of the century.

5.5.3 The energy use of the transport sector

The emissions of CO_2 are nearly proportional to the energy consumption of the transport sector. An EU-wide policy for increased energy efficiency would therefore be an alternative to a harmonized CO_2 tax.

In December 1995, a new strategy for reducing CO_2 emissions from cars was put forward by the Commission in a Communication Paper entitled *A Community Strategy to reduce CO_2-emissions from passenger cars and to improve fuel economy (COM/95/689)*. The proposed strategy was a mix of fiscal and non-fiscal measures. It included voluntary agreements between the Commission and the European car industry and car importers to cut the average emissions by 25% from new cars by 2005 (base year: 1990). The study also contained the idea of developing an EU framework for national fiscal measures to promote low-consumption cars. The aim was that new petrol-driven cars would be able to drive 10 km on only 0.5 litre by 2005 and diesel driven cars on 0.45 litre. These goals were, however, considered by the car industry as being too ambitious. The industry has therefore been lobbying for an extension of the limit.

The critical question is, however, to what extent this proposal is compatible with the contemporary political will to liberalize the energy markets of the member states *(Acid News,* 2, April 1996). In a White Paper entitled *An energy policy for the European Union* (dated January 1996 - *COM/95/682*), the Commission presented three strong arguments for liberalizing and harmonizing the energy markets of the member states for the next 25 years: 1/ the need to keep the EU competitive 2/ the need to secure energy supplies 3/ the need to protect the environment. The Commission expects the energy demand from industry to be stabilized at present levels, and the domestic sector will probably show a slight decline. In contrast, transportation will continue to use steadily more energy (despite the expected increase in vehicle efficiency).

In a remarkably sharp report (entitled *Road Transport and the Environment - Energy and Fiscal Aspects*), the Eurostat confirmed, by July 1996, that there was an increasing demand for energy in the transport sector in the Union. The transport's share of the total final energy consumption was 30.8% in 1994, and this share was increasing. Road transport consumed 82.3% of this share in 1994. Transport was also, by far, the largest consumer of petroleum products (64% in 1994), and its share is still growing. The Eurostat therefore claimed that this increase was a serious obstacle to the attainment of the objectives of the Common Transport Policy. The increasing demand for energy was characterized as 'unsustainable' by the report.

5.5.4 The Auto/Oil Programme

After the middle of 1990s, one easily gets the impression that the Commission has found it more attractive and more effective to make agreements directly with industry than to negotiate with the member states on legal frameworks. The initiative of December 1995 just discussed is one example. The so-called "Auto Oil Programme" is another. The Commission seems to be testing the possibility of using some kind of technology forcing even if the agreements with the industry are said to be "voluntary".

In October 1996, the Commission presented the final version of its long-awaited *Auto Oil Programme* aiming at a reduction of certain emissions from motorized vehicles (COM/96 /248). Its introduction runs: 'The Commission's proposed strategy for the control of vehicle emissions is designed to achieve extremely rigorous air quality objectives for carbon monoxide, benzene, nitrogen dioxide, particulate matter and low-level ozone'.

The idea was, thus, that the oil industry and the car industry should be committed to deliver more environmentally friendly products in the future. The car and the oil industries were therefore invited to meetings with the Commission. In these meetings, they evidently argued for less strict rules.

After the final decision of the Commission, the two industries began to dispute with each other. The car industry, represented by ACEA, argued that it would be easier to achieve improvements in air quality immediately with cleaner fuels than through new car technology (see *ACEA, Newsletter* 36, 1996). The oil industry, represented by EUROPIA, claimed, on the other hand, that the most cost-efficient way of reducing pollution is to produce more energy-efficient cars. This dispute seems to be a clear case of *interaction failure*, which now threatens the fulfilment of the *Auto Oil Programme*.

The European Parliament has, in its turn, voted in favour of significant strengthening of the proposals for automobile emissions and fuels. The Commission claims, however, that its proposals are the most cost-efficient ones and, at the same time, technically viable. The outcome of the political process is difficult to predict (*ACEA, Newsletter* 42, 1997).

5.5.5 The environmental effects of the TEN Programme

The European Council decided in December 1993 to accelerate the development of the Trans-European Networks (TENs). The main objective was to support economic growth in the Union (see 5.2.2). After a conciliation procedure (see above, 5.4.3), the European Parliament succeeded in 1996 in including an environmental article in the final decision requiring member states to carry out environmental impact analysis (EIA) for all TEN projects (*T&E, Bulletin* 50 1996).

Guidelines for EIA were already indicated by EEC in 1985 (*COM/85/337*). Its aim is to monitor and mitigate effects of separate infrastructure projects. However, the environmental impact assessment often comes too late in the planning process. The wider questions at the level of corridors, programmes and policies are never raised.

Both environmental NGOs (for instance, *T&E, Bulletin* 46, 1996) and researchers (for instance, Sheate, 1995) have therefore pleaded for the introduction of legislation about so-called strategic environmental assessment (SEA). They maintain that such an assessment, which covers the total environmental impact of infrastructure investments, has to be applied to transport plans and programmes as well as to single projects.

In 1996, the Commission and the Parliament developed the idea of SEA in connection with the TEN programme. The amendments to the Commission's proposals submitted by the European Parliament were met, however, with an uncompromising negative reaction from the Council of Ministers. This has been interpreted as a defence of national sovereign power: 'In the Council's position can be seen the resistance of several member states to handling over decision-making power to the EU on what were regarded as, essentially, national projects. SEA was rapidly becoming a pivotal issue in the policy process, offering real prospects for environmental integration' (Richardson, 1997, p 339). Again, the ambition of the Union of enhancing a European transport system environmentally sustainable in the long term was thwarted.

5.6 A final summary and some conclusions

The results of the explorative study of the relations between national and European transport policies can now be summarized and some conclusions drawn.

National transport policies are not developed in isolation. Spontaneous imitation of elements of other European countries' transport policies might have occurred in Denmark, the Netherlands and Sweden. It would be interesting to trace the effects of such imitation but it is beyond the scope of the present study. The influence exerted by the recommendations of the European Conference of Ministers of Transport (ECMT) since 1953 have certainly been substantial. The extent of this influence is, however, poorly known today. The influence of the Common Transport Policy (CTP) of the European Union has, on the other hand, been the focus of this explorative study.

The existence of CTP has obviously aroused interest among national politicians in the three countries, particularly in questions related to the possibility of promoting sustainable transport systems. Quite a few passages in political documents from the 1990s indicate this. The texts express both some fear of loss of independence in transport policy but, more often, hopes that it will be possible, within the Community, to identify powerful policy instruments to reduce the current unsustainable character of the national transport systems. Examples of such policy instruments are the harmonization of taxes and other duties as well as the harmonization of technical standards and emission levels. The Commission's possibility of using various kinds of technology forcing to promote energy-efficient and environmentally friendly car technology also appears attractive in the national perspective.

Against this background, it appears as a negative fact that the policy-making and implementation of transport policy in EU do not seem to support the creation of environmentally sustainable transport systems in the Union. In the documents of the Commission, it is openly admitted that there is an inherent and frustrating conflict between economic growth and favourable conditions for creating environmentally sustainable transport systems. The market cannot be expected to solve this dilemma. Government initiatives are necessary.

Unfortunately, the present institutional structure of EU makes it particularly difficult to take such decisions that would reduce the present unsustainable character of road transport in the Union. The rules for decision-making are a barrier to resolute actions. Apart from this, certain important actors (car industries, oil industries, trade unions, some NGOs) influence both the decisions and their implementation in a way which is seldom in favour of environmental sustainability.

This conclusion was, finally, tested by reviewing a number of current transport and environmental issues in the Union. Apart from the decision on the mandatory rule that new cars should be equipped with catalytic converters from January 1st 1993 in the entire Union, these issues have not produced any success stories. After several years of negotiations, no agreement on a harmonized CO_2 tax in the Union (mandatory or voluntary) is in sight. The outcome of the Commission's initiative to reduce the energy use of the transport sector is all but promising. The realization of the Auto Oil Programme is still uncertain due to disagreement between the two main industrial actors concerned. The hope that strategic environmental assessment will be carried out in the case of the TEN projects is, after all, very weak. This negative result is in contrast not only to the "miracle of 1989" but also to successful achievements in other fields of EU politics. This contrast cannot be explained by a bias in the selection of examples. In fact, it would be difficult to identify other success stories in the field of transport and environment in the decade after 1989.

Referring to this experience, the present Deputy Secretary-General of ECMT, Jack Short, has very strong arguments when he pleads for a more appropriate balance between national and international actions:

> Many countries, and Denmark is no exception, insist that international actions are needed, especially to solve the CO2 problem.... So countries wait for action at EU level. However, such action is very slow to emerge. In 1989 proposals to deal with the CO2 issue were promised. Only very recently, after six years, has a strategy emerged and a very weak one at that... Precisely the same difficulty arises with introducing fiscal incentives in the European Union. Here unanimity is required amongst the member states and therefore agreement will be at the lowest level - totally unsatisfactory for those countries who want to move faster to resolve environmental problems. There is a clash between the so-called single market objectives and environmental objectives and the environmental ones are the losers. In my view, it is not enough to wait for agreement at European level. Countries' interests are different and environmental concern varies. More flexibility is needed to allow actions at national and local level (Short, 1996, p12sq).

My conclusions from the same historical evidence are somewhat different: First, there is reason to doubt that the national politicians are able to establish the suggested balance between national and European transport policy. They cannot solve the problems of the present unsustainability of the transport systems at the national level as
- the environmental problems are not confined within the frontiers of any nation
- their possibilities of using more radical policy instruments are restricted by the present rules of the Union and
- even successful transport policies in some countries will not be enough to solve the problem of current unsustainable transport systems in Europe.

Second, the national politicians' possibilities of acting at the European level are circumscribed by the facts that
- a proposal may be rejected with reference to the Principle of Subsidiarity
- a decision may have unanimous support as its precondition and
- the implementation of a decision may be blocked by a number of influential actors.

Therefore, I draw the conclusion *that national politicians seem to have been caught in a kind of a social trap when they try to enhance environmental sustainability in transport policy.* The present institutional arrangements of the European Union have to be blamed for this dilemma. It can be characterized as an *institutional failure*.

In my view, the creation of transport systems in Europe which are efficient, safe, equitable and sustainable in the long term requires the allocation of more political power to genuine European institutions such as the European Parliament and the Commission - *as far as transport policy for environmental sustainability is concerned*.

In the absence (or anticipation) of a reshaping of the institutional structure of the Union, I think, however, that there are still some policy options available for reducing the unsustainable character of the national transport systems. I will return to this theme in the final chapter. First, however, follows a critical evaluation of the current transport policies in Denmark, the Netherlands and Sweden.

6 A Critical Evaluation: Success or Failure?

6.1 Introduction

The assessment of the results of a certain policy can be carried out in different ways. Bartlett has distinguished between three general categories in the evaluation of *environmental* policies: 1/ outcomes 2/ processes and 3/ institutions (Bartlett, 1994). Institutions are evaluated as to their general, direct and indirect effects. Processes may be evaluated as being participatory, cooperative, integrative, cost-effective, or the contrary. Evaluations of outcomes deal with the real impact of policies.

In this chapter, I will present the result of an assessment of the real *outcome* of Danish, Dutch and Swedish *transport policies* in the period 1987-1997 with special reference to environmental sustainability. Thereby, it will be possible to answer the question of the main title of the book: *Towards environmental sustainability?*.

6.2 A critical evaluation of present national transport policies

In the Danish, Dutch and Swedish political documents, I identified some *intermediate objectives* which may be interpreted as steps towards the goal of reduced environmental unsustainability. This identification was somewhat arbitrary but I refer to my arguments above (4.4.1 - 4.4.5). Some *timetabled quantitative targets* for the reduction of emissions from traffic were, on the other hand, explicitly defined in the political texts. I will deal with the intermediate objectives first (6.2.1) and then with two of the quantitative targets (6.2.2).

6.2.1 Intermediate objectives aiming at environmental sustainability

The more or less well articulated, intermediate objectives aiming at environmentally sustainable transport were the following:

- a political will to influence transport volumes (in terms of size and/or distribution among different transport modes)
- a political will to influence the level and/or composition of energy consumption
- a political will to influence the technical standard of the fleet of motor vehicles
- a political will to influence the environmental adaptation of new infrastructure.

The outcome of these political ambitions can, in most cases, be evaluated by quantitative methods. There are, however, a number of problems associated with the attempts to measure the real outcome of these policies. The first problems have to do with the *availability* of quantitative data and with their *reliability*. Secondly, as we shall see below, the *comparability* of the figures describing the emissions is also sometimes problematic. All figures presented should therefore be interpreted with great caution. Finally, the possibility of regarding figures describing broken trends as being results of transport policy and not of other factors is far from being self-evident. All figures have therefore to be interpreted and commented on.

Attempts to influence transport volumes and/or the distribution among different modes. There are some indications in the Danish, Dutch and Swedish policy documents that there was a certain political will in the period studied to influence transport volumes in terms of size and/or modal split. The actual development of *road and rail passenger km (and the growth of GDP)* in the period 1986-1995 appears from the following table:

Table 6:1 The development of GDP (index 1986=100) and road passenger km (cycle km not included) and rail passenger km (index 1986=100) in the three countries

Country	1986		1992		1995	
	GDP	road+rail	GDP	road+rail	GDP	road+rail
Denmark	100	100	106	119	115	130
Holland	100	100	117	116	124	121
Sweden	100	100	106	113	111	118

Sources: Statistisk Årbog 1995, p 526, and 1997, p 521; *Natur og Miljø* 1997 (with personal communication); RIVM, Bilthoven (with personal communication); *Transportprognos år 2005 och 2020* ed. by the National Road Administratr. et al

Transport volumes normally increase with economic growth. The first remarkable fact in the table is that the Dutch increase in passenger transport volumes in this period was somewhat lower than its economic growth. *This might be interpreted as an effect of the Dutch political will to influence the transport volumes.*

The second fact is that the Danish growth in road and rail passenger kms was remarkably fast, even in relation to economic growth in the years 1986-1995.

The Swedish development of mobility in the years 1992-1995 was more in line with its economic development in the same period (the figures for 1995 are, however, only estimates).

In this context, *car ownership and car density* are parameters of importance - see table 6:2.

Table 6:2 The number of cars (in ten thousands) and the car density (number of cars per 1000 inhabitants) in the three countries for five selected years

Country	1987	1989	1991	1993	DK 97/S 96
Denmark	1.64 (321)	1.65 (323)	1.65 (320)	1.67 (323)	1.80 (350)
Holland	5.12 (348)	5.37 (361)	5.57 (368)	5.76 (375)	na
Sweden	3.37 (400)	3.58 (419)	3.62 (419)	3.57 (410)	3.70 (413)

Sources: *World Road Statistics, Trafikredegørelse* 1997, p 115 and *Bilismen i Sverige 1997*, pp 11sq

Economic growth leads regularly to increased car ownership, even if the development of the two curves is seldom quite parallel. The weak Swedish economic development in the middle of the 90s is easy to trace in the figures for Swedish car density. The Danish development is characterized by a sudden jump in the expansion between 1993-1997. The Dutch figures indicate a smoother but constant expansion.

Increased car density strengthens the role of the automobile in the transport systems. Accordingly, increasing numbers of cars transport increasing numbers of people (both car drivers and car passengers).

This is the case in Denmark and Holland in the period between 1987-1997 - see table 6:3 (the figures of 1986 defined as index 100).

Table 6:3 The development of passenger km by car (drivers and passengers) in the three countries compared with the development of GDP (index 1989=100)

Country	1986 GDP	1986 km	1990 GDP	1990 km	1992 GDP	1992 km	1995 GDP	1995 km
Denmark	100	100	104	115	106	120	114	130
Holland	100	100	113	107	117	110	125	118
Sweden	100	100	108	115	106	117	112	121

Sources: GDP: *Statistisk Årbog* 1995, p 526, 1993, p 526 and 1997, p 521 ed. by Danmarks statistik. TRANSPORT: Denmark: *Natur og Miljø 1997* (with personal communication). The figure of 1995 is estimated. Holland: *Beleidseffectrapportage 1993*, p 60 and *1995*, p 74. Sweden: *Transportprognos år 2005 och 2020* ed. by the National Road Administration et al

The number of passenger km increases often at a somewhat higher rate than the growth in GDP. The Danish and the Swedish figures are in harmony with this general rule (the Danish increase in passenger km between 1986 and 1992 is even remarkably high) but *again, Holland seems to have been able to restrain the increase in passenger km by car in the period in line with its transport policy objectives*.

Despite this fact, an evaluation in the Netherlands in 1994 drew the conclusion that attempts to restrain car mobility in the long run were like "swimming against the tide" (see 4.5.1). The expected increase in car mobility in the period 1986 to 2010 should be halved (from 70% to 35%) according to the *Second Transport Structure Plan* of 1990. It remains to see if this target will be attained.

The question of modal split is closely related to the question of transport and traffic volumes.

The Danish Plans of 1990 and 1993 indicated a political will to influence the modal split by making public transport more attractive and by stimulating the use of bicycles *(Transport Action Plan* of 1990, p 13). The Dutch Plan of 1990 expressed a political will to make public transport a real alternative to the private car *(SVV2,* p 10). The Swedish Government emphasized the importance of combining private and public transport in its bill on transport policies as early as 1979 (3.4.1) and repeated this in the bill of 1988 (3.4.2).

A comparison of the *relation between private transport and public transport* in the three countries may be seen as an indicator of the results of these attempts.

Table 6:4 The relation between public (bus+rail+ship) transport (figures to the left) and private (car+soft modes) transport (figures to the right) in the three countries (in percent of passenger km) for three selected years

Country	1986	1992	1995
Denmark	23/77	21/79	21/79
Holland	13/87	16/84	19/81
Sweden	20/80	17/83	18/82

Sources: For Denmark and Holland: *World Road Statistics* (IRF). For Sweden: *Transportprognos år 2005 och 2020* ed. by the National Road Administratr. et al

If these figures are reliable, the Danish public transport sector decreased its share of the total land transport slightly (possibly as a result of the development of costs, which was less favourable for public transport than for private transport), while the Dutch public transport sector has increased its share somewhat. The Swedish development is fairly stable. The three countries seem to approach the same relation (approximately 20/80) between public and private transport.

The role of the bicycle should not be underestimated in the three countries in the analysis of passenger km per year.

Table 6:5 The percentage of passenger km by cycle in the three countries for three selected years (the Swedish figures are estimated)

Country	1986	1990	1995
Denmark	7.8%	7.8%	na
Holland	7.7%	7.6%	7.1%
Sweden	2.0%	1.9%	1.8%

Sources: Denmark: *Transportstatistik 1995*, p 129. Holland: *Beleidseffectmeting 1995*, p 74. Sweden: *Transportprognos år 2005 och 2020* ed. by the National Road Administration et al

The impressive role of the cycle in Denmark and the Netherlands is brought into relief in comparison with Sweden. On the other hand, there are no indications of an increasing role of cycling in any of the countries. One circumstance is, however, remarkable. In the only Danish metropolitan area (Copenhagen), *the role of the bicycle is impressive*. According to a study of commuters to 19 working places in the city *(På cykel til og fra arbejde i København* 1996), the trips made by bicycle (34% of the number of trips) exceeded both trips by car (31%) and trips by public transport (31%). The average bicycle trip was almost 7 km. Around 70% of the cyclists stated that they used the cycle during the winter.

Attempts to influence the level and/or composition of the energy consumption. A political will to influence the level of energy consumption in the transport sector had been expressed in several political documents, and some interest in a transition from fossil fuels to alternative fuels had also been indicated (see 4.4.3). The actual outcome is not in line with this political ambition - see table 6:6.

Table 6:6 Energy consumption (in Mtoe) in the total transport sector and in road transport (consumption of diesel and petrol in parenthesis) in the three countries in three selected years

Country	1980		1985		1993	
	transp sector	road transport	transp sector	road transport	transp sector	road transport
Denmark	3.6	2.4(2.3)	4.2	2.9(2.8)	4.5	3.4(3.4)
Holland	8.8	7.0(6.2)	9.0	6.9(6.0)	11.8	8.8(7.8)
Sweden	6.1	5.2(5.2)	6.6	5.5(5.5)	7.5	6.3(6.3)

Source: OECD Environmental Data 1995, p 227 and p 229

There was a stable upward trend in the use of energy in the transport sector as a whole as well as in road transport between 1980-1993 in the three countries. In none of the countries is there any sign of fossil fuels losing the dominant position. The Danish increase in energy consumption is in line with the increase in motorized transport (cf table 6:3). The Dutch figures are remarkably higher than expected in relation to the increase in motorized transport (see table 6:3). In Sweden, the diesel and petrol consumption stabilized (temporary?) in 1996 and 1997 (according to the National Road Administration).

Attempts to influence the technical standards of motor vehicles. In all three countries, the political interest in influencing the technical standard of the national fleet of motor vehicles has been heavily emphasized. Here, I think it is reasonable to compare the development of 1/ the percentage of cars equipped with catalytic converters 2/ the average energy efficiency of cars in use and 3/ the percentage of cars weighing more than 1100 kg (service weight) - see tables 6:7, 6:8 and 6:9.

Table 6:7 The percentage of cars in use equipped with catalytic converters for four selected years

Country	1987	1990	1992	1996
Denmark	0%	2.5%	12.5%	45%
Holland	0%	17%	33%	56%
Sweden	0.3%	20.5%	31%	46.4%

Sources: Denmark: The figures are estimated on the basis of data in *Mere miljøvenlige biler*, p 52 and *Transportstatistik* 1995, p 90. For the year 1996, the source is *Trafikredegørelse 1997*, p 119. Holland: CBS, Voorburg/Heerlen. Sweden: *Bilismen i Sverige 1997*, p 11 and 17

The energy efficiency of new cars is also of importance. It is, however, well-known that different countries use different ways of calculating new car fuel economy. The data can therefore not be directly compared. On the other hand, the data describing the trend in each country are comparatively reliable (a higher index figure indicates a better fuel economy in comparison with the situation in 1985):

Table 6:8 The average energy efficiency of new petrol-driven cars measured as number of km driven per litre of fuel

Country	1985	1992	1994	1995
Denmark	100	108	104	na
Holland	100	100	102	92
Sweden	100	104	101	102

Sources: Denmark and Sweden: *Transportation Energy Data Book Ed. 17* (table I-8). Holland: CBS, Voorburg/Heerlen

The weight of the cars is also of importance.

Table 6:9 The percentage of cars weighing 1100 kg or more for three selected years

Country	1986	1991	1994
Denmark	11%	11%	12%
Holland*	10%(1985)	20%	29%
Sweden	61.5%	64.3%	67.6%

* The Dutch data refer to the percentage of *new* cars weighing more than *1150* kg

Sources: Denmark: *Transportstatistik 1995*, p 90. Holland: CBS, Voorburg/Heerlen. Sweden: SCB and *Bilismen i Sverige 1997*, p 13

Summing up these observations, it is possible to state the following: Cars gradually became cleaner in the period studied (more cars are equipped with catalytic converters). On the other hand, the trend towards increased energy efficiency was broken. The number of heavier cars (traditionally a great percentage of the total Swedish fleet of cars) increased somewhat in Denmark and, in the case of new cars, significantly in Holland. This change in the Danish and Dutch car fleets becomes more obvious if the figures of cars lighter than 800 kg are compared for 1980 and 1996, which corresponds to a reduction from 45% to 20 % in Denmark *(Trafikredegørelse* 1997, p 117). In Holland, the share of new cars lighter than 850 kg decreased from 45% in 1985 to 16% in 1995 (CBS, Voorburg/Heerlen).

Attempts to influence the environmental adaptation of new infrastructure. The Danish and Swedish transport policies in the 1990s have been very much concerned with the expansion and upgrading of road and rail infrastructure.

The Dutch policy has been more selective in expanding the national road net-work for fear of a successive fragmentization of the landscape but some expansion took place nevertheless. The construction of motorways represents substantial interference in the landscape. In all three countries there has been a political interest in influencing the environmental adaptation of the infrastructure and in mitigating a possible negative environmental impact (see 4.4.5).

180 Towards Environmental Sustainability?

There was a substantial *increase in the length of motorways* in the first half of the 1990s - see tables 6:11 and 6:12.

Table 6:10 The expansion of motorways in the three countries between 1990 and 1994 in absolute (km) and relative (%) numbers

Country	1990	1994	Change (km)	Change (%)
Denmark	604	786	182	30.0%
Holland	2092	2167	75	3.5%
Sweden	929	1061	132	14.0%

Sources: World Road Statistics and, for Sweden, the National Road Administration

This expansion of the motorways is *a continuation of a historical trend*. In the period 1970-1989, the expansion of motorways in the three countries had also been impressive.

Table 6:11 The expansion of motorways in the three countries beween 1970 and 1989 in absolute (km) and relative (%) numbers

Country	1970	1989	Change (km)	Change (%)
Denmark	200	600	400	200%
Holland	980	2070	1090	111%
Sweden	400	930	530	132%

Source: Banister and Rothengatter 1993, p 28 (the Swedish figure of 1989 is estimated)

Thus, all three countries exhibit a substantial increase in the length of motorways in the period 1970-1994. This building of motorways has lead to *the loss of more or less productive soil*. It is estimated that the construction of 1 km motorway corresponds to a loss of an area of 6 ha (Banister, 1993, p 55). The total losses (until 1994) and the losses in the period 1970-1989 and 1990-1994 respectively are therefore important - see table 6:12.

Table 6:12 Losses of more or less productive soil (in ha) in the three countries totally (until 1994) and during two different periods: 1970-1989 and 1990-1994

Country	total losses	1970-1989	1990-1994
Denmark	4716	2400	1092
Netherlands	13002	6540	450
Sweden	6366	3180	792

Sources: as in table 6:11

There are, thus, impressive losses of more or less productive soil as an effect of motorways in the Netherlands but the expansion of the road infrastructure has, however, been much slower in the 90s. In contrast, Denmark and Sweden have continued their infrastructural expansion at a high rate. Apart from losses of soil, the motorways have increased the barriers to the mobility of several species of animals with unknown effects on the function of ecosystems (for instance, Bolund, 1996).

In order to reduce or mitigate the environmental effects of different investment projects, environmental impact assessment (EIA) has been applied since the middle of the 1980s in the three countries. Most researchers seem to agree that EIA has not been used as an appropriate instrument for an environmental adaption of new road infrastructure. This is the view taken in a recent evaluation of projects in UK, Denmark and Sweden (Nielsen, 1998). The credibility of assessments *ex ante* is modest. Monitoring programmes are rare. Furthermore, the EIA procedure is disappointing to some interest groups, which leads to opposition to large-scale infrastructure projects.

The Swedish way of applying the instrument of EIA has been exposed to serious criticism (Kjellerup, 1997). According to this study, there is no appropriate method of selecting projects for assessment nor of determining what affects should be seen as significant. Moreover, the opportunities for the citizens (for instance the local population) to participate in the procedure has been far from satisfactory.

The Dutch procedure has not been able to realise the objective of performing assessments both *ex ante* and *ex post*. It has appeared to be very difficult. Therefore, in reality, very few *ex post* evaluations have been made (Arts, 1994). Economic interests have, as a rule, been more important than environmental considerations (Bressers and Plettenburg, 1997, p 128).

6.2.2 Two timetabled targets

The three countries have all defined timetabled quantitative targets for reductions of the emissions of NOx, CO2 and other substances. Particular difficulties emerge when one has to interpret and compare figures from the three countries describing the emissions of different substances.

The models used differ in the way vehicles are categorized, the annual trip length, speed, average trip length, amount of fuel consumption are estimated, and in the assumptions concerning the variation of emission factors under different circumstances. In Sweden, for instance, the monitoring methods used by the Swedish Environmental Protection Agency have been exposed to criticism by the car industry and transport stakeholders. The following figures should therefore be interpreted with great caution. I will deal only with NOx and CO2 - see tables 6:13 and 6:14.

Table 6:13 The development of emissions of NOx from road traffic in the three countries for four selected years

Country	1986	1990	1993	1995
Denmark	100	105	95	86.5
Holland	100	101	96	91
Sweden	100	97	81	77

Sources: Denmark: *Natur og Miljø 1997* (with a personal communication). Holland: *Beleidseffectrapportage* 1993, p 38 and 1995, p 52. Sweden: *Environmental report 1996*, ed. by the Swedish National Road Administration, p 12 (together with personal communication)

All three countries have strived for a reduction of the emission of NOx from traffic. The Dutch target for 1995 (a reduction of 20% of the figures of 1986) was not met. It is still uncertain whether the very ambitious target for 2010 (a reduction of 75%) will be met. It seems probable that the Danish (less ambitious) target for 2010 (a reduction of 40% of the figures of 1988) will be met.

The data are, however, uncertain. This is clearly illustrated by a conflict in Sweden about the achievements between 1980 and 1995. The Swedish Parliament had decided that the emissions of NOx should be reduced by 30% between 1980 and 1995 (with 1980 as the basis year). A general interpretation of this decision was that the road traffic also should reduce its emissions of NOx by 30%. According to a model used by the Swedish Environmental Protection Agency (SEPA), the reduction was actually 26%, but according to a model used by the Association of Automobile Manufacturers and Wholesalers, the reduction was as much as 39%. Two independent researchers were therefore entrusted with the task of assessing the results. They found that the reduction was approximately 30%, given the data used and the construction of the model (used by SEPA) combined with measurements of local traffic emissions, but that the uncertainty was + - 10% (Grennfelt and Holmberg, 1997).

The Swedish achievement in reducing NOx from road traffic seems therefore to be outstanding, if the optimistic figures are reliable. The key factor behind this success story is the rapid introduction of catalytic converters in Sweden (see table 6:7). The Swedes began to introduce cars equipped with catalytic converters as early as 1987. A more rapid introduction of catalytic converters has, however, taken place in the Netherlands (see the same table). How these facts can be interpreted will be discussed below (6.2.3).

It should be added, however, that the introduction of catalytic converters reduces the emissions of NOx but, at the same time, increases the emissions of SO_2, namely at the units producing the material to the converters. Factories producing platinum and other metals used in many catalytic converters emit substantial amounts of SO_2, particularly in Russia, an important producer of these metals. A car has to drive a world average around 5 000 km before there is any net effect in terms of reduced acidification and 25 000 km, if the platinum is produced in Russia *(New Scientist*, September 20, 1997, p 13).

It should also be taken into consideration that a reduction of the emissions is just one part of the story. First, a reduction of the emissions is not the same as the elimination of the impact of the emissions. Second, the timescale of nature's recovery is of importance. This depends very much on the amount of the environment's historical exposure to various noxious substances and on the character of the soil. Acidification is a serious problem, for instance, in the Netherlands and Sweden, but not as so serious in Denmark as its soil is rich in lime. Eutrophication is, on the other hand a serious problem in all three countries.

A recent scientific report based on the "Gårdsjön Roof Project" in Sweden (where the deposition of various substances was hindered by a "roof" above a certain area) presented some general conclusions about the short-term and long-term effects of totally eliminated acid deposition. The results of the project are summarized in the following way:

> Recovery starts quickly, but its rate soon becomes limited by some rather slow ecosystem processes. It is these very processes which have protected ecosystems from rapid acidification under the influence of acid deposition, and this 'acidification debt' must now be paid. Quite how long this will take is still uncertain.

How these results translate into the wider landscape of Europe is not very clear at present. Soils which can absorb and desorb sulphate (like the soil at Gårdsjön) are very common in acid-affected areas, and might be expected to react in a rather similar way. Some illustrative scenario modelling might clarify the picture for policy-makers. But improvements will not be immediate and dramatic as far as water quality is concerned, and still less so for forest health. This contrasts with mechanisms where pollutants affect organisms directly - the effect goes away quickly once the pollutant is removed. The unmanaged soils of Europe have had to cope with increasing amounts of deposition from the atmosphere since the Industrial Revolution began in around 1780. It is likely to take natural processes a similar amount of time to restore the pre-industrial *status quo* - if that is what we want to do. If a faster response is required, direct intervention to restore ecosystems will be necessary. It will be essential to do this with sensitivity (Hultberg et al. 1998, pp 458sq).

Stabilization of the emissions of CO_2 has also been a prioritized political target in Denmark, the Netherlands and Sweden.

Table 6:14a Emissions of CO_2 from road traffic in the three countries for four selected years (index 1986=100)

Country	1986	1990	1992	1995
Denmark	100	106	108	114
Holland	100	112	117	123
Sweden	100	106	109	108

Sources: Denmark: *Natur og Miljø* 1997 (with a personal communication). Holland: *Beleidseffectrapportage* 1993, p 42 and 1995, p 56. Sweden: *Environmental report 1996*, ed by the Swedish National Road Administration, p 12 (together with personal communication)

If these figures are correct, there is a remarkable deviation in the Dutch figures, not only from the national target (see below), but also from the national development of passenger km by car (see table 6:3). If, instead, the data of the development of vehicle km in total Dutch road traffic is compared with the data of the CO_2 emissions, this deviation is less pronounced.

Table 6:14b Emissions of CO2 from road traffic in Holland compared to the number of vehicle km

Holland	1986	1990	1992	1995
CO2 emissions	100	114	126	127
Vehicle km	100	na	121	129

Source: RIVM, Bilthoven (with personal communication)

The targets for the reduction of CO_2 seem to be very difficult to reach in all three countries. The Danish *Transport Action Plan* of 1990 aimed at stabilization of the emissions at the level of 1988 by the year 2000 and a reduction of 25% by 2030 (a target confirmed by the Danish Parliament in 1996). The Dutch *Second Transport Structure Plan* of 1990 set the target for stabilization at the level of 1986 by 1995 and for reduction of 10% by 2010. The Swedish ambition was originally to stabilize the emissions of CO_2 at the level of 1990 by the year 2000. This target was postponed to 2010 in the bill of 1998 (*bill no 1997/98:56*, p 27).

The emissions of CO_2, the most important greenhouse gas, should also be seen in a somewhat more extended perspective. It is reasonable to compare the total emissions of CO_2 per capita in the three countries, the role of the transport sector and, finally, the emissions per capita in transport. These figures are available.

Table 6:15 Total emissions of CO2 (in Kt) per capita, the percentage of the total emissions contributed by the transport sector (%) and per capita emissions (in Kt) in the transport sector in the three countries

Country	1990			1994		
	per cap total (Kt)	per cent transp.	per cap tr. (Kt)	per cap total (Kt)	per cent transp.	per cap tr. (Kt)
Denmark	10,4	25,4%	2.6	12.4	21.4%	2.7
Holland	10.8	19.0%	2.1	11.4	20.1%	2.3
Sweden	6.2	40.0%	2.5	6.3	40.0%	2.5

Source: *Emissions from Transport* 1997 (ECMT/ OECD), p 26

The low Swedish total per capita emissions (in comparison with the Danish and Dutch figures) are due to the role of hydroelectric and nuclear power in the Swedish energy system. There is no indication of reduced emissions of CO_2 in any of the countries between 1990 and 1994, neither in the total emissions nor in the emissions from the transport sector. In a future national strategy for reduced emissions, the Swedish transport sector will be particularly exposed as a consequence of the great percentage of CO_2 emissions attributed to the transport sector.

Finally, it should be remembered that much more dramatic reductions of the emissions of CO_2 are necessary if the risks of the greenhouse effect are taken into consideration and the notion of ecospace is interpreted seriously. The present global distribution of coal sinks is based on the principle of "grandfathering" (see above 2.2.4). In the future it may be based on a more egalitarian principle.

Assuming around 2050 a global population of 10 billion human beings the future egalitarian share of a Danish citizen will be 0.5% (5 million people of 10 billion) of the emissions of carbon dioxide from the transport sector, the share of the Dutch citizen will be 1.5% (15 million people of 10 billion) and the Swedish share may be set at 0.9% (around 9 million people of 10 billion). It has been estimated (Steen et al. 1997, pp 41sq) that an acceptable amount of per capita emissions of CO_2 in the transport sector could be 0.4 tons per year by 2050 if the world community strives for a stabilisation of the concentration of CO_2 in the atmosphere at 450-550 ppmv in the atmosphere (see above 2.4.2) Such a level represents a drastic reduction of the present per capita emissions from the transport sector in Denmark, the Netherlands and Sweden.

Table 6:16 A comparison of current per capita emissions of CO_2 in the transport sector in the three countries (in the year 1994) and a globally equitable share of the per capita emissions in the same sector by 2050

Emissions of CO_2 per capita in the transport sector	in 1994	by 2050	% reduction
Denmark	2.7 tons	0.4 tons	85%
Holland	2.3 tons	0.4 tons	83%
Sweden	2.5 tons	0.4 tons	84%

Sources: as above

6.2.3 General conclusions: few successes, more failures

The evaluation of Danish, Dutch and Swedish transport policies in the preceding section is based on data that have to be interpreted with great caution. It is obvious, however, that there is no reason to talk about a great number of success stories in terms of a reduction of the current unsustainable character of the national transport systems. There are, however, two undeniable successes.

One of them is associated with the reduction of certain emissions, above all the emissions of NOx. In all three countries there were substantial reductions between 1986 and 1995 (see table 6:13). The Swedish achievement seems (if the figures are reliable) to be superior to that of Denmark and that of Holland. The immediate cause of the success is, of course, the spreading of cars equipped with catalytic converters in accordance with political decisions at both the national and the European level. This spreading was particularly rapid in the Netherlands (see table 6:7). The Dutch reduction NOx emissions was, however, not so substantial as one could have expected. This fact also gives rise to some doubts about the reliability of the Swedish (or the Dutch) figures, as the introduction of catalytic converters was not so rapid in Sweden as in Holland.

The original cause of the first success story is not to be found in the national or European transport policies but in the use of technology-forcing by the US federal government which compelled the automotive industry to develop some technical device to prevent the negative impact of the emissions of NOx and some other substances. The Europeans introduced the mandatory rule of catalytic converters much later than USA and Japan (see 5.5.1).

The second success story is the Dutch attempt to initiate a certain decoupling of economic growth and increased individual mobility, above all by car (see table 6:1 and table 6:3). The background of this success is to be found in the national transport policy of 1990. It is, however, only a partial success. The problems of still increasing car traffic are a source of great concern.

The number of transport policy failures in the perspective of environmental sustainability is, in contrast to the number of successes, impressive. These failures relate to four intermediate objectives identified above (4.4.1):

1 Despite the political will to influence the transport volumes in terms of size and/or distribution among different transport modes
- transport volumes are still increasing (somewhat less rapidly in the Netherlands) - see table 6:1

- car density is still increasing (with the temporary exception of Sweden, as an effect of weak economic development) - see table 6:2
- passenger kilometres by car are still increasing - see table 6:3
- the share of public transport versus private transport is not being strengthened - see table 6:4
- the role of the bicycle is not being strengthened - see table 6:5.

2 Despite the political will to influence the energy consumption of the transport sector
- the use of energy in the transport sector shows a stable upward trend (with a temporary (?) exception in Sweden 1996 and 1997) - see table 6:6
- the dominance of fossil fuels is still unbroken - see table 6:6
- the per capita emissions of CO_2 are far from acceptable from a global perspective - see table 6:16.

3 Despite the political will to influence the technical standard of the fleet of motorcars
- the trend towards improved energy efficiency has been broken - see table 6:8
- the percentage of heavier cars has increased - see table 6:9
- the emissions of CO_2 from the transport sector have increased significantly - see table 6:14.

4 Despite the political will to influence the environmental adaptation of new infrastructure
- losses of productive soil are still substantial as an effect of the building of new motorways (to a somewhat lesser degree in the Netherlands where the total losses are, however, impressive) - see tables 6:10-12
- the attempts to apply environmental impact assessment in road building have been a failure (see above).

There are, thus, not many success stories but quite a few failures in the political efforts to reduce the present unsustainable character of the national transport systems in the three countries. So there is good reason now to consider how one can explain these failures of national transport policies. I believe that the explanation is fairly complex and includes several factors.

6.3 Explanations of the failures

6.3.1 A theoretical approach

Among economists, the traditional way of explaining the problems of the transport sector is to talk about 'market and government failures'. An example is offered by an OECD report from 1992 entitled *Market and Government Failures in Environment Management: the Case of Transport*. The market failure explanation is based on the view that the external costs of traffic (pollution, noise, accidents, congestion, etc) are not internalized and not paid for to their full extent. Many economists and environmentalists therefore recommend governments to increase the costs of transport.

The role of governments is, according to economists, to eliminate the imperfections of the market. A 'government failure' is the result of their neglecting this role. It should be added that, even if the external costs are successfully internalized, this will not necessarily reduce the problems of congestion, accidents, environmental impact, etc to acceptable levels.

My approach to the problem of transport policy failures is different. I also intend to use the concept of 'government failure' but in another sense. I will look upon government failures in the perspective of political science. I will identify possible shortcomings in the policy-making process and in the implementation of the policies. This will primarily be done in a national setting, but I also intend to return to the question of how the institutional structure of the European Union influences the role of the national politicians as far as policies for sustainable transport are concerned.

I will also consider the role of important collective actors (such as industries, public agencies, NGOs etc) and the role of the citizens in their capacity as voters and consumers. Doing so, I will apply the same ways of reasoning as in a previous study (Tengström et al. 1995). The collective actors were there assumed to have different views of the problems and the possibilities of the transport system. These views can be seen as 'social representations' of the real world (on this concept see 1.2.2). These representations have been shaped (through omissions, additions and perversion) in a way that satisfies the needs and interests of the different collective actors. The interactions between these actors and between them and the government are influenced by the differences in social representations of the real world. The result is often an 'interaction failure' (an expression introduced by Tengström et al. 1995). Today, no collective actor is strong enough to impose its own interpretation of the problems of the transport system against the will of the other actors.

In the case of the ordinary citizens, there is a similar situation. First, it can be assumed that most citizens are concerned with the practical problems of their own everyday transport and probably spend very little time on thoughts about the long-term problems of the national or European transport system, even if many of them might be aware of the existence of these problems. Their attitude can be understood in the perspective of Habermas. The citizens are mostly concerned with the problems of their own "life-world" and very little concerned with the long-term problems of systems such as the transport system, the climate system or the terrestrial and maritime ecosystems. This "system-world" is mostly distant, and their own "life-world" is always present. It can be concluded that, in their eyes, problems of increasing costs, poor efficiency, deficient safety and remaining inequalities (for instance, between the sexes and between various income groups) take priority over the problems of long-term unsustainability of the transport systems.

Secondly, most of the ordinary citizens do not seem to be inclined to integrate new and alarming statements from transport experts into their present social representations of the transport system. This attitude results in a situation where they do not approve the use of efficient political instruments in transport policy (for instance, substantially increased fuel prices). This situation is aggravated by the fact that the present use of public information on the part of the government is regarded as inappropriate, and the results of public information campaigns in general have been insignificant (Palm, 1994).

The combination of the citizens' primary concern with their "life world" and their unwillingness to modify their social representations of the problems of the transport system leads to what I would like to classify as 'acceptance failures', which also contribute to the current shortcomings of transport policy.

To explain the current failures of national transport policies , I will now discuss

- the role of governments
- the role of organised interests and, finally,
- the role of ordinary citizens.

6.3.2 The role of governments

When environmental sustainability is introduced as a new goal in transport policy, it could be interpreted as a rhetorical statement without any serious intention behind it. In my view, such an interpretation is, however, oversimplified. Political positions deserve to be taken seriously.

I believe that the present government failures can be explained by a number of shortcomings in the national policy-making. Referring to the result of the evaluation in the preceding section, I claim that the politicians in these countries have failed
- to analyse the inherent conflicts between the new goal of environmental sustainability and the traditional goals in transport policy
- to consider the possibility that the attainment of a new goal requires quite a new package of policy instruments
- to make a realistic analysis of the problems of the implementation of policy instruments supporting the goal of environmental sustainability and, finally,
- to analyse how to develop an ecological modernization capacity (EMC) in transport.

The unwillingness of the policy-makers to openly acknowledge the conflicts between the different goals in transport policy is striking. The goal of national transport policies in the post-WorldWar II period was to set up transport systems which were efficient, safe, and equitable. The introduction of the new goal of sustainability significantly widened the scope for conflict between different goals in transport policy.

Promoting sustainability may lead to conflicts with efficiency. If, for instance, the costs of environmental damage are internalized, the cost-efficiency of transport decreases or, if the speed of motor vehicles is subjected to new restrictions, the time efficiency of transport is re-duced. The other way round, political efforts to increase efficiency may fail to establish sustainability, since higher efficiency would encourage higher speed, in turn leading to higher energy consumption, or call for more motorways. The result is a greater impact on the environment.

Striving for sustainability may also result in conflicts with the goals of social equity in transport: a sustainable transport system is not necessarily compatible with the demand of underprivileged groups for increased mobility and increased use of cars. More equitable traffic leads, in its turn, to greater traffic volumes, which means, *ceteris paribus*, significantly more pollution and higher energy consumption.

The goal of sustainability may also threaten the possibilities of reaching the targets of safety: The use of light or very light vehicles to save energy and reduce pollution could jeopardize the safety of the car users (unless all cars are made lighter at the same time). Increased use of vehicles that are safer for car users means, in contrast, heavier vehicles (given the technology of today), which leads to higher energy consumption and more pollution.

An obvious conclusion to be drawn from this is that, as a rule, the politicians have not been willing either to articulate the basic conflicts of modern transport (Dutch politicians were the exception) or to analyse the conflicts in a way permitting the selection of priorities. We must admit, however, that the conflicts of transport *are* complex and that they highlight the present crisis of modernity (1.2.1).

The *second* aspect of present government failures has to do with the unwillingness or inability of the policy-makers to consider the possibility that a new goal in transport policy requires a new policy package. This is a view taken by the ECMT/OECD project group on urban travel and sustainable development in its final report entitled *Urban Travel and Sustainable Development* (1995). Here, it is claimed that 'awareness of the impracticability of catering for forecast volumes of car travel, concern about resource consumption and anxieties about the possibility of climate change' have led to 'the identification of a new set of policy objectives' (p 133). To reach these objectives, traditional measures are considered to be insufficient: a number of policy instruments are therefore recommended in the report (pp 147sqq). The key sentence of this part of the report runs: '*Widespread agreement exists about the need for a new approach*' (p 147, the italics are original). This agreement does not seem to be fully shared by the Danish, Dutch and Swedish governments.

Thirdly, I claim that a part of the explanation of the present government failures in transport policies is associated with the inability or unwillingness of the policy-makers to analyse the institutional and actor-orientated aspects of the implementation process. Politicians are, of course, well aware of the fact that there are a number of barriers to any attempt to transform the transport systems in the direction of sustainability. The very first condition for success seems, however, to be a political analysis of how the main actors will react to different measures necessary for the creation of long-term sustainable transport systems. There will be some winners but also some losers. Win-win solutions are rare. I have not been able to identify any attempts to perform such an analysis of the problems associated with the implementation of a policy for sustainable transport.

This statement brings us back to the fact that the ability of the Danish, Dutch and Swedish governments to establish an ecological modernization capacity in transport has not been impressive (see above 4.6). Such a capacity is based on four elements:
- economic performance (a condition which is fulfilled at least by Denmark and the Netherlands but not by Sweden as a consequence of the economic recession in this country in the first half of the 1990s)
- strategic proficiency, partly realised only by the Dutch government
- innovation capability, realised to some extent by the Dutch government and, finally,

- consensus ability, not appropriately realised by any government, even if the Dutch approach seems to be more promising than the Scandinavian ones.

All these shortcomings are evidently due the national governments themselves. Environmental and transport policy are, however, also being dealt with within the European Community as a whole. Here, other circumstances emerge as important explanatory factors.

The national politicians face a difficult situation, as was claimed in the previous chapter. On the one hand, they cannot solve the problems of present unsustainable transport systems exclusively at the national level, because
- the environmental problems are not confined within the frontiers of the nation and
- a national environmental decision may be interpreted by the Commission as introducing a new trade barrier.

On the other hand, any efforts made by the national politicians to realise their transport policy goals at the European level are circumscribed by the possibility that
- a proposal concerning a harmonized transport policy may be rejected with reference to the principle of subsidiarity or
- a decision about harmonization of rules and fees may not receive unanimous support.

Therefore, I draw the conclusion *that, in the present European context, national politicians are caught in a social trap in their efforts to create sustainable transport systems.* To some extent, the present institutional structures of the European Union have therefore to be blamed for this situation. It can be characterized as an 'institutional failure' of the European Union.

6.3.3 The role of organized interests

However, the national governments and the institutional structure of the European Union cannot alone be blamed for the present failures to move towards environmental sustainability in transport in the three North-European countries. The structure and function of a country's transport system is only partly decided at the national (and European) political level.

There are a number of important actors besides the national governments that are able to influence the expansion of the transport infrastructure, the composition of the vehicle fleets, the consumption of fuels (type, quality and quantity) and the development of individual mobility patterns. Such actors are governmental agencies, local political bodies, producing industries, automotive industries, transport companies, tourist organizations, producers and distributors of fuels, trade unions and other non-governmental organizations.

The collective actors' own perceptions of the problems and possibilities of the present transport systems are important realities (see 6.3.1). There are (to my knowledge) no empirical studies of how different collective actors actually perceive the problems of the present unsustainable character of the national transport system. However, it may be assumed that there is little disagreement about the goal of sustainable transport but a host of diverging ideas about when and how to realise this goal and how to define it.

These diverging ideas have their roots in the various social representations of the problems and possibilities of the present transport systems. Important actors are therefore unable to cooperate with their government and with each other in the national interest of reducing the unsustainable character of the transport system and its threats to the climate system and the function of terrestrial and maritime ecosystems.

Unfortunately there exists, at present, no institutional framework within which the different collective actors would be able to modify their social representations of the reality of the transport system. The creation of such a framework would be an extraordinary proof of political innovation capability and an essential element in the building of an ecological modernisation capacity in the field of transport. The objective of the new institution would be to develop a national consensus.

6.3.4 The role of ordinary citizens

Besides the governments and a number of strong collective actors, the ordinary citizens influence both transport policy and transport practices. In their capacity as individual transport users, the citizens determine, to a large extent, the number of trips undertaken and the modal split, and their vehicle preferences influence the real outcome of any political attempt to reduce the negative environmental impact of transportation. In their role of voters, they also define the action potential of the policy-makers. Thus, the citizens contribute to the failures in transport policy in their double role as consumers and voters.

In the theoretical approach to this section, I argued that there are circumstances that can explain the attitudes of the citizens which result in what I called 'acceptance failures'. This factor aggravates the other forces explaining the failures of the national politicians in their attempts to enhance environmental sustainability of transportation.

At the same time, there are probably quite a few citizens who really have modified their views of the problems and possibilities of the transport system. Their changed perceptions do not lead, however, to any behavioural change in transport matters. This situation is easily explained by the well-known sociological theory of 'social dilemmas'. The individual citizen finds it meaningless to alter his/her behaviour as long as he/she does not believe that a substantial number of other citizens will do the same.

Besides this, some citizens may have very ambiguous attitudes, for instance, to car use. They like to drive their cars very much but they are also aware of the negative environmental impact of mass automobility. According to the psychological theory of 'cognitive dissonance', they tend to belittle the negative aspect of car use - as long as they can. In the following chapter, I will elaborate on the role of social dilemmas and cognitive dissonance further.

Finally, it should be emphasized that the acceptance failures have something to do with the cultural role of the automobile in Westernized countries. In the perspective of social anthropology, the motor car is a well-known carrier of cultural values such as freedom, status, wealth, togetherness, masculinity etc. It is therefore understandable that transport policies questioning the present expansion of car use appeal neither to current nor to potential car users.

Therefore, the problems of the current unsustainable transport systems in countries such as Denmark, the Netherlands and Sweden expose their citizens to questions of a deep existential nature concerning their relation to the artifact called "the automobile". The answers to these questions will be crucial for the future prospects for transport policies aiming at the creation of long-term sustainable transport systems.

6.3.5 Concluding remarks

In this section, I have tried to explain why Danish, Dutch and Swedish transport policies have failed to reduce the unsustainable character of present transport systems. I have done this in the belief that such explanations may contribute to new efforts to promote sustainable transport. My argumentation has been based on an interdisciplinary approach combining perspectives in political science, sociology, psychology, social psychology and social anthropology.

After all, I do believe that there is a way out of the present dilemma. This will be the theme of the very last chapter.

7 Policy Options for the Future

7.1 Introduction

The present political inability to reduce the unsustainable character of the transport sector and to approach sustainability, the declared new goal of transport policy, justifies a final discussion about policy options for the near future.

As was shown in the first chapter (1.1.3), many recent studies deal with the question of how to promote environmental sustainability in the transport sector. Some influential institutions have also taken initiatives in the same direction.

The World Bank published a study in 1996 entitled *Sustainable Transport: Priorities for Policy Reform*. Here, the question of how to achieve economic, environmental and social sustainability in the transport sector is addressed. The report ends by redefining the role of governments in the transport sector. Its conclusions are applicable to all kinds of societies, particularly Third World Countries.

The "OECD Group on Pollution Prevention and Control" has focused an essential part of its work on the transport sector (*Environmental Criteria for Sustainable Transport* 1996).

OECD has also organised a number of workshops on the question of sustainable consumption and individual travel behaviour, inviting social scientists from many countries to participate. The reports from these workshops (*Values, Welfare and Quality of Life* 1996) contain analyses and recommendations to policy-makers about how to influence the travel behaviour of the general public to promote transport sustainability.

At the European level, the EU Commission has financed a two-year project "Policy Scenarios for Sustainable Mobility" (POSSUM), initiated in September 1996. A number of alternative scenarios have been elaborated to serve decision-making on the Common Transport Policy (CTP) and concerning the Trans-European-Network (TEN) programme. A set of assumptions was presented regarding the future impact of major infrastructure and policy options.

The study also involved discussions of criteria for sustainable mobility and of how to tackle conflicting goals associated with the implementation of policy scenarios. It intends (in the second half of 1998) to present ideas about how to realise the scenarious by means of backcasting. The following should be seen in this policy-orientated context.

7.2 The importance of an underestimated policy instrument

The creation of long-term sustainable passenger transport systems necessitates, in my view, the involvement of the ordinary citizens. To achieve their involvement, traditional policy instruments seem to be inappropriate. More importance needs to be attached to an underestimated policy instrument, namely communication.

In the case of environmental policy, a similar position is taken by Martin Jänicke, who claims that '(i)n contrast to the attention accorded to technology and legal regulation, the significance of information and communication as policy instruments for environmental change has been neglected' (Jänicke, 1996, p 80). As to transport policy and practices, the same opinion has been voiced in the USA. A study entitled *Toward a Sustainable Future* (1997), published by the Transportation Research Board, emphasizes that

> (c)hanges in transportation policies, technologies, and practices...often require broad and deep public support. Because the risk of climate change and the other ecological effects of transportation are at present largely imperceptible to the public, special efforts are needed to enhance public awareness and understanding of these risks in order to spur dialogue and debate about opportunities for addressing them (p 12).

To be sure, information/communication is often mentioned in political documents. In the Danish *Transport Action Plan* of 1990, information campaigns are mentioned briefly (p 182). In a recent publication, entitled *Lokal agenda 21* (August 1997), the Danish Ministry of Energy and Environment recommended local authorities to initiate a dialogue with the general public on environmental problems such as emissions of carbon dioxide. The Swedish Commission on a National Plan for Transport and Communications analyses, at some length, the possibilities of information strategies in order to influence the attitudes of the citizens (*SOU 1997:35*, pp 455sq) but it also says, very briefly, that it is very important that 'information develops into a dialogue with the public and business sectors' (p 456, my translation).

The Dutch *Second Transport Structure Plan* of 1990 discusses communication and education as strategic factors at some length, on the basis of theoretical reasoning about the value of communication and education as strategic factors in transport policy (*SVV2*, pp 81sq). Communication should therefore be a key factor in creating political acceptance of more radical policy instruments. 'On the basis of a communication plan, action will be undertaken over the next few years with a view to increasing public knowledge, promoting awareness and ultimately altering behaviour' *(SVV2,* p 82).

However, in political documents, the distinction between information and communication is not always strictly observed. Information is certainly a kind of communication but is has one-way direction: from the sender to the receiver. This policy instrument is generally regarded as being inefficient (Palm, 1994; Windahl, 1997). Ideas for developing efficient environmental information strategies are sometimes suggested by researchers (for instance, Nitsch, 1996).

Communication is a more complex interaction between, at least, two participants. The official view of communication as a political instrument, if distinguished from information, is, however, often technocratic. The ordinary citizens are seen as objects of educational efforts rather than subjects with minds of their own. I believe that policy-makers and their experts have to change this view, if they want the ordinary citizens to become more involved in the necessary transformation of the transport system. Genuine communication is therefore, in my view, an underestimated instrument in transport policy.

There are a number of well-known difficulties associated with the use of communication as a political instrument. The pessimistic view is that, if communication can go wrong, its goes wrong. Secondly, communication is a time-consuming process, even when it is successful. Thirly, it is easier to initiate communication at the local level than at the national level.

The channels between the politicians and the general public are sometimes non-existent, sometimes difficult to use. In the Netherlands, there is therefore a growing interest (see 3.3.4) in the role of "intermediate groups" (such as NGO:s). After all, communication is the key method of problem-solving in modern democracies such as Denmark, the Netherlands and Sweden.

The entire idea of the involvement of the ordinary citizens in transport policy can be linked to Giddens' theory of 'life-politics'. According to him, the global problems of environmental sustainability necessitate not only coordinated global responses but also 'reaction and adaptation on the part of every individual' (see above 1.2.5).

Individual responses to transport problems as part of the crisis of modernity (1.2.1) could lead to a gradual change in lifestyles and would also stimulate the emergence of new political forms.

Referring to these ideas, I repeat that the creation of a sustainable society necessitates the involvement of the ordinary citizens, maybe also their deep commitment. "The sustainability transition" has to be a democratic process (cf O'Riordan, 1996). I believe that the transformation of the passenger transport system could be used as a process of collective learning. The reason for this last view is that most decisions concerning if, when and how to move from one place to another are taken individually.

The role of communication can also be related to the theory of J. Habermas about *'das kommunikative Handeln'* (Habermas, 1981). This concept refers to a linguistic interaction without coercion between citizens and an exchange of rational arguments. According to Jänicke, the ecological question has already 'led to the development of new integrative mechanisms such as quasi-institutional dialogue structures' (Jänicke 1996, p 77).

Habermas' theory has been applied to an analysis of modern society from the point of view of decision-making by a Norwegian sociologist (Eriksen, 1993). Modern society is assumed to have a potentiality for reasoning (p 35). In such a society, decisions are taken on the basis of a free debate by means of arguments (p 27). The communicative process results, when it is successful, in mutual understanding (p 31). Under such circumstances, people are supposed to be able to act both in the general interest and in their self-interest (p 47). However, some actors may be able to manipulate information in a strategic way (p 38). In reality, therefore, the power relations in a society often determine the actual outcome of the decision-making process.

Objections have therefore been raised against Habermas' view mainly on the grounds that there is an obvious tension between the normative and the real (Flyvbjerg, 1998b). To increase the understanding of social change in democratic societies in an effort to develop procedures for dealing with conflicts that cannot be solved by argumentation, the discourse ethics of Habermas have to be contrasted, according to Flyvbjerg, with the power analysis and ethics of Foucault.

In the case of environmentally sustainable transport, there is possibly general agreement about the necessity to develop transport systems that are sustainable in the long term, but ideas do diverge about how and when to reach this goal. Conflicts between collective actors may, however, become constructive, particularly if these collective actors consist of reflecting citizens.

I draw the conclusion from these arguments that the use of genuine communication as a political instrument will initiate both dialogues and conflicts, some of which will be constructive.

A possible effect of a period of intense communication and conflict is a reconstruction of the *social representations* (on this concept, see 1.2.2) concerning the problems and possibilities of passenger transport. After such a reconstruction, the ordinary citizens may be willing to accept a more innovative transport policy than that of the 90s. At the same time, the behaviour of industrial and commercial actors may be modified as a consequence of the new involvement of the ordinary citizens/consumers. Finally, the same citizens are the only ones that are able to develop long-lasting solutions to the conflict between sustainability and the other goals of transport policy by adopting new ways of defining welfare and the quality of life. Under favourable circumstances, such development may lead to new patterns of mobility and new, less mobile and less car-dependent, lifestyles at all levels (see 1.2.5).

Communication and conflict can also inspire such public actions that have been characterized as "history-making" in a recent American study of 'entrepreneurship, democratic action and the cultivation of solidarity' (Spinosa, Flores and Dreyfus, 1997). Taking a political action group called "Mothers Against Drunk Driving" as a paradigmatic example, the authors found that the shared personal experience of the participants helped them to identify disharmonies in accepted practices (i.e. drinking before driving) and to involve other groups of citizens (physicians, lawyers, educators, executives etc) in their efforts to alter the law (*op. cit.* pp 88sqq).

The role of the general public in the development of transport policy and transport planning in Britain, Norway and the Netherlands is recently treated in an empirical study by three authors (Zwanenberg et al. 1998). One of their general conclusions is that '(i)t seems that any serious attempt to move towards sustainable transport systems is going to involve challenges to core assumptions about the desirability and inevitability of increasing mobility' (*op.cit.* p 142). They also claim that 'transport policy is a technocratic endeavour in which such assumptions are rarely open for negotiation' (*ibid.*).

They identify, however, some promising initiatives in the Netherlands. In the 1980s, a dialogue between environmental groups and the engineers was developed and several discussion platforms for this dialogue were created. The discussions of those days aimed at increasing public awareness and mobilizing public support for or against specific projects (*op.cit.* p 138). This procedure was often time-consuming.

In the 1990s, a more promising initiative was taken. A semiautonomous subdepartment (RWS) of the Dutch Ministry of Transport and Communication established "Infralab", a special devision entrusted with the task of overcoming the gap between the authorities, experts and society: 'The working method of Infralab is to find concrete ways of organizing dialogue between RWS and other groups in society, thus bringing more creativity into the planning phase and shortening the process of decision-making' (*ibid.*). The process begins with defining the problem. The participants in the dialogue are treated as persons, not as representatives of organizations (*op.cit.* p 139). The maximum timescale of the process is one year. The method has been applied to some large infrastructure projects (*op.cit.* pp 139sqq).

To summarize: My main thesis in this chapter is that there is reason to believe that a period of intense communication and conflict initiated by the policy-makers will change the preconditions for more radical policy options aiming at reduced environmental unsustainability in the medium term (2005-2020) and aiming at the creation of sustainable transport systems in the long term (2020-2050). It should be added that applying genuine communication as a policy instrument will naturally not render other policy instruments obsolete.

7.3 Four possible topics for dialogue or conflict

A variety of questions could be addressed by the participants in such a communicative process but, here, I would like to draw attention to four possible topics or policy options. These options cover transport-related activities that are within the control of the citizens of a single nation:

- reducing speed on the entire road-net
- increasing the use of carbon-neutral or carbon-free fuels
- stabilizing present motor vehicle transport volumes for individual mobility
- reducing the use of private cars

7.3.1 Lowering speed limits on the entire road-net

An appropriate first topic for dialogue or conflict is the question of a general reduction of speed limits on the entire road-net as well as a reduction of the actual speeds. Such reductions, if attained, would not only increase road safety to a significant extent but also cut down the energy consumption and the emissions of noxious fumes substantially.

A discussion of this issue could be initiated by the authorities through an intense information campaign similar to the one which preceded the change-over from driving on the left side of the road to the right side, which occurred amazingly smoothly in Sweden in 1967. The reasons for a speed reduction should be spelled out in the perspective of increased safety and reduced unsustainability. Good arguments are easily available.

In a recent Dutch report entitled *Time to tame our speed?* (1996), it is argued that it is possible to define the optimum speed limit in a socio-economic sense. This is defined as 'the limit in which the balance of social costs (travelling time) and social benefits (less external costs in terms of injuries, fatalities and the environment) reaches a maximum' (p 2). As there is no consensus on the estimates of these costs and benefits, the authors calculate with two alternatives: one where they assume average external costs and one where they assume high external costs.

Under these assumptions, they identify a number of direct effects of applying optimum speed limits (reduced energy consumption, reduced emissions and reduced injuries and fatalities) as well as indirect effects (a reduction of vehicle kilometres due to longer travelling times).

To present their results, they compare four scenarios:

1 a *basic scenario* representing the actual speeds on the Dutch road-net
2 a scenario where the *present speed limits are scrupulously observed*
3 a scenario where the optimum speed limit is defined on the assumption of *average external costs* and
4 a scenario where the optimum speed limit is defined on the assumption of *high external costs*:

Table 7:1 Estimates of direct and indirect effects of three different scenarios of speed reduction in Holland compared to the actual figures (=basic scenario)

	basic	present speed limits observed	optimum average costs	optimum high costs
vehicle km	100	94	91	86
energy	100	89	79	68
CO_2	100	89	79	68
NO_x	100	85	64	48
injuries	100	85	83	73
fatalities	100	79	75	60

Source: *Time to tame our speed?*, p 4

The suggested lowering of speed limits will not be dramatic on the Dutch road-net. In the optimum scenario based on the assumption of high external costs, they would be 90 km/h on motorways, 70 km/h on present 80 km/h roads and 40 km/h on present 50 km/h roads (given that the speed limits are scrupulously observed).

Lowering speed limits on the road-net seems to be politically feasible. There are already organizations pleading for such a reform (for instance, the "Swedish Association for Traffic Safety" in its periodical publication

Säker trafik, 1997:3). Many citizens are probably able to identify disharmonies in established practices in terms of a high level of fatalities and limited saving of time. I believe that quite a few citizens could be mobilized in a drive for speed limits. The time they lost through reduced speed would have a negligible impact on their life patterns. A new traffic culture would instead offer some advantages in terms of reduced stress.

The majority of the voters could probably also accept more rigid ways of controlling actual speeds, if this turns out to be necessary. The Dutch study recommends two methods: a prompt punishment policy or the gradual compulsory introduction of various technical devices such as cruise control and speed limiters.

7.3.2 Increasing the use of carbon-low, carbon-neutral or carbon-free fuels

The present dependence of the transport sector on fossil fuels is not sustainable in the long term, possibly not even in the medium term (see above 2.5). In order to carry out the step-by-step replacement of fossil fuels, it is necessary to use a number of measures. Some of these are available and politically feasible now. An intensified dialogue between politicians and experts, on the one hand, and the ordinary citizens, on the other, would probably make this process more viable than it is today.

A *first step* in the replacement process is to reduce the present consumption of fossil energy. The technical possibilities of reducing the specific energy use of the individual car per km are considerable. In the period until 2010 a major part of the present car fleet will have been replaced by new cars. It has been estimated by the Swedish Environment Protection Agency that, if new energy-saving cars (of the same size) replace older cars in 50% of the Swedish households, this would mean a 5% saving on fuel (*Biff och bil?*, pp 48sq).

It has also been estimated by the same Agency that if 50% of all car-owning households in Sweden carried out 20% of their local journeys by other means than the car, this would already reduce the transport fuel consumption of Swedish households by another 5% (*ibid.*). The possibilities of saving fuel by reducing the speed were discussed above on the basis of Dutch figures. A real speed reduction on the Swedish motorways from 110 to 90 km/h has been estimated to correspond to a reduction of fuel consumption of 25% per km, provided that the cars are optimized for these two levels of speed respectively (Steen et al. 1997, p 186).

A *second step* in the replacement process is to increase the use of carbon-low, carbon-neutral or carbon-free fuels. A voluntary introduction of such fuels seems to be viable in the near future (before 2015) even if the taxes are of decisive importance (*SOU* 1997:35, pp 366sqq). The significance of such an introduction is not so much its impact on the actual energy consumption but rather that it increases the public awareness of the necessity of replacing fossil fuels. It will help to improve the mental readiness of the population to face possible non-linear developments in the future, for instance, in terms of international agreements on substantial national reductions of emissions of carbon dioxide from the transport sector, or in terms of various forms of turbulence on the oil market (price shocks etc).

In the case of cars, one way to replace some fossil fuels today is probably to use rape oil methyl ester (RME) in diesel-fuelled vehicles and, in petrol-fuelled vehicles, to use a mixture of petrol and alcohols (ethanol or methanol) made from renewable energy sources. Blending can be done at a refinery or at the depot *(Implementing of Alternative Fuels in Sweden,* 1997). The potential production of biofuels in Sweden has recently been estimated to have capacity to cover the future demand of the transport sector (Johansson, 1996).

The possibility of a broad introduction of ethanol was demonstrated in Brazil in the 70s. It was essential to entrust the oil companies with the task of distributing the new fuel. It was (and still is) used both mixed (22%) with petrol and as neat ethanol (100%). The latter is most convenient in specially constructed cars. The crucial problem of the Brazilian case (which is based on sugar cane) is the variability of world sugar prices. When the price is high, it is more profitable for the producers to produce sugar instead of ethanol.

Hybridecars (fuelled by petrol and electricity) are seen, particularly by the car industry, as an alternative, at least for the near future. When driven on "clean" electricity, they contribute both to a substantial reduction of local pollution and a minor reduction of emissions of greenhouse gases. The future of the pure electric car is, however, still (spring 1998) obscure. Another option for the consumer is to buy a flexible fuel vehicle (FFV). The technical and political possibilities of introducing various kinds of environmentally friendly cars have recently been assessed in Denmark (*Mere miljøvenlige biler - tekniske muligheder og politiske tiltag*, 1997).

A *third and final step* in the replacement process would be to increase the use of non-fossil fuels substantially in the period 2015-2040. The feasibility of a long-term replacement programme has recently been studied by a group of scientists at Stockholm University (Steen et al. 1997). The group has analysed the possibility of creating a sustainable transport system in Sweden around 2040 and has arrived at the conclusion that, by 2040, Sweden could have a transport system based only on renewable energy amounting to 35 TWh. Despite this, they estimate that leisure time mobility will have increased by 20% compared with today's levels.

However, the main conclusion drawn from this future study was that a sustainable transport system in Sweden cannot be based only on technical change. A successful transition will also necessitate
- stabilized transport volumes
- planning for reduced mobility by means of conscious urban planning and increased use of information technology
- the public acceptance of strong economic measures and new principles of urban planning and the idea of sustainable development (*op.cit.* p xi).

7.3.3 Stabilizing the motor vehicle transport volumes for individual mobility

In the three countries under investigation, the growth in road transport volumes is generally expected (see above 3.2.4; 3.3.3 and 3.4.4) to continue in the short (1998-2005) and medium (2005-2020) term. Increased mobility by car threatens, however, to undo any of the benefits gained by enforcing other measures to deal with the problems of the transport system. The increased energy efficiency of the individual vehicle risks being outweighed by a growth in traffic. With increasing transport volumes, congestion problems become more serious in many areas. When traffic intensifies, so does the problem of trying to reduce the total environmental impact.

The necessity of breaking the tendency of increasing mobility has been emphasized by many scientists, for instance, the British Royal Commission on Environmental Pollution, which recommended in its Report (1994) that 'the aim of future planning policies must be to reduce the need for movement (instead of stimulating ever more mobility, as has been for too long the case). This will involve a gradual shift away from lifestyles which depend on high mobility and intensive use of cars' (*Report on Transport and the Environment*, p 233).

No "natural" saturation levels are in sight today. Suppose that the average growth in GDP will be something between 1-2.5 % in the next two decades in the OECD countries, the task will be to decouple transport growth from economic growth in the same way as energy growth was decoupled from economic growth in the 70s (Peak and Hope, 1994). Historical experience shows, however, that it is difficult for politicians to influence traffic growth by means of traditional policy instruments.

Stabilization can, I am convinced, be achieved by a conscious rationalization of individual trips - if the general public is committed to this objective. It is reasonable to assume that the potential for rationalization of individual trips is substantial. At present, the incentives for such a rationalization are weak. Rationalization may be realised 1/ by means of better planning of one's own mobility, 2/ by increased use of public transport, car sharing, and soft modes (cycling and walking), and 3/ by increased use of information technology.

After a period of intensive dialogue between politicians and transport experts, on one hand, and the ordinary citizens, on the other, it would be possible for the governments in the three countries (supported by majorities in the Parliaments) to *enter into a social contract* with the population stipulating 1/ that the total passenger transport volumes should be stabilized by voluntary means also in periods of economic growth and 2/ that, if the volumes are not stabilized by voluntary means, strong economic instruments to reach the target should be accepted by the voters.

The citizens can be assumed to accept a voluntary rationalization of trips associated with production and reproduction (which makes access to various services necessary) more easily than trips associated with their leisure. Trips of the first category have seldom any value in themselves and a reduction of them would not mean any loss of traditional welfare. People can therefore be assumed to be willing to consider ways of reducing the number of such vehicle-km. Everyday commuting may, for instance, be rationalized through initiatives taken by the employers or by the organizations of the employees.

The willingness to stabilize the number of vehicle-km covered in periods of leisure can be assumed to be much less. The proportion of domestic trips made in "free" time (not for production nor reproduction purposes) is considerable in many countries. It corresponds to around 40-50% of all trips (measured in length and time but not in frequency). It should be emphasized that traditional statistics do not include international trips, estimated to correspond to 15 % of the overall mobility in the case of the Swedish population (Frändberg, 1998, p 51). International trips by Swedes are dominated by tourist trips both with regard to frequency and trip length. This kind of tourist mobility corresponds on average to 5 km/a day per capita (*op.cit.* pp 49sq). Among the tourist trips, the 10% longest trips accounted for around 60% of the energy used for tourist travel (*op.cit.* p 84). In the perspective of sustainability, the volume of such trips and its present increase are particularly problematic, as the annual average improvement in fuel efficiency cannot be expected to compensate for the increase in energy consumption and corresponding increase in emissions of carbon dioxide and NOx. The latter substance emitted in the upper troposphere contributes relatively more to global warming than NOx which is emitted at the ground level (*op.cit.*

82sqq).

Any stabilization of transport volumes in free time challenges basic values of modern welfare (in terms of quality of life) and modern lifestyles. At present, a high degree of mobility in free time is regarded by many as an important element of their welfare. Basic values can hardly be changed by political means in a democracy. It is therefore only the citizens themselves who are able to reorientate their priorities and preferences. To reflect on the environmental consequences of one's actions seems, however, to become a new element in the existential situation of modern man (cf above 1.2.5). The individual's mobility in free time is, indeed, an urgent matter for such reflection. A less mobile lifestyle may make more room for values which are underestimated today (see Berg, 1996). In my view, any stabilization of the use of motor vehicles would also necessitate a reorientation of the lifestyles in leisure time. Globalization of the current international tourist mobility of people in many countries like Denmark, the Netherlands and Sweden would be unsustainable.

7.3.4 Reducing the use of private cars

A fourth topic for dialogue and conflict would be the possibility of changing the role of the *private* car in national transport systems. A reduction in the number of cars and in the number of trips made by car would help to solve many traffic problems (such as congestion, increasing energy consumption, emissions of carbon dioxide and other substances).

Successful implementation of this reduction would not conflict with the goal of efficiency, at least not at the societal level, as congestion would decrease. At the individual level, efficiency (measured in terms of time, not in terms of money) would sometimes decline. On the other hand, such a change in the role of the car would not necessarily conflict with the goal of striving for social equity in transport, not even with regard to equal access to car use (see below).

What makes it very difficult to break the historical trend of increasing car use is not only the obvious advantages associated with the practical and convenient use of the private car but also the cultural embeddedness of this remarkable vehicle (see above 1.2.5). Therefore, certain political risks are involved when challenging the role of the automobile, not only as a part of the national transport system, but also as a part of the entire social and cultural context of modern men and women.

The ownership of a private car is sometimes regarded as a human right by politicians, for instance, by the former Swedish Prime Minister

Ingvar Carlsson in an interview in the newspaper *Dagens Nyheter* (1989-08-21). His successor, the Conservative Prime Minister Carl Bildt, when asked about the problems connected with a globalization of car ownership at the Rio Summit in 1992, replied that the Chinese people should consider the possibility of developing public transport instead of introducing mass automobility (*Dagens Nyheter* 1992-06-13).

The ethical arguments for and against automobile use have been recently evaluated with reference to John Stuart Mill's theory of freedom (Meaton and Morrice, 1996). The authors arrive at the conclusion that a total ban on private automobile use would be justifiable in ethical terms but not advisable at present.

Any attempt to reduce the role of the car in a more permanent way necessitates an intense public debate about the key problems of the transport system. Messages from national and local political authorities and their experts must be relevant to their audience (deal with the health and safety of the citizens and with the future life conditions of their children, with land-use and energy consumption) and relate to the experience of the citizens (the economic costs of car use). Messages should also emphasize practical and positive alternatives. These are the recommendations made by an the OECD panel of social scientists (7.1).

There is fortunately one easy way of reducing the role of the car substantially and of doing it in a socially acceptable way. It is by creating incentives for the spreading of a new form of car sharing that has begun to emerge through grass roots initiatives in several European countries. I refer to privately owned car-pools or "clubs", where individuals may become members.

This kind of car club has been set up particularly in Germany (in 50 cities) and Switzerland (40 cities). There are also some examples to be found in Austria, the Netherlands and Sweden, and there is some interest in Denmark. A European umbrella organization called "European Car Sharing" (ECS) has been established (in 1994) to stimulate the spreading of the idea, now also supported by the "Car Free Cities Network". In Sweden a tenant-owners association (HSB) has recently (October 1997) initiated a programme in which its more than half a million members will be given the opportunity to join such car-pools.

There are a number of individual advantages associated with the arrangement according to a brochure (*City Car Club: Carfree but carefree*), published by the "Car Free Cities Network" in cooperation with the organization "European Car Sharing". A member of the car pool does not need to be responsible for the maintenance of the car, he/she can choose between cars of different types and sizes for different purposes. As a rule, the member has to pay a membership fee (with a deposit), a monthly contribution and, of course, cover the costs of the use of a vehicle (varying according to the size of the car).

There are some disadvantages, too. A member does not have the same immediate access to a car as the private car owner. The demand for cars might also sometimes exceed the supply of cars (for instance, at beautiful weekends in springtime). If predicted, this increased demand can, however, be met by a temporary extra-supply of cars hired from car-renting firms. The members also have access to cars belonging to other clubs in more than 250 European cities.

The cost/driven km is reduced substantially (one example is described in *City Car Club: Carfree but carefree*). The greater economic saving for the household is, however, represented by the elimination of unnecessary car use. The reduced cost for having access to a car would probably be a strong argument among quite a few present car users. On the other hand, previously careless people often join the clubs (Hovgesen and Norre, 1998). This favours, however, increased equity in the transport system.

The policy instrument that political decision-makers at the national level could use is to facilitate the creation of car pools by adapting the present systems of regulations and taxes in order to provide incentives for people to organize or join them. At the local level, the authorities may support the initial promotion of the service by offering parking facilities to the club. They may also hire unused cars in the daytime for their own employees in order to reduce the costs of car club members (this is the case in Örebro, Sweden).

The creation of a major number of car clubs would reduce the role of the car in the transport system quite substantially. According to the estimates of the "European Car Sharing", every car used by the members of the clubs can eliminate 4-6 private cars on the roads. Such a happening would, in its turn, mean less pressure on the existing infrastructure, less pollution and less energy consumption in the transport sector. Larger areas could be used for other purposes than parking. The total energy consumption per capita of a member of a car club who is a previous ordinary car user is estimated by the Swiss office for energy affairs to be reduced by 50% (including energy consumption covering the use of car and the use of public transport).

The introduction of numerous car clubs would also mean that the socio-cultural role of the car would be modified. To break the personal relationship between the car and its user would reduce the symbolic importance of the automobile and transform it into a purely practical vehicle. Certainly, many individuals would stick to the old values associated with private car use. At the same time, however, a new trend in terms of changed attitudes and behaviour in relation to car use would prepare the ground for new lifestyles. A less car-dependent Western lifestyle would have a further effect: it will offer new models for the growing economies in the Third World and contribute to the creation of a new global pattern of mobility, compatible with the climate system and ecological systems.

7.4 The potential socio-political basis for the suggested policy options

The next question to address is whether there is, or could be, a socio-political basis for the suggested policy options in Denmark, the Netherlands and Sweden. A recent study indicates that a substantial proportion of the Swedish population is prepared even today to change their life-styles in a way that is less harmful to the environment. This leaves a certain amount of room for political action (Bennulf, 1996). However, the same study also shows that ordinary citizens are not very willing to change their car use but that well informed people such as politicians, journalists and those responsible for local environmental protection agencies are better motivated (*op.cit.* p 166).

The following discussion of the potential socio-political basis for policy options leading to sustainable transport is inspired by a classification of different attitudes among the citizens suggested by the POSSUM project. Here, a distinction is made between three approaches:

1. the idealistic approach
2. the responsible citizens' approach, which is divided into two sub-groups
   a/ those who actively work for a solution of the problems of the transport systems (grassroots initiatives - bottom-up strategies)
   b/ those who passively accept a solution to the problems of the transport systems (political initiatives - top-down strategies)
3. the self-interest approach (which are supposed to be negative to any strategies for long-term sustainable transport)

With this categorisation in mind, I will discuss the potential socio-political basis for the suggested policy options in Denmark, the Netherlands and Sweden.

7.4.1 The core group: environmentally concerned people

The core group providing the socio-political basis for a transport policy aiming at a reduction of present unsustainability consists of people who claim to be environmentally concerned. They are to be found among the voters of all political parties. A substantial percentage of these people are also members of various environmental NGO:s. Spokespeople of these organizations have openly articulated their criticism of present national transport policies.

In Denmark, the organization "Dansk Naturfredningsforening" ("Danish Association for the Protection of Nature") has collaborated with the Centre for Alternative Social Analysis in publishing a critical review of the Danish Transport Action Plan "Trafik 2005" (*Trafik 2005. Det grønne korrektur*, 1994). Taking the concept of sustainability and the Precautionary Principle as their points of departure, they argue for a transport policy aiming at a reduction of transport volumes by 10% before 2005, a modal shift to more environmentally friendly transport modes and a reduction (in relation the 1988 level) of emissions of carbon dioxide of 20% before 2005, of 40% before 2025 and of 60% before 2040.

In order to achieve these targets, they recommend (among other things) raising the price of petrol (by one Danish crown per year in ten years), increasing financial support to public transport, introducing road pricing, reducing the need of transport through more regulatory physical planning and through the development of local mobility planning (with the stakeholders involved) and, finally, initiating a public debate on sustainable transport.

The environmental organizations in the Netherlands have also expressed their criticism of current Dutch transport policy. "Stichting Natuur en Milieu" is an example (Tengström et al. 1995 p 73). It is an umbrella organization representing twenty national and regional associations, which are, in their turn, said to comprise some 700 000 members. In relation to transport, it has focused on the possibilities of trend breaches in both freight transport and private car use.

Another organization, called "Vereniging Milieudefensie" (the Dutch section of "Friends of the Earth"), consists of some 100 local groups and has its head office in Amsterdam. It organizes campaigns concerning a number of questions related to the environment. On road transport, the organization published a study entitled *Schoon op Weg: naar een trendbreuk in het personen verkeer* as early as 1989 (a short English version entitled *The Netherlands travelling clean* is available).

In a trend-breach scenario for 2010, a considerable reduction in the total number of passenger kilometres was envisaged (from 137 billion pkm by 1984 to 106,2 billion pkm by 2010) together with a drastic change in the modal split:

212 Towards Environmental Sustainability?

Table 7:2 Modal split in Holland (in percentage of total number of passenger km) for two years: actual figures for 1984 and estimated figures for 2010

	bike/walking	public transp	motor vehicle	other
1984	11.8%	12.2%	75.1%	0.9%
2010	23.4%	48.7%	26.8 %	1.1%

Source: *The Netherlands travelling clean* p 8 and 11

The same organization published a study entitled *Actieplan Nederland Duurzaam* in 1992 (entitled *Sustainable Netherlands* in an abbreviated English version). Taking the concept of 'environmental space' and the equity principle as its points of departure, the organization draws a picture of a sustainable Netherlands compatible with the needs of the Third World. With regard to mobility, it is necessary to halve the amount of carbon dioxide resulting from vehicle emissions (*Sustainable Netherlands*, p 24). This means that every Dutch citizen would be entitled to use one litre of petrol per day for transport by 2010. At this energy cost, he/she would be able to go 25 km by car (now 15 km) or 65 km by train (now 60 km) or 50 km by bus (now 38 km) or 10 km by aeroplane (now 10 km) - if the expected increase in energy efficiency is realised by that time. Such a target is far beyond the objectives of the current Dutch transport policy.

In Sweden, there has been an anti-car movement among Green organizations since the middle of the 1960s (Tengström 1992, pp 83sqq). A current proposal about the role of transport in a sustainable Sweden has been put forward by "Friends of the Earth Sweden" in a recent study (*Mål och beräkningar för ett hållbart Sverige*, 1997).

The following changes are suggested for the period up to 2010:

- funds should be allocated to the railway instead of to road infrastructure
- light rail should be introduced into a number of middle-sized cities
- a number of economic policy instruments should be used to restrict car use (taxes and tolls)
- the speed on the roads should be reduced (by means of automatic speed control)
- planning at the level of municipalities should aim at a reduction of traffic
- private car pools may be an alternative for some people
  prices for air trips should be increased (pp 72-74).

The "Swedish Association for the Protection of Nature" presented, also in 1997, its view of the problems of the transport sector in a publication in Swedish entitled *Ett hållbart transportsystem* (in translation "*A sustainable transport system*"). The publication includes four basic principles of transport policy and a detailed action programme. The four principles are: 1/ to reduce transport demand by means of physical planning 2/ to make transport more efficient by increasing the load factor 3/ to favour energy-efficient and space-efficient transport modes and 4/ to improve engine technology and switch to renewable fuels.

These examples are enough to show that environmental organizations in the three countries have already expressed views which are in line with the suggestions presented above (7.3).

7.4.2 The role of women in changing transport patterns

The Green organizations represent the idealistic approach according to the POSSUM classification. In order to identify the second category, responsible citizens, I will follow two lines of approach: 1/ to look for differences in attitudes and behaviour between the sexes in relation to car use and mobility and 2/ to look for factors representing potential changes of transport behaviour in parts of the entire population.

In a recent study of the mobility of men and women in Sweden (Polk, 1996), it was found that women's mobility patterns, at the time of the study, were more environmentally benign than those of men. Women travel fewer kilometers than men, they also travel fewer kilometers than men as the sole occupant of the car, and they use high energy intensive modes to a lesser degree than men. These differences in mobility patterns reflect, probably to a large degree, current differences between the sexes in socio-economic matters.

A similar view is taken in another recent study (Carlsson-Kanyama, Lindén and Thelander, 1998, forthcoming). The authors have arrived at results and explanations which are very close to those of Polk, and they have also estimated the 1996 average emissions of CO_2 from men's mode of transportation to be 53% higher than those generated by women. A difference of this magnitude is equal to that between average Paraguayans and average Belgians as regard the emissions of greenhouse gases. The authors of this article share the view that not only social and economic factors but also cultural patterns and lifestyles help to explain a difference of this magnitude.

Women (at least Swedish women) seem to be more concerned about the environment than men (Bennulf, 1994). They seem also to show a greater propensity to change their car use than men, at least in terms of stated willingness (Polk, 1998). Men are also more inclined than women to prefer technological solutions to the environmental problems of car use, while women show more support for alternatives which entail using other forms of transportation than the car (*op.cit.*)

It is therefore reasonable to assume that many women form part of the potential socio-political basis for a transport policy aiming at a reduction of the unsustainability of present transport systems. The average woman will probably accept some of the options suggested above more easily than the average man.

7.4.3 The role of people at present caught in a social dilemma

The responsible citizen's approach is also represented by all sorts of people who are not actively concerned with the environmental issues but who are ready to modify their behaviour in transportation if this could contribute to a better and more sustainable passenger transport system in their local community or in their country. People of this kind do not find it meaningful, however, to alter their own travel behaviour as long as they distrust other people's willingness to change their behaviour. Their own individual contribution seems to be (and is of course) very unimportant.

This attitude is described and explained by the well-known sociological theory of 'social dilemmas' referred to above as a factor underlying what was called "acceptance failure" (6.3.3). Such dilemmas have also been demonstrated to be an important factor behind the unwillingness of the general public in many countries to change their travel behaviour and their mobility patterns. A recent study describes this situation in Denmark (Norre, 1996).

Present mobility patterns *are*, however, changeable. Some empirical studies in psychology have investigated under what conditions citizens' perceptions, attitudes and behaviour are open to change (for instance, Vlek et al. 1993). A theoretical model of how habits and behaviour may be changed has been constructed by another psychologist (Biel,1996). There is also some, albeit weak, empirical evidence that young people in Sweden today do not want to imitate the transport patterns of their parents (Andréasson and Sjöberg, 1996). They are also very critical about their parents' lack of reflection. If the attitudes of these young people persist (which is far from certain), they will probably be interested in supporting transport policies aiming at sustainability.

Thus, social dilemmas constitute the main barrier to radical changes in transport practices. Such dilemmas can, however, be dissolved if there is a political will to take the lead and mobilize public support for a certain measure (Dawes, 1980). The establishment of a social contract between the government and the population about the voluntary stabilization of transport volumes (suggested above 7.3.3) could be such a political initiative.

7.4.4 The role of people at present suffering from cognitive dissonance

Another theory was mentioned above as an explanatory factor underlying the unwillingness of the general public to accept radical measures in transport policy, namely the theory of cognitive dissonance (6.3.3). It may be also cited when mapping the potential socio-political basis for a transport policy of the kind suggested above. The psychological theory of 'cognitive dissonance' developed by Festinger is able to explain behaviour associated with phenomena which include both positive and negative aspects (Festinger,1957). A high level of mobility and the use of a car are examples of such phenomena. For many people, it is very positive to be highly mobile, and it is very positive for many of them to have access to a comfortable, speedy and attractive automobile. At the same time, a number of negative effects (accidents, environmental impact etc) are associated with high mobility and with a frequent use of cars. These conflicting aspects of mobility and cars constitute an obvious case of cognitive dissonance.

In a recent Danish inquiry, Mette Jensen used both qualitative and quantitative methods to study the attitudes to cars and the environment among different categories of Danish transport users. Actual as well as potential car users demonstrated an ambiguous attitude to the role of the car in the transport system and its effects on the environment (Jensen 1997:I-II). Only people classified as "passionate car users" and certain cyclists were less ambiguous, but for opposite reasons (Jensen 1997 II: 81). I draw the conclusion from this study that the number of people in Denmark suffering from cognitive dissonance in relation to traffic is considerable. I assume that the same can be expected from similar studies of Dutch and Swedish citizens.

Festinger's theory also claims that people often demonstrate a strong power of action if it becomes a psychological necessity for them to dissolve the dissonance by means of some action (for instance, an smoker who has to choose between altering his/her smoking behaviour or dying suddenly). Such a necessity might emerge as a result of a dialogue between the national and local political authorities and their experts, on the one hand, and the ordinary citizens, on the other. However, if people suffering from cognitive dissonance are to change their transport behaviour, the arguments must be very convincing.

7.4.5 A Norwegian empirical study of different lifestyles in transport

There are not only theoretical arguments in support of my view that the socio-political basis for a transport policy for sustainability might be quite substantial. An empirical study on patterns of values, attitudes and actions associated with environment and transport was carried out in Norway by means of a questionnaire which was filled in by 13 700 respondents from the whole country (Berge, 1997). The identification of different lifestyles in relation to transport was based upon a distribution of the answers along two main dimensions: a modern-traditional vertical axis and a community-individual horizontal axis.

"Modern" people prefer an active life outside their home, and they have a high personal material consumption. "Traditional" people are more fond of staying at home and are less receptive to new impulses. "Community-orientated" people are concerned with care, solidarity and social responsibility. "Individually-orientated" people are more concerned with personal freedom and individual responsibility. This horizontal dimension seems also to be very much an environmental dimension.

Some important conclusions were drawn from this way of plotting the answers along the two axes. Motoring was considered as a social dilemma only by the community-orientated respondents. However, community-orientated people used the car less than average and had a low degree of car-based lifestyle. The opposite was true of those who are individually-orientated. They also believed in technical solutions to the environmental problems of transport and assumed that they would drive as much in ten years as they do today.

The community-orientated segments of the Norwegian population seemed to be most willing to change their transport patterns. However, they drive less already and they do not have a marked car-based lifestyle. People with a traditional lifestyle as well as older individually-orientated people have, in their turn, a car-based lifestyle but, on the other hand, they drive relatively little.

According the Norwegian study, the key problem - in the perspective of environmentally sustainability - is mostly associated with "modern" individually-orientated people, particularly the younger ones. They are probably not always receptive to arguments about environment and unsustainability. In the Scandinavian countries, it is difficult to find anyone who will openly admit to such views. An interesting exception to this rule is offered by a recent publication entitled *Folkets rätt att köra bil, 1997* (in translation *People's right to drive a car*). It was written by a journalist and published by "Timbro" in Sweden (a publishing house well-known for supporting conservative values).

Here, the car was said to be the "machine of freedom" of ordinary people. Automobility was regarded as the last step in a long historical process beginning with the struggle against serfdom. Ordinary people are, however, now exposed to intensive indoctrination telling them that they are doing the wrong thing when they drive their cars. This campaign against the private car is said to be run by the political elite and propagated by the media but has no popular support. The reason for this lack of support is, according to the author of the publication, that the car is no longer an environmental problem.

7.5 Concluding remarks

There are, after all, certain ways of reducing the unsustainable character of present passenger transport. Some policy options are immediately available at the national level, but the possible success of a revised transport policy demands the involvement of the ordinary citizens.

In was argued in the first section of this last chapter that such an involvement can only be initiated by means of genuine communication between the policy-makers (and their experts) and the citizens. It was also claimed that such a communication will bring about both dialogue and conflict. These forms of human interaction may, in their turn, pave the way for new measures in transport policy.

Four policy options were suggested as topics for the communication between policy-makers and the citizens.

The first option deals with how to reduce the present speed limits as well as how to reduce the actual speed on different types of roads. The result of such a change would be decreased energy consumption in passenger transport but, at the same time, a certain loss of transport efficiency measured in time.

This loss of transport efficiency would, however, be counterbalanced by reduced traffic injuries: lower speeds will increase road safety both for car users and other people on the roads. If the new speed limits were not respected, it would be possible, with the assent and political support of those accepting the reduced speed limits, to introduce the compulsory use of technical devices such as cruise control.

The second option suggested is about how to begin the transition from fossil fuels to renewable fuels. This change can not be so impressive in the period 2000-2015, as there is no consensus yet on what kind of alternative fuels should be favoured in the long term. However, a number of alternative fuels seem to be about to enter the market in the near future. The voluntary use of such fuels is within the reach of the ordinary citizens. The most important effect of such an initiative would be giving people the opportunity to prepare themselves mentally for a major change in the time to come. Such a major change cannot be ruled out in the medium term (2005-2020) but is inevitable in the long term (2020-2050).

The third option is to achieve the stabilization of transport volumes even in periods of economic growth. This could be achieved through a voluntary agreement with the citizens ("a social contract"). If successful, this initiative would mean that the necessary decoupling of economic growth and passenger transport growth would be realised and that other measures for reducing unsustainability would become more efficient (the increased energy efficiency of cars would not be eaten up by increased transport volumes). Any resulting deterioration in welfare standards was said to be marginal in countries like Denmark, the Netherlands, and Sweden. If this initiative fails, it would be possible, with the assent and political support of those citizens who were willing to achieve the objective by voluntary means, to introduce severe economic instruments to prevent the increase in passenger transport.

The fourth option is to propagate and support the idea of converting private car ownership to membership of car clubs. This measure would reduce the transport volumes and the energy consumption substantially even if many car-less people join the clubs. It would also improve the economy (and the service capacity) of public transport. Such a change in the role of the private car in the transport system would be crucial for creating long-term sustainable transport systems at the national level. It would reduce transport efficiency in some cases (through switching from car use to use of public transport or cycling/walking) and increase the same efficiency in other cases (through reduced congestion). It would also favour road safety and, possibly, increase the equity of the transport system. The total effect would probably be an improvement in social well-being if measured in the entire population. The success of the fourth initiative cannot be secured by compulsory measures but would be substantially facilitated by economic incentives.

In the final section of the chapter, an attempt was made to map the potential socio-political basis for the suggested policy options. First, it was possible to claim that the core group comprises people who are environmentally concerned in a conscious way. Many of these people are members of environmental organizations. It was shown that Danish, Dutch and Swedish environmental organizations have expressed views which seem to be in support of the suggested policy options.

Secondly, it was claimed that quite a few citizens can be expected to support the same policy options - if their feeling of being caught in a social dilemma is dispersed by the policy-makers. Some of those who are now suffering from cognitive dissonance in relation to their car use could also be expected to support the same options if they are deeply convinced of the negative effects of an unsustainable transport system. Arguments were presented indicating that women in general seem to show more support for transport solutions which entail using other forms of transport than the car. A Norwegian study of lifestyles in transport gave some empirical confirmation of the theoretical arguments used.

Finally, it is reasonable to claim that a transport policy revised in the way described above seems to be a very important feature in democratic societies confronting "the sustainability transition". Transport policy may even become a paradigmatic case of this process if based upon the involvement and commitment of the citizens.

Sources and Literature

1 Primary sources

1.1 Official documents
(the documents are, within each category, enumerated in a chronological order)

Denmark:

Trinvis udbygning af motorveje i "det lille h" (1976), Danish Road Dirrectorate.
'Trafikpolitisk redegørelse' (1987), in *Folketingstidende* 1986/87, col. 9290-9305.
Trafikpolitisk Handlingsplan (1987), Ministry of Public Works.
Færdselsikkerhetspolitisk handlingsplan (1988), Betænkning afgivet af Færdselsikkerhetskommissionen.
Regeringens transporthandlingsplan før miljø og udvikling (1990), Ministry of Transport.
The Danish Transport Action Plan for Environment and Development, an English summary (1991), Ministry of Transport (January 1991).
Danmark på vej mod år 2018. I: Analyse og vision (1992), Ministry of the Environment.
Danmark på vej mod år 2018. II: Resumé og handling (1992), Ministry of the Environment.
Trafik 2005: Trafikpolitisk redegørelse (1993), Ministry of Transport (December 1993).
Trafik 2005: Problemstillinger, mål og strategier (1993), Ministry of Transport (December 1993).
The Danish Government's White Paper on Transport and the Traffic Plan "Traffic 2005", a summary in English (1994), Ministry of Transport.
Evaluering af Trafik- og Miljøpuljen (1995), Miljøstyrelsen.
Natur- og miljøpolitisk redegørelse (1995), Ministry of Energy and the Environment.
Danmarks Energifremtider (1995), Ministry of Energy and the Environment.

Forslag til Landplanredegørelse: Danmark og europæisk planpolitik (1996), Ministry of Energy and the Environment
Regeringens handlingsplan for reduktion af transportsektorns CO_2-udslip (1996), Ministry of Transport
Dansk økonomi: forår 1996 with an English summary (1996), The Economic Council.
Status for den Færdselssikkerhetspolitiske handlingsplan af 1988 (1996), afgivet af Færdselsikkerhetskommissionen.
Hver olycke er én for meget. Regeringens handlingsplan for trafiksikkerhed (1997), Ministry of Transport.
CO_2-reduktioner i transportsektoren, Hovedrapport (1997), Ministry of Transport.
Trafikredegørelse (1997), Ministry of Transport.
Transportpolitisk redegørelse (1997), Vejle *amt* (county).
Lokal Agenda 21 (1997), Ministry of Energy and the Environment.

The Netherlands:

Structuurschema Verkeer en Vervoer, deel a: beleidsvoornemen (1977), Ministry of Transport and Public Works and the Ministry of Housing and Physical Planning (March 1977).
Structuurschema Verkeer en Vervoer, tekst van de na parlementaire behandeling vastgestelde pkb (1981), Ministry of Transport and Public Works and the Ministry of Housing and Physical Planning
Tweede Struktuurschema Verkeer en Vervoer: deel a beleidsvoornemen (1988), Ministry of Transport and Public Works (November 1988).
Zweiter Strukturbericht zur Verkehrsentwicklung in den Niederlanden: Teil a Diskussionsentwurf 1988, a German translation of the preceeding text (1989).
Rekening rijden: Road Pricing in the Netherlands (1989), Ministry of Transport and Public Works.
To Choose or to Lose: National Environmental Policy Plan (1989), Ministry of Housing, Physical Planning and the Environment.
Second Transport Structure Plan, part d: Government Decision (1990), Ministry of Transport and Public Works and the Ministry of Housing, Physical Planning and the Environment.
The Environment: today's Touchstone: the Netherland's Second Environmental Policy Plan (1994), Ministry of Housing, Physical Planning and the Environment.
Towards a Sustainable Netherlands: Environmental Policy Development and Implementation (1994), Ministry of Housing, Physical Planning and the Environment.

Sweden:

1 Government bills, etc.:

Regeringens proposition (Government bill) no.1963:191.
Regeringens proposition (Government bill) no.1978/79:99.
Regeringens proposition (Government bill) no.1987/88:5.
Regeringens proposition (Government bill) no.1990/91:87.
Regeringens proposition (Government bill) no.1990/91:90.
Regeringens proposition (Government bill) no.1991/92:100 app. 7.
Regeringens proposition (Government bill) no.1992/93:176.
Regeringens proposition (Government bill) no.1992/93:100 app. 7.
Regeringens proposition (Government bill) no.1993/94:100 app. 7.
Regeringens proposition (Government bill) no.1993/94:111.
Regeringens proposition (Government bill) no.1993/94:100 app. 15.
Regeringens proposition (Government bill) no.1994/95:100.
Regeringens proposition (Government bill) no.1996/97:53.
Regeringens proposition (Government bill) no.1997/98:56.
Minutes of the Standing Commission on Foreign Affairs (Utrikesutskottet) UU 25 1995/96.
Minutes of the Standing Commission on Foreign Affairs (Utrikesutskottet) UU 13 1996/97.

2 Reports of Investigative Commissions (SOU), etc:

Storstadstrafik 5 (SOU 1990:16).
Rapport från Klimatdelegationen, årsrapport (1994) (SOU 1994:138).
Det svenska miljöarbetet i EU (1994), Ministry of the Environment and Natural Resources (Ds 1994:126).
Rapport från Klimatdelegationen, slutrapport (1995) (SOU 1995:96).
Ny kurs i trafikpolitiken: delbetänkande 1 (1996) (SOU 1996:26).
Ny kurs i trafikpolitiken: delbetänkande 2 (1996) (SOU 1996:165).
Ny kurs i trafikpolitiken: slutbetänkande (1997) (SOU 1997:35).
Sammanställning av remissyttranden över Kommunikationskommitténs betänkande "Ny kurs i trafikpolitiken" (1997), Ministry of Transport.

Documents and reports published by the European Conference of Ministers of Transport (ECMT):

On Transport and Environment, a resolution of the ECMT (no. 66) (1989), ECMT, Paris.

Transport Policy and the Environment (1990), ECMT and OECD, Paris.
Transport Policy and Global Warming. A Report from a Seminar (1992), ECMT, Paris.
The European Conference of Ministers of Transport 1953-1993 (1993), ECMT, Paris.
Urban Travel and Sustainable Development (1995), ECMT and OECD, Paris.

Documents and reports published and/or initiated by the Commission of the EU:

1992. The Environmental Dimension: the Task Force Report on the Environment and the Internal Market (1989), Economica Verlag, Bonn.
The Fifth Environmental Action Programme, a White Paper (1992), (COM/92/23).
The Impact of Transport on the Environment, a Green Paper (1992), (COM/92/46).
The Future Development of the Common Transport Policy: a Global Approach to the Construction of a Community Framework for Sustainable Mobility, a White Paper (1992), (COM/92/494).
Economic Growth and the Environment: Some Implications for Economic Policy-Making, a Communication Paper (1994), (COM/94/465).
The Citizens Network - Fulfilling the Potential of Public Passenger Transport in Europe, a Green paper (1995), (COM/95/601).
Towards Fair and Efficient Pricing in Transport. Policy Options for Internalisation of External Costs of Transport in the European Union, a Green paper (1995), (COM/95/ 691).
An Energy Policy for the European Union, a White Paper (1995), (COM /95/682).
A Community Strategy to Reduce CO2 Emissions from Passenger Cars and to Improve Fuel Economy, a Communication Paper (1995), (COM/95/689).
Auto Oil Programme, a White Paper (1996), (COM/96/248 final).
A report on the implementation of The Fifth Environmental Action Programme (1996), (COM/95/624).
Road Transport and the Environment - Energy and Fiscal Aspects, a report from Eurostat (1996).

1.2 Publications of various organizations

AIMSE. The motorway project for the Europe of to-morrow (1990), the International Road Federation (IRF), Geneva and Washington, D.C.
Alternative transport policy in Poland, 1997. Information package no.2, Institute for Sustainable Development, Warsaw.
City Car Club: Carfree but carefree (sine anno), Carfree Cities Network, Brussels.
Definition and Vision of Sustainable Transportation (1997), Centre for Sustainable Transportation, Toronto.
Ett hållbart transportsystem: Svenska Naturskyddsföreningens handlingsprogram (1997), The Swedish association for the Protection of Nature, Stockholm.
Folkets rätt att köra bil (1997), Timbro förlag, Stockholm (Timbro rapport 16/1997).
Järnvägens andra revolution (1995), Rail Forum Sweden, Ekerlid förlag, Stockholm.
Keeping Europe Mobile (1988), The European Round Table of Industrialists (ERT).
Missing Links (1985), The European Round Table of Industrialists (ERT).
Our Common Future. A Report from the World Commission on Environment and Development, chaired by G.H.Brundtland (1987), Oxford University Press, Oxford.
Mål och beräkningar för ett hållbart Sverige (1997), Miljöförbundet, Göteborg.
Säker trafik, a journal ed. by The Swedish Association for Traffic Safety.
Sustainable Netherlands (1992), Vereniging Milieudefensie, Amsterdam.
The Netherlands traveling clean (1989), Vereniging Milieudefensie, Amsterdam.
Ten Times Better: Fair Shares in Environmental Space (1997), Friends of the Earth Netherlands
The Need for Renewing Transport Infrastructure in Europe (1989), The European Round Table of Industrialists (ERT).
Trafik 2005. Det grønne korrektur (1994), The Danish Association for the Protection of Nature.
Transport in Europe, 1997, a book written by C. Gerondeau, Artech House, Boston and London.

1.3 Statistical handbooks etc

Beleidseffectmeting Verkeer en Vervoer, annual reports ed. by Ministerie van Verkeer en Waterstaat 1993 and 1995.
Beleidseffectrapportage see - Beleidseffectmeting Verkeer en Vervoer
Bilismen i Sverige (="Automobility in Sweden") (1997), The Swedish Association of Automobile Manufacturers and Wholesalers, Stockholm.
Emissions from Transport (1997), ECMT and OECD, Paris.
Environmental Report (1996), The Swedish National Road Administration, Borlänge.
Holten-Andersen, J. et al. (1998), *Natur og Miljø: Påvirkninger og tilstand 1997. Faglig rapport*, Ministry of Energy and the Environment together with Danmarks miljøundersøgelser, Copenhagen.
Natur og Miljø: Påvirkninger og tilstand 1997. Faglig rapport - see J. Holten-Andersen et al.
OECD Environmental Data (1995), OECD, Paris.
På cykel til og fra arbejde i København. En undersøgelse af transportvaner for medarbejdere på 19 københavnske arbejdplatser (1996), Stadsingeniørens Direktorat, Vejavdelningen, Copenhagen.
Statistisk Årbog: 1990, 1995, 1997 ("Statistical Yearbook"), Danmarks Statistik, Copenhagen.
Trafikredegørelse (1997), Ministry of Transport, Copenhagen.
Transportation Energy Data Book, Ed. 17 (1997), prepared by Oak Ridge National Laboratory for the U.S. Department of Energy.
Transportstatistik 1995 ("Transport Statistics 1995"), Danmarks Statistik, Copenhagen.
Transportprognos 2005 och 2020 (sine anno), The Swedish National Road Adminstration et al. Borlänge.
World Road Statistics 1990-1994, International Road Federation (IRF), Geneva and Washington, D.C.

2 Secondary sources

2.1 Bibliographies

Sustainability in Transport (1991-1994), Current topics in transport no. 81, 1995, Library Services at the Transport Research Laboratory, Crowthorne, Berkshire.

Sustainability in Transport Update (1995-1997), Current topics in transport no. 81.1, 1997, Library Services at the Transport Research Laboratory, Crowthorne, Berkshire.

2.2 Scientific literature and reports

A Study of Global Change, a booklet published by the International Geosphere-Biosphere Programme (1989), International Council of Scientific Unions, Paris.

Aburish, S.K. (1995), *The Rise, Corruption and Coming Fall of the House of Saud*, Bloomsbury, London.

Als, J. (1994), 'Environmental Impact Assessment: from Ex Ante to Ex Post Evaluation', in H.Voogd (ed.), *Issues in Environmental Planning*, Pion, London, pp 145-163.

Andersen, M.S. (1994), *Governance by Green Taxes. Making Pollution Prevention Pay*, Manchester University Press, Manchester.

Andersen, M.S. (1997),' Denmark', in M. Jänicke and H. Weidner (eds), *National Environmental Policies. A Comparative Study of Capacity-Building*, Springer Verlag, Berlin, pp 157-174.

Andersen, M.S. and Hansen, M.W. (1991), *Vandmiljøplanen: Fra forhandling til symbol*, NICHE, Århus.

Andersson-Skog, L. and Ottosson, J. (1994), *Institutionell teori och den svenska kommunikationspolitikens utformning - betydelsen av ett historiskt perspektiv (with a summary in English)*, Umeå and Uppsala Universities, Departments of Economic History, Umeå and Uppsala (Working Papers in Transport and Communication History 1994:1).

Andréasson, H. and Sjöberg, A. (1996). *Ungdomars syn på kollektivtrafik och bil: en etnologisk intervjuundersökning kring attityder, resvanor och framtidsbilder*, Trafikkontoret, Göteborg (Göteborgs stad Rapport 1996:9).

Anshelm, J. (1995), *Socialdemokraterna och miljöfrågan: en studie i framstegtankens paradoxer*, Symposion, Stockholm.

Azar, C. and Rodhe, H. (1997),'Targets for Stabilization of Atmospheric CO_2', in *Science*, vol. 276 (20 June 1997), pp 1818-1819.

Banister, D. (1993), 'Policy Responses in the UK', in D. Banister and

K. Button (eds), *Transport, the Environment and Sustainable Development*, E & FN SPON, London, pp 53-78.
Banister, D. and Berechman, J. (1993), *Transport in a Unified Europe: Policies and Challenges*, North-Holland, Amsterdam (Studies in regional science and urban economics 24).
Banister, D. and Button, K. (eds) (1993), *Transport, the Environment and Sustainable Development*, E & FN SPON, London.
Barde, J.-P. and Button, K. (eds) (1990), *Transport Policy and the Environment: six case studies*, Earthscan, London.
Bartlett, R.V. (1994), 'Evaluating Environmental Policy - Success and Failure', in N.J. Vig and M.E. Kraft (eds), *Environmental Policy in the 1990s. Towards a New Agenda*, 2nd ed. CQ Press, Washington, D.C.
Beck, U. (1992), *Risk Society. Towards a New Modernity* (translated by M. Ritter), Sage, London.
Beck, U. Giddens, A. and Lash, S. (1994), *Reflexive Modernization: Politics, Tradition and Aestetics in the Modern Social Order*. Stanford University Press, Stanford, Calif.
Bennulf, M. (1994), *Miljöopinionen i Sverige*, Dialogos, Lund (Göteborg studies in politics 30).
Bennulf, M. (1996), 'Det gröna handlingsutrymmet', in L.J. Lundgren (ed.), *Livsstil och miljö: Fråga, forska, förändra*, Byggforskningsrådet etc, Stockholm, pp 153-169.
Berg, P.G. (1996), *Rörlighet och rotfasthet. Ett humanbiologiskt perspektiv på framtidens transporter och kommunikationer*, Liber-Hermod, Malmö.
Bergdahl, J.N.H. (1996), *Nationella miljöpolitiska åtgärder och den Europeiska Unionen*, Nordplan, Stockholm (Meddelanden 1996:3).
Berge, G. (1995), 'The Battle of Images: Cultural Conceptions of Different Transport Modes in Oslo', in A. Lohmann-Hansen (ed.), *Proceedings of Trafikdage på AUC*, 21-22 August 1995, Aalborg University, Aalborg, pp 711-724.
Berge, G. (1997), *Livsstil, miljøbevissthet og transportatfærd*, Transportøkonomisk Institutt, Oslo (report 366).
Berner, B. (1981), *Teknikens värld. Teknisk förändring och ingenjörsarbete i svensk industri* (with an English summary), Arkiv för studier i arbetarrörelsens historia, Lund.
Bertills, U. and Hanneberg, P. (1995), *Försurningen i Sverige - vad vet vi egentligen?* (with an English summary), Naturvårdsverket, Solna (report 4421).
Biel, A. (1996), 'Väljer människor att agera miljövänligt?', in L.J. Lundgren (ed.), *Livsstil och miljö: Fråga, forska, förändra*, Byggforskningsrådet etc, Stockholm, pp 54-66.

Biff och bil? - om hushållens miljöval, (1996), Naturvårdsverket, Stockholm (report 4542).
Bijker, W.E., Hughes, T.P. and Pinch, T. (eds) (1987), *The Social Construction of Technological Systems. New Directions in the Sociology and History of Technology*, The MIT Press, Cambridge, Mass.
Bjørnland, D. (1993), *Transport Policy and Transport Development in the European Community (EC) compared with the Norwegian and Swedish Development*, Göteborg University, School of Economics and Commercial Law, Göteborg.
Bleijenberg, A.N. and Dings, J.M.W. (1997), *European transport: emission trends and policy responses*, Centre for Energy Conservation and Environmental Technology, Delft.
Bolin, B. (1993), *Hotet om klimatförändring*, Scandinavian University Press, Stockholm.
Bolin, B. (1997), 'Växthuseffekten skapar risker', in G. Jervas et al. (eds), *2000-talets stora utmaningar: Aktuella resurs- och miljöproblem i ett konfliktperspektiv*, SNS, Stockholm, pp 170-196.
Bolund, P. (1996), *Ecological Problems Caused by Roads and Railroads*, University of Stockholm, Department of System's Ecology, Stockholm (examensarbete 1996:20).
Bressers, H.T.A. and Plettenburg, L.A. (1997), 'The Netherlands', in M. Jänicke and H. Weidner (eds), *National Environmental Policies. A Comparative Study of Capacity-Building*, Springer Verlag, Berlin, pp 109-132.
Brokking, P. et al. (1997), *An Environmentally Sustainable Transport System in Sweden. A scenario study*, The Swedish Transport and Communications Research Board, Stockholm (report 1997:3).
Button, K. and Rothengatter, W. (1993), 'Global Environmental Degradation: The Role of Transport', in D. Bannister and K. Button (eds), *Transport, the Environment and Sustainable Development*, E & FN SPON, London, pp. 19-52.
Campbell, C.J. and Laherrère, J.H. (1998), 'The End of Cheap Oil', in *Scientific American*, March 1998, pp 60-65.
Carlsson-Kanyama, A. et al. (1998), 'Gender differences in environmental impacts from patterns of transportation - a case study from Sweden', forthcoming in *Society and Natural Resources*.
Chaib, M. and Orfali, B. (eds) (1996), *Sociala representationer: Om vardagsvetandets sociala fundament*, Daidalos, Göteborg.
Christiansen, P. M. (ed.) (1996a), *Governing the Environment: Politics, Policy, and Organization in the Nordic Countries*, Nordic Council of Ministers, Copenhagen (Nord 1996:5).
Christiansen, P. M. (1996b), 'Denmark', in P.M.Christiansen (ed.), *Governing the Environment: Politics, Policy, and Organization in the*

Nordic Countries, Nordic Council of Ministers, Copenhagen (Nord 1996:5), pp 29-102.
Christoff, P. (1996), 'Ecological Modernisation, Ecological Modernities', in *Environmental Politics*, vol.5:3, pp 476-500.
Clercq, le F. (1985), 'Dynamics in Transportation Planning: an Overview', in G.R.M. Jansen, P. Nijkamp and C. Ruijgrok (eds), *Transportation and Mobility in an Era of Transition*, North Holland, Amsterdam, pp 1-11.
Clercq, le F. (1987), 'Policy Cycles and New Planning Issues', in P. Nijkamp and S. Reichman (eds), *Transportation Planning in a Changing World*, Gower, Aldershot, pp 93-108.
Climate Change 1995: The Science of Climatic Change. Contribution of Working Group I to the Second Assessment Report of the Intergovernmental Panel on Climate Change, (1996), ed by J.T. Houghton et al. Cambridge University Press, Cambridge.
Climate Change 1995. Impacts, Adaptations and Mitigation of Climate Change: Scientific-Technical Analyses. Contribution of Working Group II to the Second Assessment Report of the Intergovernmental Panel on Climate Change, (1996), ed by R.T. Watson et al. University Press, Cambridge.
Climate Change 1995: Economic and Social Dimensions of Climate Change. Contribution of Working Group III to the Second Assessment Report of the Intergovernmental Panel on Climate Change (1996), ed. by J.P. Bruce et al. Cambridge University Press, Cambridge.
Dansk Transportpolitik - en oversigt (1993), The Danish Transport Council, Copenhagen (report no. 93-01).
Dawes, R.M. (1980), 'Social Dilemmas', in *Annual Review of Psychology* 31, pp 169-193.
Deaking, E. (1993), 'Policy Reponses in the USA', in D. Banister and K. Button (eds), *Transport, the Environment and Sustainable Development*, E & FN SPON, London, pp 79-101.
DeCicco, J. and DeLucchi, M. (eds) (1997), *Transportation, Energy, and Environment: How Far Can Technology Take Us?*, American Council for an Energy-Efficient Economy, Washington, D.C.
Diekstra, R. and Kroon, M. (1997). 'Cars and behaviour: psychological barriers to car restraint and sustainable urban transport', in R. Tolley (ed.), *The Greening of Urban Transport: Planning for Walking and Cycling in Western Cities*. 2nd ed. Wiley, Chichester, pp 147-157.
Downs, A. (1972), 'Up and Down with Ecology - the 'Issue-Attention' Cycle', *Public Interest* 28, pp 38-50.
Dreborg, K. and Jungmar, M. (1994), *Sambandet mellan väginvesteringar och samhällsutveckling - en kunskapsöversikt*, Miljövårdsbered-

ningen, Stockholm (report 1994:6).
Dugonjic, V. et al. (1993), 'The Links Between Mobility and Environmental Sustainability', in D.Banister and J.Berechman (eds), *Transport in a Unified Europe: Policies and Challenges*, North-Holland, Amsterdam, pp 195-219.
EF's Transportpolitik - en oversigt, 1993, Danish Transport Council, Copenhagen (report 93:02).
Erdmenger, J. (1984), *Vers une politique des transport pour l'Europe*, here quoted in a Swedish translation (which is an updated version of the French original) entitled *EGs transportpolitik - mål, program, genomförande* 1986, Industriförbundets förlag, Stockholm.
Eriksen, E.O. (1993), *Den offentlige dimensjon. Verdier og styring i offentlig sektor*, Tano, Bergen.
Eriksson, E. et al. (1995), *Transporters miljöpåverkan i ett livscykelperspektiv*, Chalmers University of Technology, Industrial Technology, Göteborg (Reforsk FoU 126).
Eriksson, G. (1997), 'Trafikverkens ansvar för miljön', in H.E.B. Andersson (ed.), *Trafik och miljö: Forskare skriver om kunskapsläge och forskningsbehov*, Studentlitteratur, Lund, pp 50-57.
Erlandsson, L. and Laveskog, A. (1997), 'Miljömässiga krav på fordon och drivmedel', in H.E. B. Andersson (ed.), *Trafik och miljö: Forskare skriver om kunskapsläge och forskningsbehov*, Studentlitteratur, Lund, pp 356-365.
Festinger, L. (1957), *A Theory of Cognitive Dissonance*, Standford Univ. Press, Standford, Calif.
Flink, J.J. (1975), *The Car Culture*, The MIT Press, Cambridge, Mass.
Flyvbjerg, B. (1984), 'Implementation and the Choice of Evaluation Methods' in *Transport Policy Decision Making* 2, pp 291-314.
Flyvbjerg, B. (1991), *Rationalitet og Magt I-II*, Akademisk Forlag, Copenhagen.
Flyvbjerg, B. (1998), *Rationality and Power: Democracy in Practice* (translated by S.Sampson), University of Chicago Press, Chicago.
Flyvbjerg, B. (1998b), 'Habermas and Foucault: Thinkers for Civil Society', forthcoming in *The British Journal of Sociology*.
Frändberg, C. (1998), *Distance Matters. An inquiry into the relation between transport and environmental sustainability in tourism*, Göteborg University, Department of Interdisciplinary Studies, Göteborg (Humanekologiska skrifter 15).
Gajewska, E. (1994). *Polackerna och deras bilar: En studie av den polska bilismens framväxt och aktuella situation*, The Swedish Transport and Communications Research Board, Stockholm (report 1994: 12).
Gajewska, E. (1998), Transportsystemet i Polen under transformation:

En studie med focus på privatbilens expansion (working paper), Göteborg University, Department of Interdisciplinary Studies, Section of Human Technology, Göteborg.

Gakenheimer, R. (1995), Motorizing in China (available to the author of this book only in a manuscript).

Gallopin, G. et al. (1997), *Branch Points: Global Scenarios and Human Choice*, Stockholm Environment Institute, Stockholm.

Gerentz, S. (1995), *Vägverket och företrädarna för bilism och närings-Liv:ett nätverks betydelse för transportpolitik och transportutveckling efter kriget*, Umeå and Uppsala Universities, Departments of Economic History, Umeå and Uppsala (Working papers in Transport and Communication History 1995:3).

Giddens, A. (1991), *Modernity and Self-Identity: Self and Society in the Late Modern Age*, Polity Press, Cambridge, UK.

Global Change, Local Challenge: Proceedings of a Scientific Symposium 1995 (1996), The International Social Science Council, Geneva.

Global Energy Perspectives to 2050 and Beyond (1995), IIASA/World Energy Council, sine loco.

Global Transport Sector Energy Demands towards 2020 (1995). A report made by the Norwegian oil company Statoil for World Energy Council, World Energy Council, London.

Global Warming: Economic Dimensions and Policy Responses (1995), OECD, Paris.

Goodwin, P. et al. (1992), *Modyfying our volume of traffic the primary route to sustainable transport*, University of Oxford, Transport Studies Unit, Oxford.

Graedel, T.E. et al. (1995), 'Global emissions inventories of acid-related compunds', in *Water, air, and soil pollution*, vol. 85:1, pp 25-36.

Grennfelt, P. and Holmberg, B. (1997), Vägtrafikens kväveoxidemissioner. En granskning av metoder att bestämma emissioner från vägtrafik etc (unpublished manuscript).

Gudmundsson, H. and Höjer, M. (1996), 'Sustainable Development Principles and Their Implications for Transport', *Ecological economics*, vol.19, pp 269-282.

Habermas, J. (1981), *Theorie des kommunikativen Handelns*. I-II. Suhrkamp, Frankfurt am Main.

Hagman, O. 1999. *Bilen, naturen och det moderna: Om natursynens omvandlingar i det svenska bilsamhället*, Göteborg University, Department of Social Anthropology, Göteborg.

Hajer, M.A. (1997), *The Politics of Environmental Discourse:Ecological Modernization and the Policy Process*. 2nd. ed. Clarendon, Oxford.

Haq, G. (1997), *Towards Sustainable Transport Planning: a Compari-*

son between Britain and the Netherlands, Avebury, Aldershot.
Hardoy, J.E. et al. (1992), Environmental problems in Third World cities, Earthscan Publications, London.
Helby, P. (1997), 'Energi som säkerhetsfråga', in G. Jervas et al. (eds), 2000-talets stora utmaningar: Aktuella resurs- och miljöproblem i ett konfliktperspektiv, SNS, Stockholm, pp 88-134.
Heurgren, V. (1995), Bilen i familjen och livsloppet - ur genusperspektiv, Nordiska museet, Stockholm (Bilprojektet).
Himanen, V. et al. (1992), 'Environmental Quality and Transportation Policy in Europe', in Transportation Research, vol. 26A, pp 147-157.
Holmberg, J. et al. (1994), Socio-Ecological principles for a Sustainable Society: Scientific background and Swedish experience, Göteborg University and Chalmers University of Technology, Institute of Physical Ressource Theory, Göteborg.
Holmberg, J. and Råde, I. (1997), 'Bärkraftighet - krav på det framtida transportsystemet', in H.E.B. Andersson (ed.), Trafik och Miljö: Forskare skriver om kunskapsläge och forskningsbehov, Studentlitteratur, Lund, pp 158-172.
Holmgren, B. (1994), Svensk trafikpolitik: ett kompendium, Göteborg University, Department of Human and Economic Geography, Göteborg.
Holzinger, K. (1995), 'A Surprising Success in EC Environmental Policy: The Small Car Exhaust Emission Directive of 1989', in M. Jänicke and H. Weidner (eds), Successful Environmental Policy. A Critical Evaluation of 24 Cases, Sigma, Berlin, pp 197-202.
Hovgesen, H.H. and Norre, S. (1998), 'Odense bilklub: En metode til at dæmpe væksten i byerne?', in H. Lahrmann and A. Pittelkow (eds), Proceedings of Trafikdagar på AUC, 24-25 August 1998. To appear in a supplement volume, Aalborg University, Aalborg.
Hultberg, H. et al. (1998), 'Reversal of Acidification: Policy Implications Derived from the Roof Project', in H. Hultberg and R. Skeffington (eds), Experimental Reversal of Acid Rain Effects: The Gårdsjön Roof Project, Wiley, Chichester, pp 447-459.
Hållbara transportsystem i USA (1996), A report in Swedish by A. Wingqvist, Sveriges tekniska attachéer, Stockholm (report 9603).
Hägerstrand, T. (1974), The impact of transport on the quality of life: transport in the 1980-1990 decade, OECD, Paris, pp 1-51.
Implementing of Alternative Fuels in Sweden (1997), A report to the Governmental Commission on Transport and Communications, The Swedish Transport and Communications Research Board, Stockholm.
Jamison, A. et al. (1990), The Making of the New Environmental Consciousness. A Comparative Study of the Environmental Movements in

Sweden, Denmark and the Netherlands, Edinburgh University Press, Edinburgh.

Jensen, H. (1993), *Sustainable Development in Transportation: Preparations for the 21. Century*, the Nordic Council of Ministers, Copenhagen (Nord 1993:25).

Jensen, M. (1997), *Bensin i blodet. I Kvalitativ del*, Faglig rapport fra DMU, no. 191; *II. Kvantitativ del*, Faglig rapport fra DMU, no. 200, Ministry of the Environment and Energy and Danmarks Miljøundersøgelser, Copenhagen.

Jones, P. et al. (1993), 'Transport Policy: the European Laboratory', in I. Salomon et al. (eds), *A Billion Trips a Day: Tradition and Transition in European Travel Patterns*, Kluwer Academic, Dortrecht, pp 167-187.

Johansson, B. (1996), *Energibalanser. Möjligheter att ersätta bensin och diesel med drivmedel från svenska biobränslen*, The Swedish Transport and Communications Research Board, Stockholm (meddelande 1996:22).

Johansson, T. B. (1997), 'Beyond Climate Change: 'Energizing Development'', in *E-notes: Quarterly newsletter of the International Institute for Energy Conservation*, December 1997, p 3.

Jongh, de P.E. (1996), Netherland's approach on Environmental Policies: Integrated environmental policy planning as a step towards sustainable development, Washington D.C.: Center for Strategic and International Studies, Washinton D.C. (unpublished manuscript).

Jänicke, M. (1990), 'Erfolgsbedingungen von Umweltpolitik im internationalen Vergleich', in *Zeitschrift für Umweltpolitik*, No. 3, pp 213-231.

Jänicke, M. (1996), 'Democracy as a condition for environmental policy success: the importance of non-institutional factors', in W.M. Lafferty and J. Meadowcroft (eds), *Democracy and the Environment: Problems and Perspectives*, Edgar Elgar, Cheltenham, pp 71-85.

Jänicke, M. and Weidner, H. (eds) (1995), *Successful Environmental Policy. A Critical Evaluation of 24 Cases*, Sigma, Berlin.

Jänicke, M. and Weidner, H. (eds) (1997), *National Environmental Policies. A Comparative Study of Capacity-Building*, Springer Verlag, Berlin.

Keeling, C.D. et al. (1995), 'Interannual extremes in the rate of rise of atmospheric carbon dioxide since 1980', in *Nature*, vol. 375, pp 666-670.

Kerver, W. et al. (1993), 'The Netherlands: Ground Travel below Sea Level', in I. Salomon et al. (eds), *A Billion Trips a Day: Tradition and Transition in European Travel Patterns*, Kluwer Academic, Dortrecht, pp 329-348.

Kjellerup, U. (1997), 'MKB-proceduren - offentlighet och aktörer', in H.E.B.Andersson (ed.), *Trafik och miljö. Forskare skriver om kunskapsläge och forskningsbehov*, Studentlitteratur, Lund, pp 375-387.

Kleebinder, H.-P. (1995), *Internationale Public Relations: Analyse öffentlicher Meinungsbildung in Europa zum Thema Mobilität*, Deutscher Universitäts Verlag, Wiesbaden.

Kristianssen, J. (1995), *Transportinfrastrukturens regionala udviklingseffekter*, Aalborg University, Department of Development and Planning, Aalborg (report 165).

Kroon, M. (1997), 'Traffic and Environmental Policy in the Netherlands', in R. Tolley (ed.), *The Greening of Urban Transport: Planning or Walking and Cycling in Western Cities*, Wiley, Chichester, pp 161-176.

Kågesson, P. (1994), *The Concept of Sustainable Transport*, Transport & Environment, Brussels (report 1994:3).

Lélé, S. M. (1991), 'Sustainable Development: a Critical Review', in *World Development*, vol. 19:6, pp 607-621.

Lindén, A.-L. (1994), 'Livsstil och konsumtionsmönster. Drivkrafter och motkrafter i energianvändning', appendix 5 to the *Report of the Swedish Climate Delegation* (SOU 1994:138).

Liniado, M. (1996), *Car Culture and Countryside Change*, The National Trust, Cirencester.

Lundvist, L.J. (1980), *The Hare and the Tortoise: Clean Air Policies in the United States and Sweden*, The University of Michigan Press, Ann Arbor.

Lundvist, L.J. (1996a), 'Environmental Politics in the Nordic Countries: Policy, Organisation, and Capacity', in P.M.Christiansen (ed.), *Governing the Environment: Politics, Policy, and Organization in the Nordic Countries*, Nordic Council of Ministers (Nord 1996:5), Copenhagen, pp 13-28.

Lundvist, L.J. (1996b), 'Sweden', in P.M. Christiansen (ed.), *Governing the Environment: Politics, Policy, and Organization in the Nordic Countries*, Nordic Council of Ministers (Nord 1996:5), Copenhagen, pp 259-336.

Lundqvist, L.J. (1997), 'Sweden', in M. Jänicke and H. Weidner (eds), *National Environmental Policies. A Comparative Study of Capacity-Building*, Springer, Berlin, pp 45-71.

Lööv, T. and Miegel, F. (1989), *The Notion of Lifestyle. Some Theoretical Considerations*, Lund University, Department of Sociology, Lund.

Market and Government Failures in Environment Management: the Case of Transport 1992, OECD, Paris.

Maruo, K. (1992), *Japanerna och deras bilar. En studie av bilismen i*

Japan (with a summary in English), The Swedish Transport Research Board, Stockholm (report 1992:22).

Masser, I. et al. (1992), 'From Growth to Equity and Sustainability: Paradigm Shift in Transport Planning?', in *Transportation Planning and Technology*, vol. 17:4, pp 319-330.

May, T. (1993), 'Transport Policy and Management', in D. Banister and K. Button (eds), *Transport, the Environment and Sustainable Development*, E & FN SPON, London, pp 232- 247.

Meaton, J. and Morrice, D. (1996), 'The Ethics and Politics of Private Automobile Use', in *Environmental Ethics*, vol.18:1, pp 39-54.

Menes, E. (1997), 'Poland - the private car and public transport in conflict', in E. Tengström and M. Thynell (eds), *Towards Sustainable Mobility: Transporting people and goods in the Baltic Baltic Region*, University of Uppsala, Baltic university programme, Uppsala.

Mere miljøvenlige biler - tekniske muligheder og politiske tiltag (1997), The Danish Transport Council, Copenhagen (report 97-04).

*Miljökonsekvensbeskrivning för vägar: Handbok (*1995), The Swedish National Road Administration, Borlänge.

Miljøvurdering af transportprojekter - en casestudie (1994), The Danish Transport Council, Copenhagen (notes 94-06).

Mol, A.P.J. (1996), 'Ecological Modernisation and Institutional Reflexivity: Environmental Reform in the Late Modern Age', in *Environmental Politics*, vol.5:2, pp 302-323.

Moscovici, S. (1989), 'Des répresentations collectives aux répresentations sociales: éléments pour une histoire', in D. Jodelet (ed.), *Les répresentations sociales*, Presses Univ. de France, Paris, pp 62-86.

Nitsch, U. (1996), 'Informationsstrategier för en bättre miljö', in L.J. Lundgren (ed.), *Att veta och att göra: Om kunskap och handling inom miljövården*, Naturvårdsverket, Stockholm, pp 73-97.

Nijkamp, P. (1994), 'Roads Towards Environmentally Sustainable Transport', in *Transportation Research*, vol. 28 A:4 pp 261-271.

Nielsen, K. L. (1998), *Environmental Appraisal of Large Scale Transport Infrastructure Investments*, Aalborg University, Department of Development and Planning, PhD Dissertation, Aalborg (forthcoming).

Nolin, J. (1995), *Ozonskiktet och vetenskapen. En studie av postnormal vetenskap*, Almqvist & Wiksell International, Stockholm.

Norre, L. (1996). 'Sociale Dilemmaer på persontransportområdet', in H. Lahrmann and L.H. Pedersen (eds), *Proceedings of Trafikdagar på AUC, 19-20 August 1996*, Aalborg University, Aalborg, pp 497-507.

OECD Environmental Data Compendium (1995), OECD, Paris.

Orfeuil, J-P. and Bovy, P. (1993), ' European Mobility *is* Different: a Global Perspective', in I. Salomon et al. (eds), *A Billion Trips a Day:*

Tradition and Transition in European Travel Patterns. Dortrecht: Kluwer Academic, Dortrecht, pp 13-19.

O'Riordan, T. (1996), 'Democracy and the sustainability transition', in W.M. Lafferty and J. Meadowcroft (eds), *Democracy and the Environment: Problems and Prospects*.: Edgar Elgar, Cheltenham, pp 140-156.

Palm, L. (1994), *Övertalningsstrategier: Att välja budskap efter utgångsläge*, Lund University Press, Lund (Lund Studies in media and Communication 1).

Peak, S. and Hope, C. (1994), 'Sustainable Mobility in Context. Three Transport Scenarios for the UK', in *Transport Policy*, vol.1:3, pp 195-207.

Pemberton, M. (1988), *The World Car Industry in the Year 2000*, The Economist, London.

Pierce, D.W. et al. (1994), 'The Economics of Sustainable Development', in *Annual Review of Energy and the Environment*, vol.19, pp 457-474.

Plath, D.W. (1990), 'My-Car-isma: Motorizing the Showa Self', in *Showa: the Japan of Hirohito. A special issue of Daidalus, Journal of the American Academy of Arts and Sciences*, vol.119:3, pp 229-244.

Polk, M. (1996), 'Swedish Men and Women's Mobility Patterns: Issues of Social Equity and Ecological Sustainability', a paper presented at the National Conference on Women's Travel Issues, Baltimore Maryland, Oct.1996, forthcoming in *Proceedings from the 2nd National Conference on Women's Travel Issues*, Baltimore, Maryland.

Polk, M. (1997), 'Women and the Automobile in Sweden', in H. Lahrmann and L.H. Pedersen (eds), *Proceedings of Trafikdagar på AUC, 25-26 August 1997*, Aalborg University, Aalborg, Supplement, pp 53-62.

Polk, M. (1998), *Gendered Mobility. A Study of Women's and Men's Relations to Automobility in Sweden*, Göteborg University, Department of Interdisciplinary Studies of the Human Condition, Section of Human Ecology, Göteborg.

Pollution Prevention and Control: Environmental Criteria for Sustainable Transport (1996), OECD, Paris.

Ragin, C.C. (1987). *The Comparative Method. Moving Beyond Qualitative and Quantitative Strategies*, University of California Press, Berkeley.

Raskin, P. and Margulis, R. (1995), *Global Energy in the 21st Century: Patterns, Projections and Problems*, Stockholm Environment Institute, Stockholm.

Report on Transport and the Environment presented to Parliament by the British Royal Commission on Environmental Pollution (1994),

HMSO, London.
Richardson, T. (1997), 'The Trans-European Network: Environmental Policy Integration in the European Union', in *European Urban and Regional Studies*, vol 4:4, pp 333-346.
Rietveld, P. (1993), 'Policy Responses in the Netherlands', in D. Banister and K. Button (eds), *Transport, the Environment and Sustainable Development*, E & FN SPON, London, pp 102-113.
Roberts, J. et al. (1992), *Travel Sickness. The Need for a Sustainable Transport Policy for Britain*, Lawrence & Wishart, London.
Rodhe, H. (1997), 'Ozonskiktets nedbrytning', in G.J ervas et al. (eds), *2000-talets stora utmaningar: Aktuella resurs- och miljöproblem i ett konfliktperspektiv*, SNS, Stockholm, pp 158-169.
Rodhe, H. et al. (1995), 'Global Scale Transport of Acidifying Pollutants', in *Water, air, and soil pollution*, vol. 85:1, pp 37-50.
Sagar, A.D. (1995), 'Automobiles and global warming: alternative fuels and other options for carbon dioxide emissions reduction', in *Envionment Impact Assessment Review*, vol.15:3, pp 241-274.
Sahibzada, M. (1994), *Subsidiaritetsprincipen i Maastrichtfördraget - en princip som rör kompetensfördelningen mellan EG och medlemsstaterna*, Juristförlaget, Stockholm (Skrifter utgivna av Institutet för europeisk rätt vid Stockholms universitet 27).
Sachs, W. (1992), *For Love of the Automobile. Looking Back into the History of Our Desires*, University of California Press, Berkeley.
Sannerstedt, A. (1979), *Fri konkurrens eller politisk styrning? 1963 års trafikpolitiska beslut - debatten om innehåll, tillämpning och effekter* (with an English summary), Studentlitteratur, Lund.
Schafer, A. and Victor, D. (1997), 'The Past and Future of Global Mobility', in *Scientific American*, October 1997, pp 36-39.
Schinas, M. and Vinois, J.-A. (1993), 'Transport Policy', in P. Coffey (ed.), *Main Economic Policy Areas of the EC - After 1992*, Kluwer Academic, Dortrecht, pp 123-147.
Schipper, L. (1995), 'Determinants of Automobile Use and Energy Consumption in OECD Countries', in *Annual Review of Energy and Environment*, vol. 20, pp 325-386.
Schrama, G.J.I. and Klok, P.-J. (1995), 'The Swift Introduction of "Clean cars" in the Netherlands, 1986-1992. The Origin and Effect of Incentive Measures', in M. Jänicke and H. Weichner (eds), *Successful Environmental Policy: A Critical Evaluation of 24 Cases*, Sigma, Berlin, pp 187-202.
Sharma, A. and Roychowhury, A. (1996), *Slow murder - the deadly story of vehicular pollution in India*, Center for Science and Environment, New Dehli - a publication not available to the author of this book.
Sheate, R. (1995), 'Transport policy: a critical role for strategic envir-

ronmental assessment', in *World Transport Policy and Practice*, vol. 1:4, pp 17-24.

Short, J. (1996), 'Transport Policy and the Environment', in H. Lahrman and L.H. Pedersen (eds), *Proceedings of Trafikdage på AUC, 19-20 August 1996*, Aalborg University, Aalborg, Supplement, pp 5-18.

Skrotningspræmien: Effekter for miljø og bilpark (1995), The Danish Transport Council, Copenhagen, (report 95-04).

Sperling, D. and Shaheen, S.A. (eds), (1995), *Transportation and Energy: Strategies for a Sustainable Transport System*, American Council for an Energy-Efficient Economy, Washington, D.C.

Starkie, D. (1987), 'Configurating Change: Reflections on Transport Policy Processes', in P. Nijkamp and S. Reichman (eds), *Transportation Planning in a Changing World*, Gower, Aldershot pp 269-283.

Spinosa, C. et al. (1997), *Disclosing New Worlds: Enterpreneurship, Democratic Action and the Cultivation of Solidarity*, the MIT Press, Cambridge, Mass.

Steen, P. et al. (1997), *Färder i framtiden: Transporter i ett bärkraftigt samhälle*, The Swedish Transport and Communications Research Board, Stockholm, (report 1997:7).

Sustainable Transport. Priorities for Policy Reform (1996), The World Bank, Washington, D.C.

Tanner, J.C. (1983), *International Comparisons of Cars and Car Usage*, The Transport and Road Research Laboratory, Crowthorne, Berkshire (report 1070).

Tengström, E. (1992), *The Use of the Automobile: its Implication for Man, Society and the Environment*, The Swedish Transport Research Board, Stockholm (report 1992:4).

Tengström, E. (1993), *Private Cars and Political Decision-makers. An Historical Survey and a Critical Review of Current Transport Policy*, The Swedish Transport and Communications Research Board, Stockholm (report 1993:21).

Tengström, E. (1994), 'Mass Road Transport in the East and West Threatens the Environment of the Baltic Sea', in *A Future for the Baltic:Scientists Discuss the Future of the Baltic*, The Swedish Council for Planning and Coordination of Research, Stockholm, pp 23-42.

Tengström, E. in collaboration with E. Gajewska and M. Thynell (1995), *Sustainable Mobility in Europe and the Role of the Automobile. A Critical Inquiry*. 2nd ed., The Swedish Transport and Communications Research Board, Stockholm (report 1995:17).

Therborn, G. (1995), *European Modernity and Beyond. The Trajectory of European Societies, 1945-2000*, Sage, London.

The Ecological City, the Swedish Report to OECD (1995), The Swedish National Board of Housing Building and Planning, Karlskrona (report

1995:3).
Thynell, M. (1998), *Automobility in the Perspective of International Development Studies Illustrated by Two Case Studies: Tehran and Brasilia*, Göteborg University, Department of Peace and Development Research, Göteborg.
Time to tame our speed? A study of the socio-economic costs and benefits of speed reduction of passenger cars (1996), Primary report, Project bureau IVVS, Den Haag.
Toward a Sustainable Future: Addressing the Long-Term Effects of Motor Vehicle Transportation on Climate and Ecology (1997), American Transporation Research Board, Washington D.C. (Special report 251).
Towards an Environmentally Sustainable Transport System (1996), Final report from the Swedish EST-project, Swedish Environmental Protection Agency, Stockholm (report 4682).
Toward Clean and Fuel Efficient Automobiles (1992), Proceedings of an International Conference Berlin 25-27 March 1991, OECD, Paris.
Towards Clean Transport: Fuel-Efficient and Clean Motor Vehicles (1996), Proceedings of a Conference organised by the OECD and the IEA, hosted by the Government of Mexico, OECD, Paris.
Towards Sustainable Transportation (1997), a Summary of the Proceedings of a Conference organized by the OECD, hosted by the Government of Canada in Vancouver, March 24-27, 1996, OECD, Paris.
Urban Travel and Sustainable Development (1995), ECMT and OECD, Paris.
Uth, T. (1996), 'Definitions of Life Style and its Application to Travel Behavior', in H. Lahrmann and L.H. Pedersen (eds), *Proceedings of Trafikdagar på AUC, 19-20 August 1996*. Aalborg: Aalborg University, Aalborg, pp 531-544.
Waard, van der J. and Hoorn, van der T. (1995), 'Miles ahead (?) The Dutch national land use transport policy: a progress note after four years' (available to the author only in a manuscript).
Walker, B. (1996), 'Predicting a Future Terrestrial Biosphere: Challenges to GCTE Science", in B. Walker and W. Steffen (eds), *Global Change and Terrestrial Ecosystems*, International Geosphere-Biosphere Programme, *sine loco*, Book Series 2, pp 595-607.
Values, Welfare and Quality of Life (1996), Reports of two OECD workshops in in March and July 1996, OECD, Paris.
Wedin, J. (1982), *Spelet om trafikpolitiken*, Norstedts förlag, Stockholm (Skrifter utgivna av statsvetenskapliga föreningen i Uppsala 93).
Vedung, E. (1977), *Det rationella politiska samtalet. Hur politiska budskap tolkas, ordnas och prövas*, Aldus/Bonnier, Stockholm.

Vedung, E. (1982), *Political Reasoning* (a translation and revised edition of Vedung 1977), Sage, Beverly Hills.
Vedung, E. (1998), 'Policy Instruments: Typologies and Theories', in M-L. Bemelmans-Videc, et al. (eds), *Carrots, Sticks, and Sermons: Policy Instruments and Their Evaluation*.: Transaction Publishers, New Brunswick, pp 21-58.
Wee, van B. (1996), 'The Treatment of Traffic in the Dutch Environmental Outlooks: the role of science in poliy making and policy evaluation', in *Transportation Planning and Technology*, vol.19:34, pp 265-274.
Whitelegg, J. (1994), *Transport for a Sustainable Future. The Case for Europe*, Wiley, Chichester.
Wiman, B. (1992), 'The Ecological System Context: Complexity, Risk Perception, and Politics in a Changing Environment', in *Journal of International Association of Traffic and Safety Sciences*, vol.15, pp 19-27.
Windahl, S. (1997), 'Kommunikation, information och utbildning som styrmedel', in H.E.B. Andersson (ed.), *Trafik och miljö: Forskare skriver om kunskapsläge och forskningsbehov*, Studentlitteratur, Lund, pp 366-373.
Vlek, C. et al. (1993), 'A Social Dilemmas Analysis of Motorised Transport Problems and Six General Strategies for Social Behaviour Change', in *Proceedings of an ECMT seminar in 1992*, OECD, Paris.
Vleugel, J. et al. (1990), 'The Netherlands', in J.-P. Barde and K. Button (eds), *Transport Policy and the Environment: six case studies*, Earthscan, London, pp 121-156.
Zegras, Ch. (1996), 'Transport and Climate Change in Latin America', in *E-notes, Quarterly newsletter of the International Institute for Energy Conservation*, June 1996.
Zwanenberg, van P. et al. 'Roads to Sustainable Transportation? On Public Engagement in Infrastructure Projects in Britain, Norway and the Netherlands', in A. Jamison (ed.), *Technology Policy Meets the Public*, Aalborg Universitetsforlag, Aalborg, pp 109-145 (PESTO Papers 2), forthcoming.

2.3 Articles in newspapers and newsletters

Acid News, April 1996.
ACEA newsletter, no. 36 (1996), 41, 42 and 46 (1997).
The China Daily, 1994-07-05.
Dagens Nyheter, 1989-08-21; 1990-09-13; 1992-06-13; 1997-03-30; 1997-04-17.
Environmental Watch, Western Europe 4:21 and 22 (1995).
Global Environmental Change, X:2 (1998-01-30).
New Scientist, 1997-09-20.
T&E Bulletin, no. 32 (1994), 46, 49 and 50 (1996).
The Economist, 1997-03-01; 1997-03-08; 1997-05-10; 1997-08-16; 1997-08-23; 1997-09-06; 1997-10-25; 1997-11-15; 1997-12-13.
The Economist, 'Remapping South America: a Survey of Mercosur', 1996-10-12.
The Economist, 'Time to Let Go: a Survey of India', 1997-02-22.
Transportation, 1995:39 'What to Do with All Those Cars' (an interview with R. Gakenheimer).